CONTRACT LAW
FLOWCHARTS AND CASES

A Student's Visual Guide to Understanding Contracts

Third Edition

By

Professor Frank J. Doti
William P. Foley, II Chair in Corporate Law & Taxation
Chapman University School of Law

WEST®
A Thomson Reuters business

Mat #41188353

© West, a Thomson business, 2007
© 2009 Thomson Reuters
© 2012 Thomson Reuters
  610 Opperman Drive
  St. Paul, MN 55123
  1–800–313–9378
Printed in the United States of America

ISBN: 978–0–314–27789–3

To all my Contracts law students past and present

who challenged me to motivate them

ABOUT THE AUTHOR

Professor Frank J. Doti received a B.S. in Accountancy degree from the University of Illinois at Urbana, Illinois (1966), and earned a Certified Public Accountant certificate in 1966 in Illinois. He received his J.D. cum laude from Chicago-Kent in 1969, where he was an associate editor of the Chicago-Kent Law Review.

Professor Doti practiced law in Chicago, including five years with the law firm of McDermott, Will and Emery. For several years he served as a vice president and corporate attorney at the Leo Burnett advertising agency.

Professor Doti has been teaching law full time since 1982 and has been a full professor at Chapman University School of Law since 1996. He is a member of the American Association of Law School's Contract Law Section. He is also a member of the Teaching Taxation Committee of the American Bar Association Section of Taxation, for which he has served as an editor of the *Tax Lawyer*. Professor Doti has written numerous articles for a variety of law reviews and professional journals, including the *Denver University Law Review* and *Tax Notes*. He is author of the Federal Income Tax CD series published by Thomson West as the Sum and Substance "Outstanding Professor" Series.

He is a member of the California, Colorado and Illinois bars and is certified as a tax law specialist by the California Board of Legal Specialization. Professor Doti has been teaching contract law since 1997. He teaches tax law courses as well and founded the Tax Law Emphasis program at Chapman.

PROLOGUE

First year law students like to identify the "black letter" rules of law wherever possible. The study of any law subject can be a daunting task. Students are frustrated by the conflict between learning a myriad of rules of law and the analytical process of applying such rules to varying fact patterns. My purpose is to help you learn and retain the rules of law in a visual manner.

Some contracts rules of law are quite confusing. This is particularly true of some provisions of Article 2 (Sales) of the Uniform Commercial Code (UCC). The exasperating "battle of the forms" rules of law in UCC § 2-207 and buyer and seller's remedies are good examples. A flowchart approach helps to sort out the varying rules in an organized way.

This book is a combination of schematic flowcharts that visually plot basic rules of contract law and selected cases that apply such rules. All of the flowcharts have been modified since prior editions to more fully and accurately identify the current rules of law.

I am grateful to my many research assistants at Chapman University School of Law who helped put this edition together. They include Troy Young, Jason Armbruster and Andrew Gahan.

If you have any questions or comments about this work, please contact me at fdoti@chapman.edu. You can also write to me at Chapman University School of Law, One University Drive, Orange, CA 92866.

Frank J. Doti

TABLE OF FLOWCHARTS

TABLE OF RESTATEMENT AND UCC CONTENTS

CONTRACT LAW
FLOWCHARTS AND CASES

A Student's Visual Guide to
Understanding Contracts

Third Edition

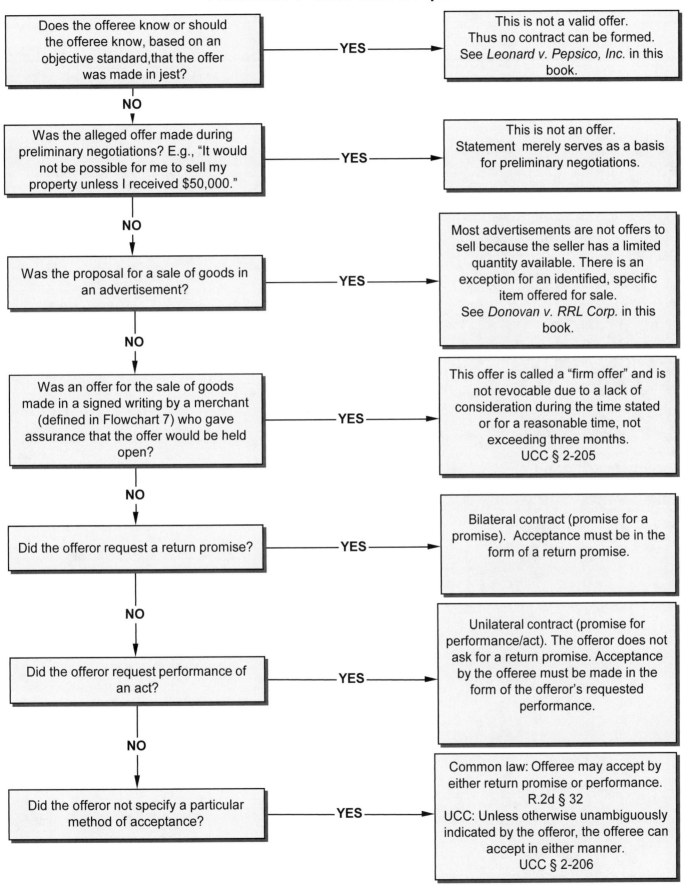

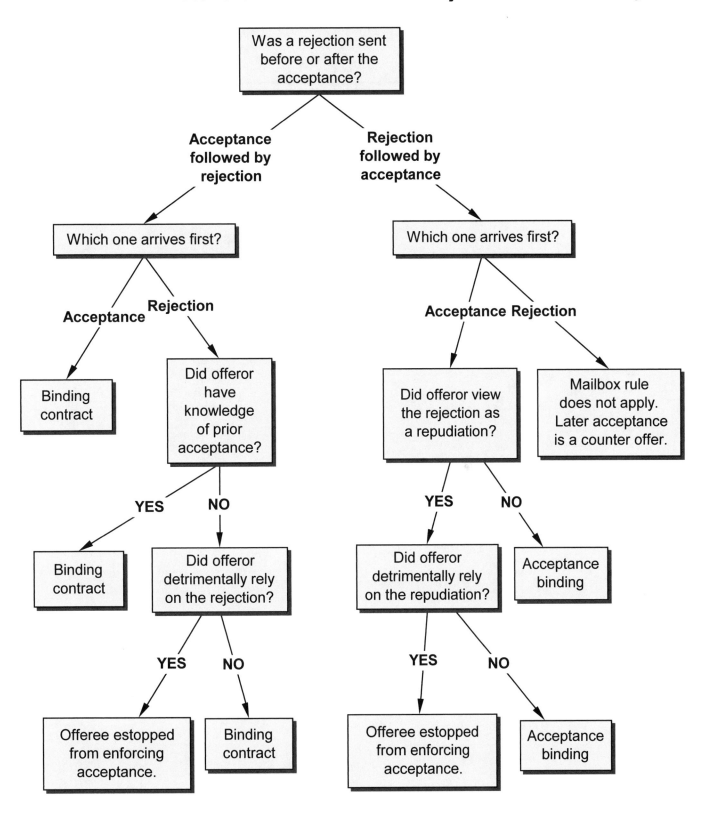

[1] This flowchart explains a situation where an offeree has sent both an acceptance and a rejection to the offeror. The general rule is that an acceptance is effective upon placement in the mail or other dispatch. A rejection is effective upon receipt by the offeror.

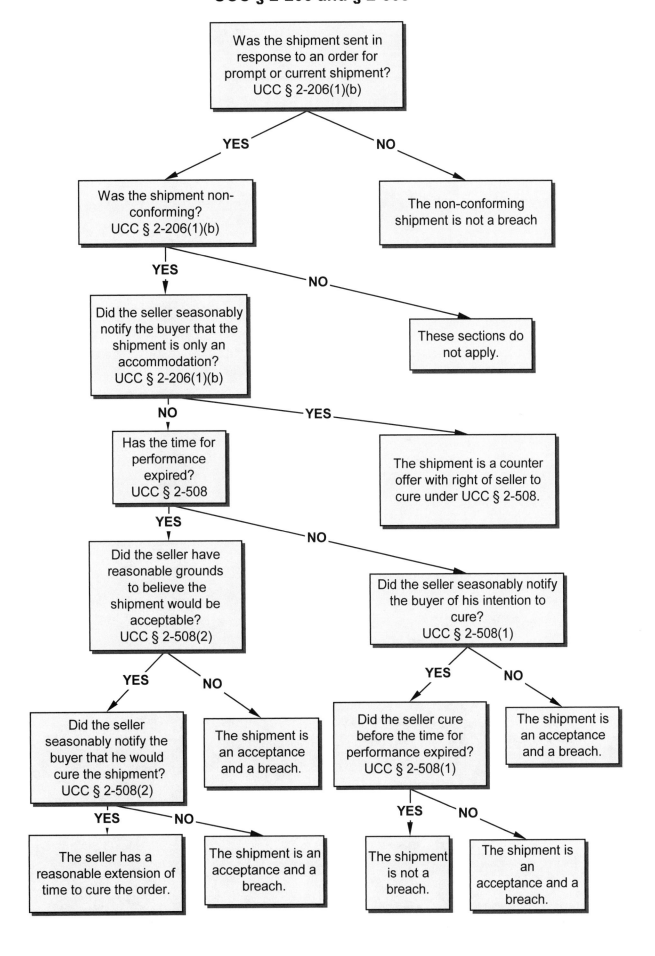

Where Both Parties Are Merchants[1]

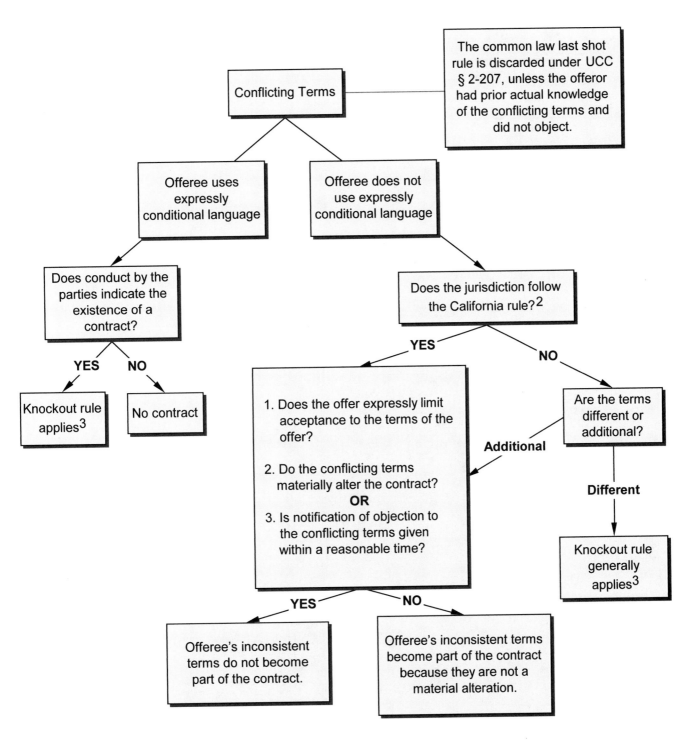

1 "Merchant" is defined in Flowchart 7. As used in this flowchart, the term " offeree" may also refer to a party who sends a written confirmation with a conflicting term.

2 The California rule refers to those jurisdictions which find no distinction between "additional" and "different" in UCC § 2-207(2). Many jurisdictions apply the rules in UCC § 2-207(2) only if the conflicting term is an additional as opposed to different term.

3 The knockout rule refers to UCC § 2-207(3), under which both parties' inconsistent terms do not become part of the contract. If UCC Article 2 has a provision which covers the matter, the applicable UCC provision is applied as a gap-filler in place of the inconsistent terms.

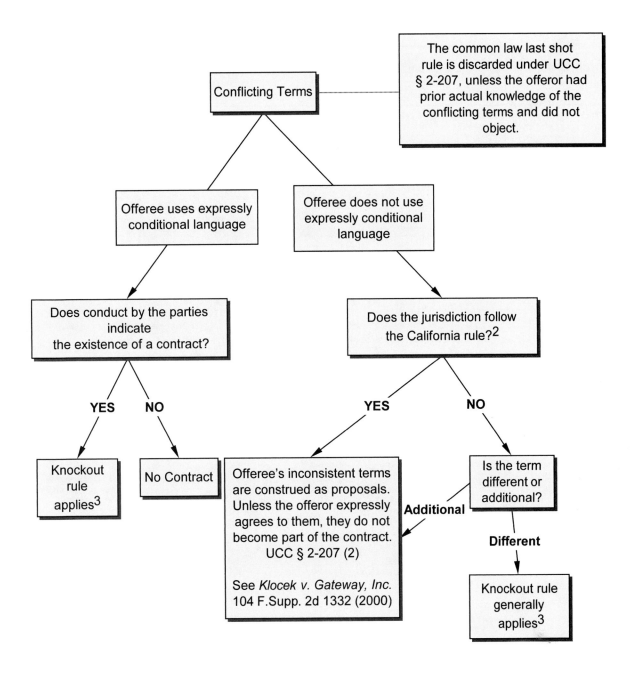

1 "Merchant" is defined in Flowchart 7. As used in this flowchart, the term " offeree" may also refer to a party who sends a written confirmation with a conflicting term.

2 The California rule refers to those jurisdictions which find no distinction between "additional" and "different" in UCC § 2-207(2). Many jurisdictions apply the rules in UCC § 2-207(2) only if the conflicting terms are additional as opposed to different terms.

3 The knockout rule refers to UCC § 2-207(3), under which both parties' inconsistent terms do not become part of the contract. If UCC Article 2 has a provision which covers the matter, the applicable UCC provision is applied as a gap-filler in place of the inconsistent terms.

Flowchart 6 Promissory Estoppel and Quasi-Contract

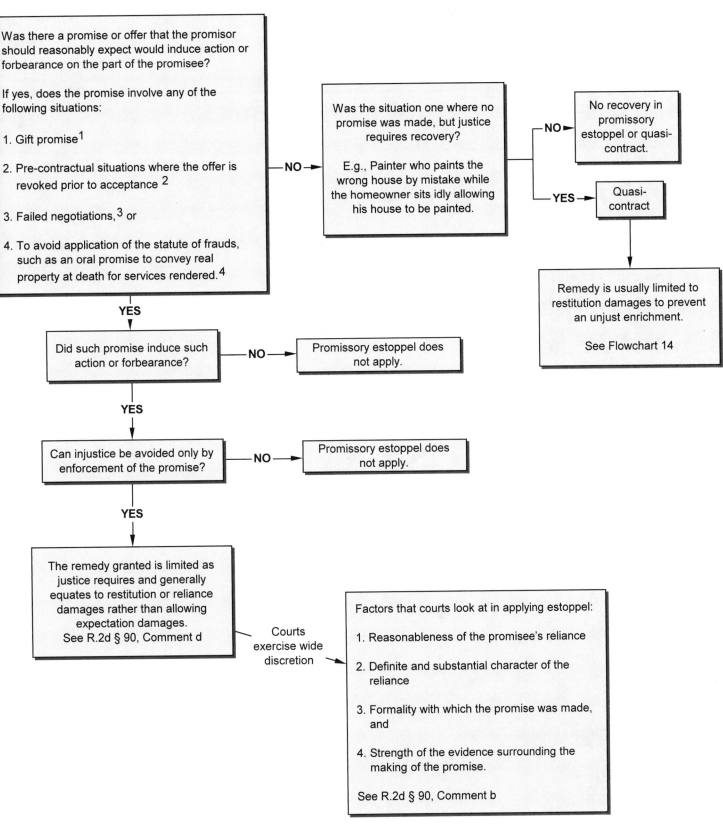

1 See *Ricketts v. Scothorn*, 57 Neb. 51 (1898).

2 See *Drennan v. Star Paving Co.*, 51 Cal.2d 409 (1958).

3 See *Hoffman v. Red Owl Stores*, 26 Wis.2d 683 (1965).

4 See *Monarco v. Lo Greco*, 35 Cal.2d 621 (1950).

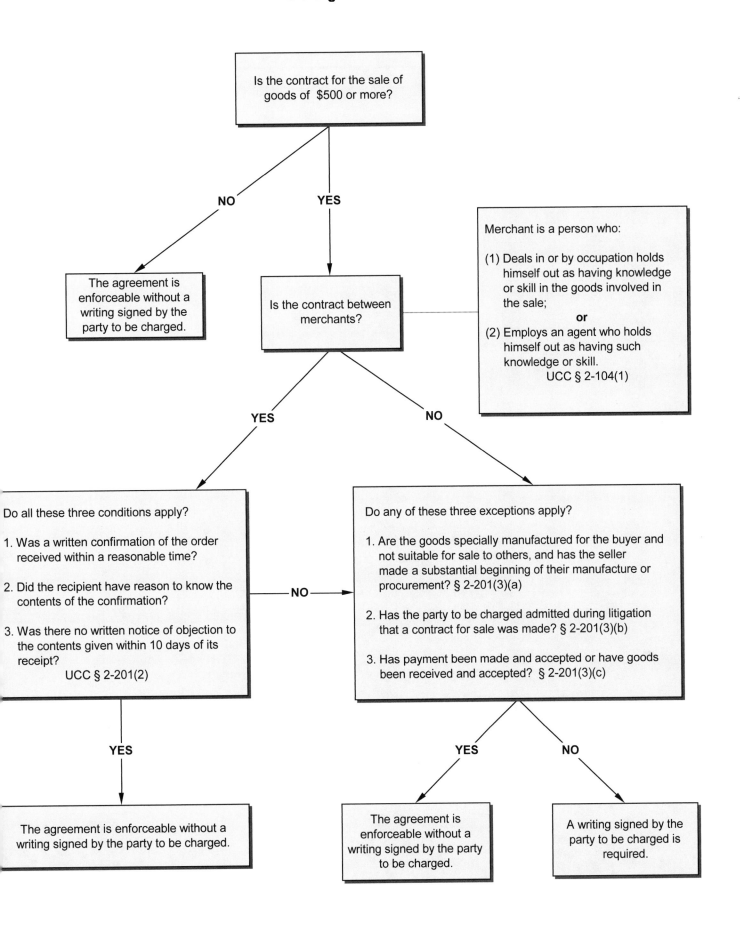

Example	Rule	Is a Writing Required?

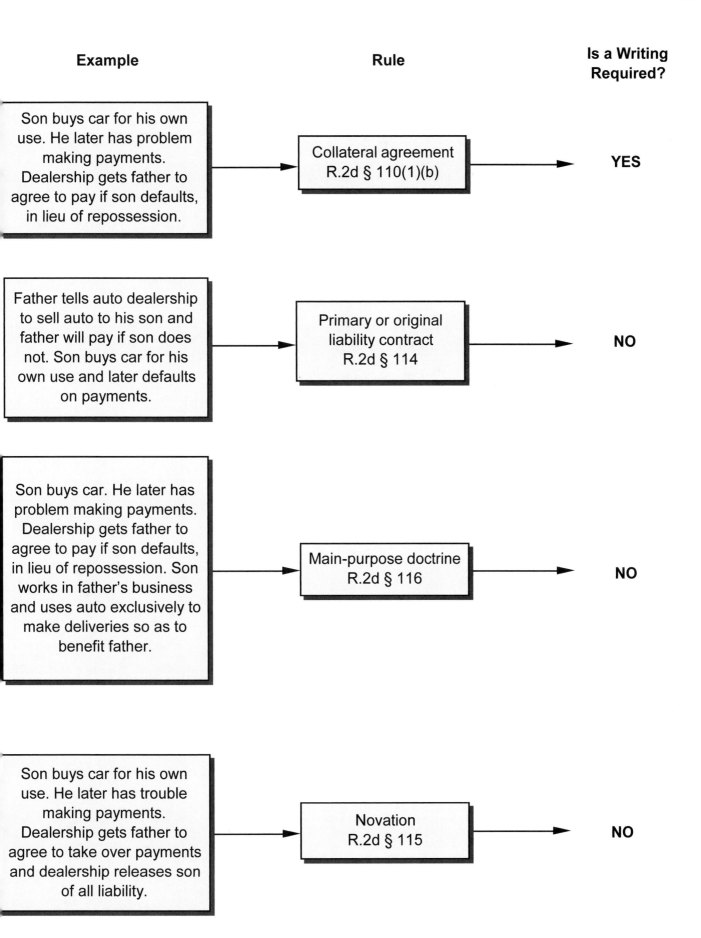

Example	Rule	Is a Writing Required?
Son buys car for his own use. He later has problem making payments. Dealership gets father to agree to pay if son defaults, in lieu of repossession.	Collateral agreement R.2d § 110(1)(b)	**YES**
Father tells auto dealership to sell auto to his son and father will pay if son does not. Son buys car for his own use and later defaults on payments.	Primary or original liability contract R.2d § 114	**NO**
Son buys car. He later has problem making payments. Dealership gets father to agree to pay if son defaults, in lieu of repossession. Son works in father's business and uses auto exclusively to make deliveries so as to benefit father.	Main-purpose doctrine R.2d § 116	**NO**
Son buys car for his own use. He later has trouble making payments. Dealership gets father to agree to take over payments and dealership releases son of all liability.	Novation R.2d § 115	**NO**

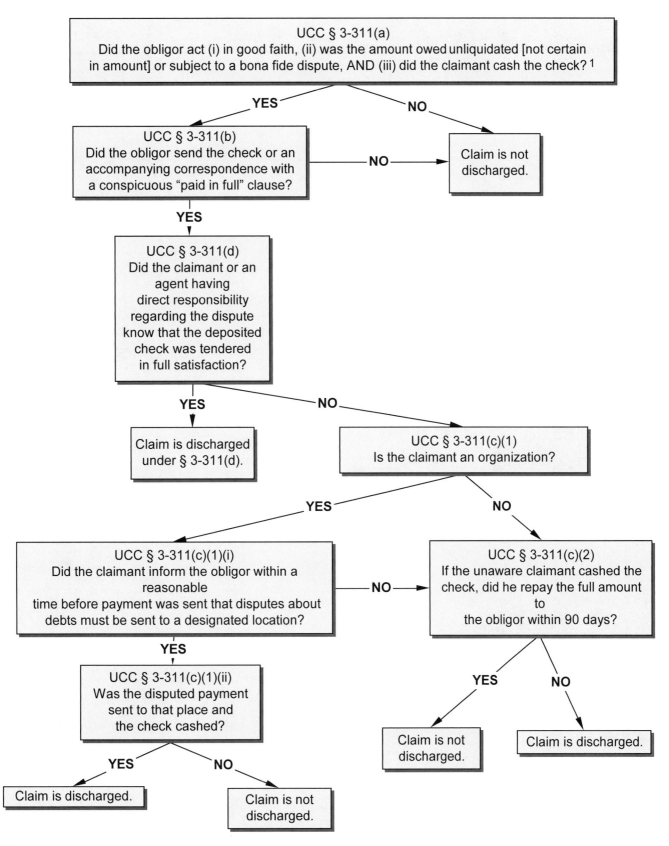

1 The obligor is the party who pays by check or other negotiable instrument. The claimant is the party who receives the check or other negotiable instrument.

Flowchart 10   Fraud and Misrepresentation

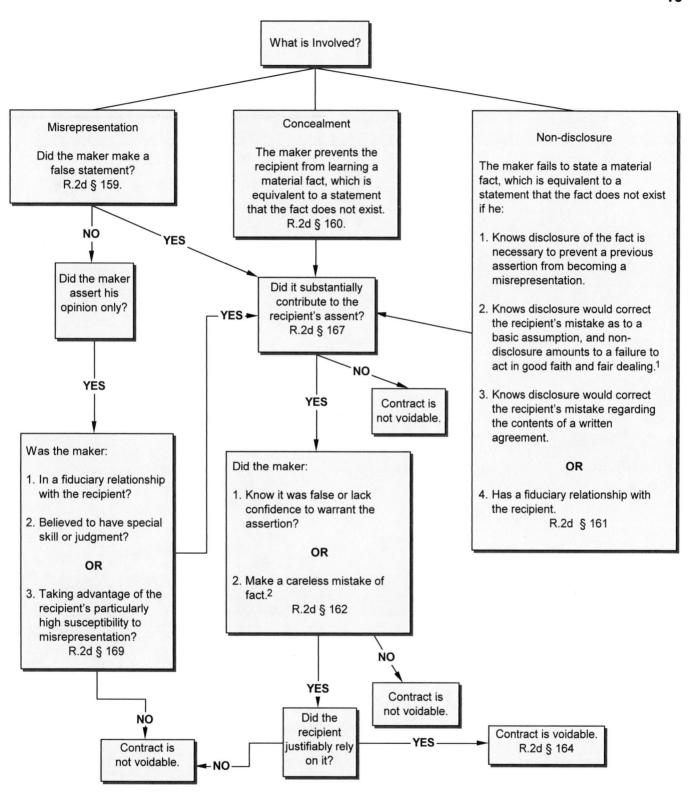

What is Involved?

Misrepresentation

Did the maker make a false statement?
R.2d § 159.

Concealment

The maker prevents the recipient from learning a material fact, which is equivalent to a statement that the fact does not exist.
R.2d § 160.

Non-disclosure

The maker fails to state a material fact, which is equivalent to a statement that the fact does not exist if he:

1. Knows disclosure of the fact is necessary to prevent a previous assertion from becoming a misrepresentation.

2. Knows disclosure would correct the recipient's mistake as to a basic assumption, and non-disclosure amounts to a failure to act in good faith and fair dealing.[1]

3. Knows disclosure would correct the recipient's mistake regarding the contents of a written agreement.

OR

4. Has a fiduciary relationship with the recipient.
R.2d § 161

NO → Did the maker assert his opinion only?

YES → Did it substantially contribute to the recipient's assent?
R.2d § 167

YES

Was the maker:

1. In a fiduciary relationship with the recipient?

2. Believed to have special skill or judgment?

OR

3. Taking advantage of the recipient's particularly high susceptibility to misrepresentation?
R.2d § 169

YES →

NO → Contract is not voidable.

NO → Contract is not voidable.

YES

Did the maker:

1. Know it was false or lack confidence to warrant the assertion?

OR

2. Make a careless mistake of fact.[2]
R.2d § 162

NO → Contract is not voidable.

YES

Did the recipient justifiably rely on it?

NO → Contract is not voidable.

YES → Contract is voidable.
R.2d § 164

---

[1] The mistake must relate to a basic assumption on which the party entered into the contract. If one of the parties has superior knowledge concerning the subject matter of the contract, generally that party has no duty to disclose the information. For example, a buyer who believes there may be valuable oil deposits under seller's land has no duty to inform the seller.

[2] A careless mistake of fact occurs when the maker does not have confidence in the truth of the assertion or knows that he does not have a basis for the assertion. Restatement 2d § 162(1)

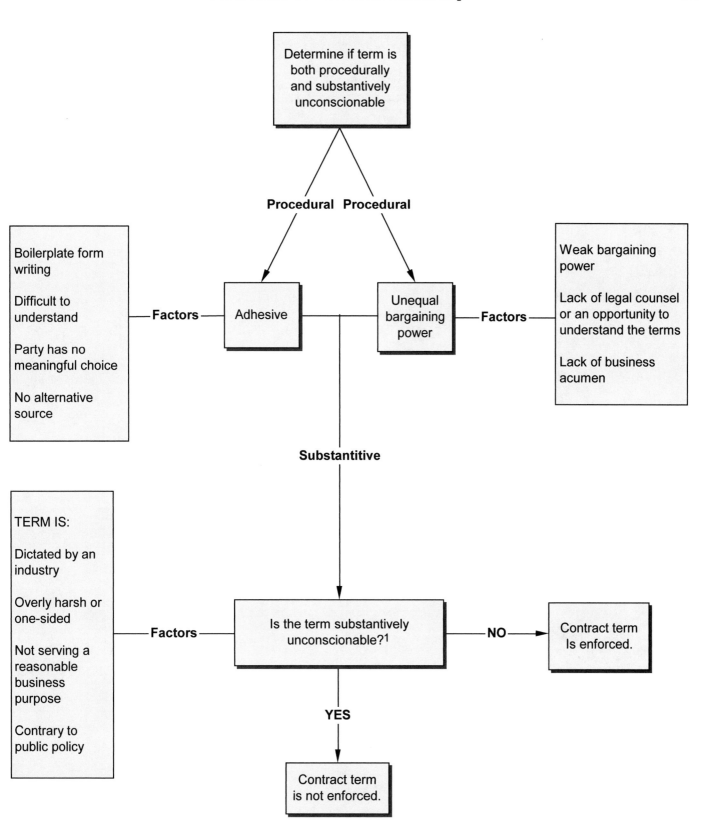

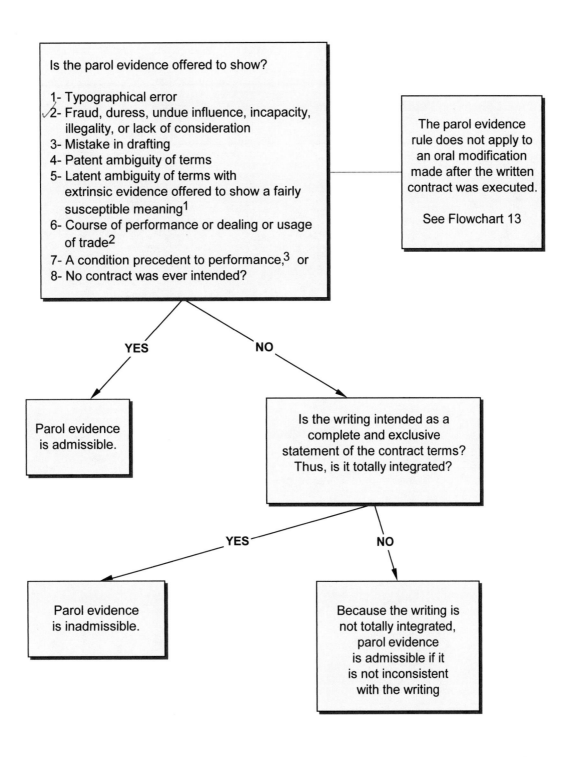

Is the parol evidence offered to show?

1- Typographical error
2- Fraud, duress, undue influence, incapacity, illegality, or lack of consideration
3- Mistake in drafting
4- Patent ambiguity of terms
5- Latent ambiguity of terms with extrinsic evidence offered to show a fairly susceptible meaning[1]
6- Course of performance or dealing or usage of trade[2]
7- A condition precedent to performance,[3] or
8- No contract was ever intended?

The parol evidence rule does not apply to an oral modification made after the written contract was executed.

See Flowchart 13

YES

Parol evidence is admissible.

NO

Is the writing intended as a complete and exclusive statement of the contract terms? Thus, is it totally integrated?

YES

Parol evidence is inadmissible.

NO

Because the writing is not totally integrated, parol evidence is admissible if it is not inconsistent with the writing

[1] If there is a latent ambiguity about the meaning of words in a writing, some courts will make a preliminary consideration of extrinsic evidence to determine if the words are fairly susceptible to an alternate interpretation. *Pacific Gas & Electric. v. G.W. Thomas Drayage & Rigging*, 69 Cal.2d 33 (1968). See also *Dore v. Arnold Worldwide, Inc.* in this book.

[2] See *Ermolieff v. R.K.O. Radio Pictures, Inc.* in this book. See also *Nanakuli Paving & Rock Co. v. Shell Oil Co.*, 664 F.2d 772 (1981) and UCC § 2-202(a), § 1-303(e).

[3] This exception does not apply if the written agreement is inconsistent with the alleged oral condition precedent.

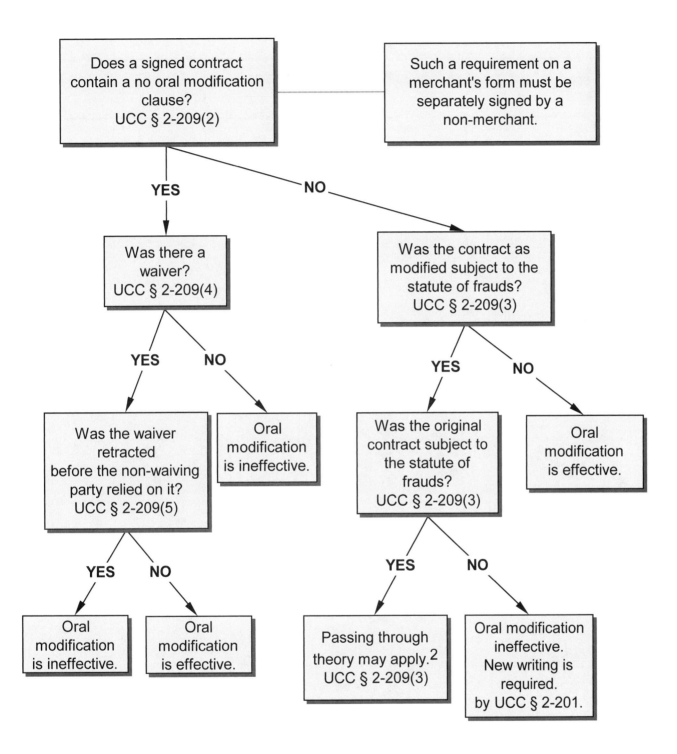

1 A modification of a non sale of goods agreement requires consideration. UCC § 2-209(1) applies to oral modifications under Article 2 of the UCC and states, unlike the common law, that no new consideration is necessary for a modification to be binding. However, the request for a modification must be made in good faith and for a legitimate commercial reason. See UCC § 2-209, Comment 2.

2 A majority of state courts require a new writing. A strong minority have adopted the "passing through theory" analysis under which a new writing is not required.

P = Non-Breaching Party   D = Breaching Party

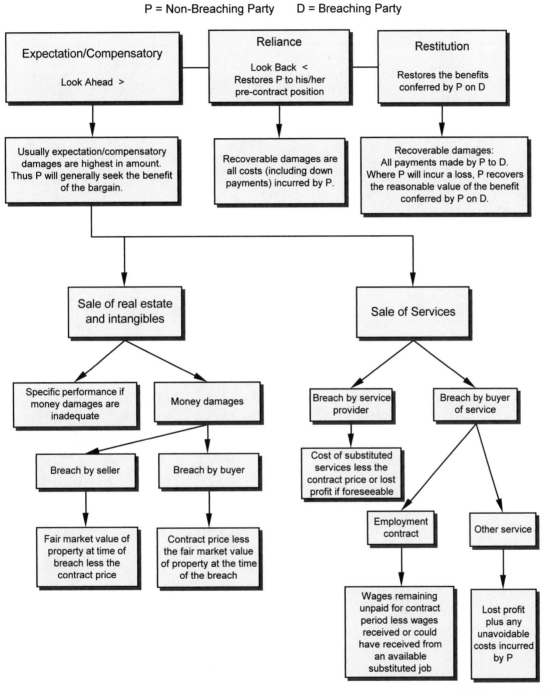

1 Consequential damages may be awarded as part of compensatory damages. They must be objectively foreseeable at the time of contracting. Substantially disproportionate consequential damages, which the breaching party would not reasonably be expected to assume, are not recoverable. *Kenford Co. v. County of Erie*, 537 N.E.2d 176 (NY 1989).

The non-breaching party has a duty to mitigate damages by avoiding costs and losses after notice of a breach.

A liquidated damages clause is enforceable if the non-breaching party can show that at the time of contracting:
(1) Anticipated damages were uncertain or difficult to prove, and (2) The agreed upon amount was a reasonable measure of expected damages.

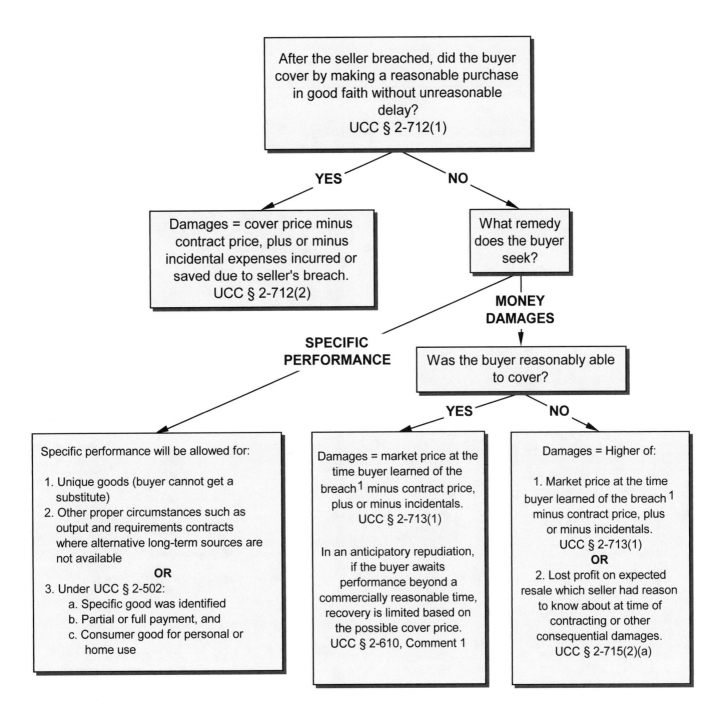

After the seller breached, did the buyer cover by making a reasonable purchase in good faith without unreasonable delay?
UCC § 2-712(1)

YES   **NO**

Damages = cover price minus contract price, plus or minus incidental expenses incurred or saved due to seller's breach.
UCC § 2-712(2)

What remedy does the buyer seek?

MONEY DAMAGES

SPECIFIC PERFORMANCE

Was the buyer reasonably able to cover?

YES   **NO**

Specific performance will be allowed for:

1. Unique goods (buyer cannot get a substitute)
2. Other proper circumstances such as output and requirements contracts where alternative long-term sources are not available
   OR
3. Under UCC § 2-502:
   a. Specific good was identified
   b. Partial or full payment, and
   c. Consumer good for personal or home use

Damages = market price at the time buyer learned of the breach[1] minus contract price, plus or minus incidentals.
UCC § 2-713(1)

In an anticipatory repudiation, if the buyer awaits performance beyond a commercially reasonable time, recovery is limited based on the possible cover price.
UCC § 2-610, Comment 1

Damages = Higher of:

1. Market price at the time buyer learned of the breach[1] minus contract price, plus or minus incidentals.
UCC § 2-713(1)
   OR
2. Lost profit on expected resale which seller had reason to know about at time of contracting or other consequential damages.
UCC § 2-715(2)(a)

[1] In the case of non-delivery, "learned of the breach" means the contract scheduled delivery date. A leading view, in the case of an anticipatory repudiation, is that "learned of the breach" means when the buyer learned of the repudiation plus a commercially reasonable time until the contract scheduled delivery date. *Cosden Oil & Chemical Co. v. Karl O. Helm Aktiengesellschaft*, 736 F.2d 1064 (5th Cir.1984).

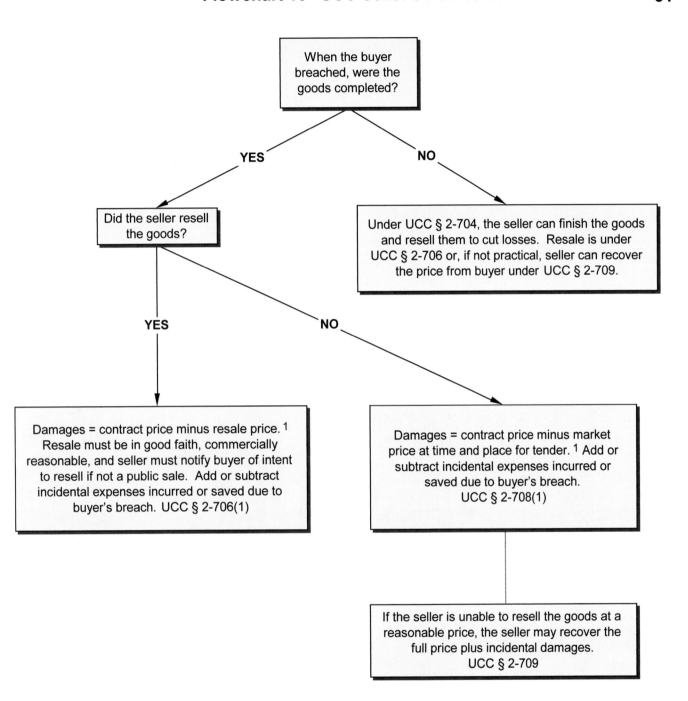

When the buyer breached, were the goods completed?

YES

NO

Did the seller resell the goods?

Under UCC § 2-704, the seller can finish the goods and resell them to cut losses. Resale is under UCC § 2-706 or, if not practical, seller can recover the price from buyer under UCC § 2-709.

YES

NO

Damages = contract price minus resale price. [1] Resale must be in good faith, commercially reasonable, and seller must notify buyer of intent to resell if not a public sale. Add or subtract incidental expenses incurred or saved due to buyer's breach. UCC § 2-706(1)

Damages = contract price minus market price at time and place for tender. [1] Add or subtract incidental expenses incurred or saved due to buyer's breach. UCC § 2-708(1)

If the seller is unable to resell the goods at a reasonable price, the seller may recover the full price plus incidental damages. UCC § 2-709

[1] A lost volume seller can recover lost profit (without reduction of overhead costs), if the contract price minus resale or market price is inadequate. A lost volume seller is one who has the demand and capacity to supply at a profit multiple units of the item to both the breaching party and another buyer. UCC § 2-708(2). *R.E. Davis Chemical Corp. v. Diasonics, Inc.*, 826 F.2d. 678 (7th Cir. 1987).

Flowchart 17   Mistake[1]

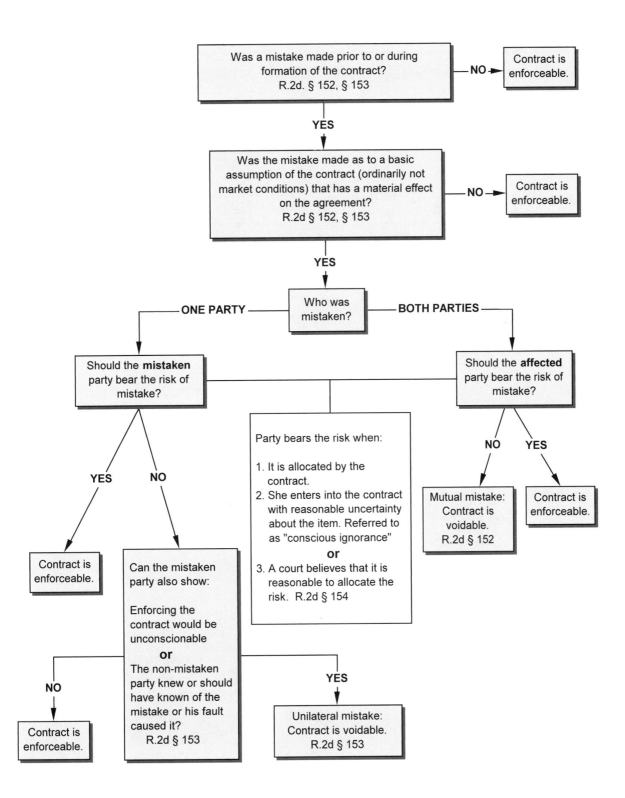

Was a mistake made prior to or during formation of the contract?
R.2d. § 152, § 153

— **NO** → Contract is enforceable.

↓ **YES**

Was the mistake made as to a basic assumption of the contract (ordinarily not market conditions) that has a material effect on the agreement?
R.2d § 152, § 153

— **NO** → Contract is enforceable.

↓ **YES**

Who was mistaken?

— **ONE PARTY** —

— **BOTH PARTIES** —

ONE PARTY:
Should the **mistaken** party bear the risk of mistake?

YES → Contract is enforceable.

NO → Can the mistaken party also show:

Enforcing the contract would be unconscionable
or
The non-mistaken party knew or should have known of the mistake or his fault caused it?
R.2d § 153

NO → Contract is enforceable.

YES → Unilateral mistake: Contract is voidable. R.2d § 153

Party bears the risk when:

1. It is allocated by the contract.
2. She enters into the contract with reasonable uncertainty about the item. Referred to as "conscious ignorance"
or
3. A court believes that it is reasonable to allocate the risk. R.2d § 154

BOTH PARTIES:
Should the **affected** party bear the risk of mistake?

NO → Mutual mistake: Contract is voidable. R.2d § 152

YES → Contract is enforceable.

---

[1] Restatement 2d § 161(b) provides that non-disclosure of a fact known to only one of the parties constitutes a misrepresentation, if there was a failure to act in good faith and in accordance with reasonable standards of fair dealing. Nevertheless, a party may reasonably expect the other party to take steps to inform himself and draw his own conclusions. For example, a buyer who believes there may be valuable oil deposits under the seller's land has no duty to inform the seller of that possibility. See R.2d § 154, Comment a, and R.2d § 161, Comment d.

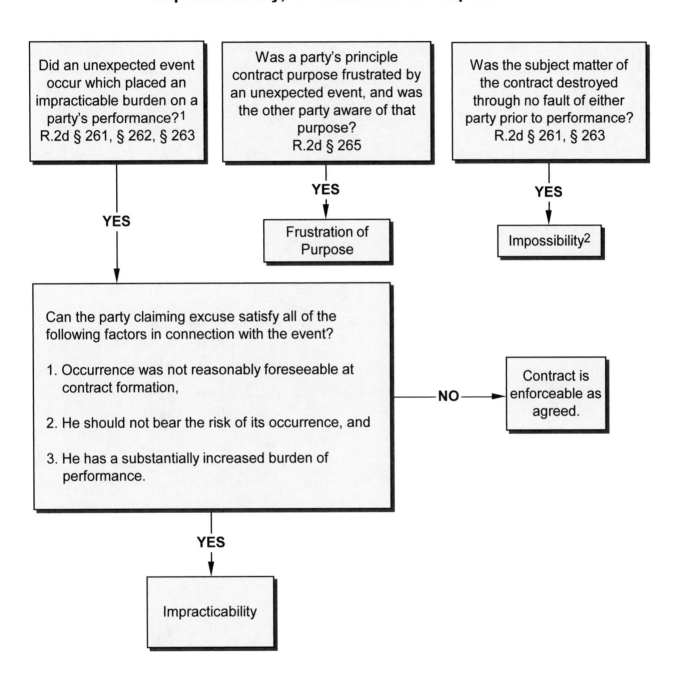

[1] Increased cost alone does not excuse performance, unless it places a great hardship on the performing party. UCC § 2-615, Comment 4. *Mineral Park Land Co. v. Howard*, 156 P. 458 (Cal. 1916). If the duty to perform a personal service cannot be delegated, death or illness of the performing party usually excuses performance. R.2d § 262. But see *Seitz v. Mark-O-Lite Sign Contractors, Inc.*, 510 A.2d 319 (N.J.Super. 1986).

[2] Restatement (Second) of Contracts merges impossibility into impracticability. R.2d § 261

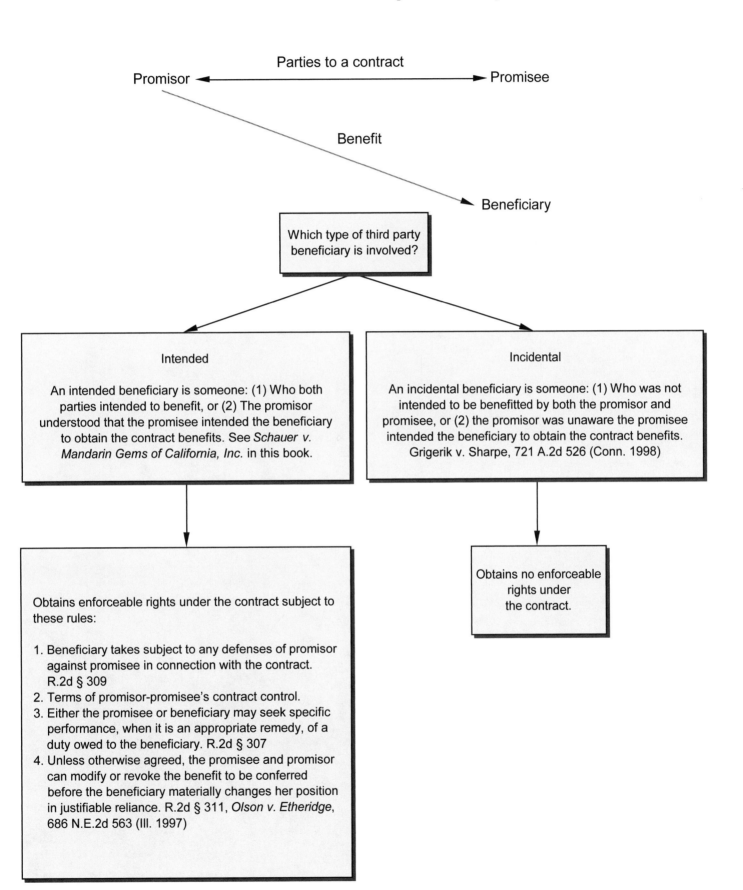

Parties to a contract

Promisor ← → Promisee

Benefit

Beneficiary

Which type of third party beneficiary is involved?

Intended

An intended beneficiary is someone: (1) Who both parties intended to benefit, or (2) The promisor understood that the promisee intended the beneficiary to obtain the contract benefits. See *Schauer v. Mandarin Gems of California, Inc.* in this book.

Incidental

An incidental beneficiary is someone: (1) Who was not intended to be benefitted by both the promisor and promisee, or (2) the promisor was unaware the promisee intended the beneficiary to obtain the contract benefits. *Grigerik v. Sharpe*, 721 A.2d 526 (Conn. 1998)

Obtains enforceable rights under the contract subject to these rules:

1. Beneficiary takes subject to any defenses of promisor against promisee in connection with the contract. R.2d § 309
2. Terms of promisor-promisee's contract control.
3. Either the promisee or beneficiary may seek specific performance, when it is an appropriate remedy, of a duty owed to the beneficiary. R.2d § 307
4. Unless otherwise agreed, the promisee and promisor can modify or revoke the benefit to be conferred before the beneficiary materially changes her position in justifiable reliance. R.2d § 311, *Olson v. Etheridge*, 686 N.E.2d 563 (Ill. 1997)

Obtains no enforceable rights under the contract.

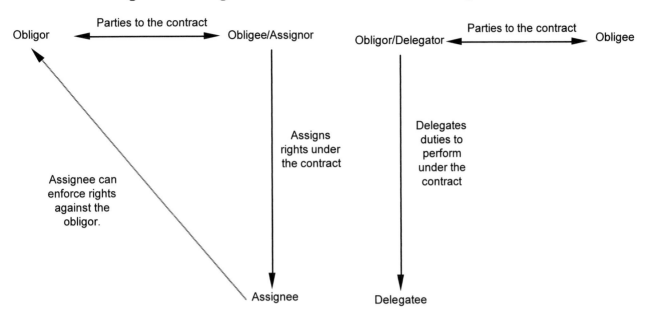

Assignment of Rights

Obligor ←—— Parties to the contract ——→ Obligee/Assignor

Assigns rights under the contract

Assignee can enforce rights against the obligor.

Assignee

Delegation of Duties

Obligor/Delegator ←—— Parties to the contract ——→ Obligee

Delegates duties to perform under the contract

Delegatee

ASSIGNMENT RULES

1. An assignment of rights without the obligor's required consent generally does not bar an assignment. R.2d § 322 and UCC § 2-210(4)

2. An assignment is ineffective if it materially:
   a. Changes obligor's duty,
   b. Increases obligor's risk,
   c. Impairs chance of return performance, or
   d. Reduces obligor's expected value.
   R.2d § 317(2)(a) and UCC § 2-210(2)

3. Obligor must know of the assignment, or obligor will be discharged if obligor provides the benefit to the assignor. R.2d § 338(1)

4. Assignee "stands in the shoes" of the assignor and takes subject to any defenses. R.2d § 336

5. Assignor cannot revoke an assignment made for value.

6. Gratuitous assignments are irrevocable if:
   a. Made in a signed writing,
   b. A document is delivered which is customarily used as evidence of ownership, or
   c. Assignee detrimentally relied on the assignment.

7. Except for irrevocable assignments, gratuitous oral assignments are terminated by:
   a. Death or incapacity of the assignor,
   b. Another inconsistent assignment, or
   c. Notification of termination.
   R.2d § 332

DELEGATION RULES

1. Non-delegation clauses are generally enforced to prevent a delegation.

2. Delegation is not allowed if the delegation materially increases the risk of proper performance.

3. Performance under a personal service contract, where there is a high degree of personal trust and confidence, cannot be delegated without the obligee's consent. Examples: Lawyer and doctor

4. The delegator remains liable, unless there is a novation whereby the obligee expressly releases the obligor/delegator of liability. R.2d § 329(2)

MAILBOX RULE FOR REJECTIONS
<u>APPLICABLE RESTATEMENT (SECOND) OF CONTRACTS</u>

§ 40. Time When Rejection Or Counter-Offer Terminates The Power Of Acceptance

Rejection or counter-offer by mail or telegram does not terminate the power of acceptance until received by the offeror, but limits the power so that a letter or telegram of acceptance started after the sending of an otherwise effective rejection or counter-offer is only a counter-offer unless the acceptance is received by the offeror before he receives the rejection or counter-offer.

Comment:

a. Receipt essential. A rejection terminates the offeree's power of acceptance because of the probability of reliance by the offeror, and there is no possibility of reliance until the rejection is received. See § 38. Hence the power continues until receipt. The same rule is applied by analogy to a counter-offer, although the reason is somewhat different: a counter-offer cannot be taken under consideration as a substitute proposal until it is received. See § 39. As to when a rejection is received, see § 68; compare Restatement, Second, Agency §§ 268-83, Uniform Commercial Code § 1-201(25) to (27).

b. Subsequent acceptance. Since a rejection or counter-offer is not effective until received, it may until that time be superseded by an acceptance. But the probability remains that the offeror will rely on the rejection or counter-offer if it is received before the acceptance. To protect the offeror in such reliance, the offeree who has dispatched a rejection is deprived of the benefit of the rule that an acceptance may take effect on dispatch (§63). The rule of this Section only applies, however, to a rejection or counter-offer which is otherwise effective. A rejection or counter-offer may be denied effect to terminate the power of acceptance if the original offer is itself a contract or if the offeror or offeree manifests an intention that the power continue. See §§ 37-39. Similarly, a purported rejection or counter-offer dispatched after an effective acceptance is in effect a revocation of acceptance, governed by § 63 rather than by this Section.

Illustration:

1. A makes B an offer by mail. B immediately after receiving the offer mails a letter of rejection. Within the time permitted by the offer B accepts. This acceptance creates a contract only if received before the rejection, or if the power of acceptance continues under §§ 37-39.

NON-CONFORMING GOODS
APPLICABLE UNIFORM COMMERCIAL CODE

§ 2-206. Offer and Acceptance in Formation of Contract.

(1) Unless otherwise unambiguously indicated by the language or circumstances

    (a) an offer to make a contract shall be construed as inviting acceptance in any manner and by any medium reasonable in the circumstances;

    (b) an order or other offer to buy goods for prompt or current shipment shall be construed as inviting acceptance either by a prompt promise to ship or by the prompt or current shipment of conforming or non-conforming goods, but such a shipment of non-conforming goods does not constitute an acceptance if the seller seasonably notifies the buyer that the shipment is offered only as an accommodation to the buyer.

(2) Where the beginning of a requested performance is a reasonable mode of acceptance an offeror who is not notified of acceptance within a reasonable time may treat the offer as having lapsed before acceptance.

* * *

§ 2-508. Cure by Seller of Improper Tender or Delivery; Replacement.

(1) Where any tender or delivery by the seller is rejected because non-conforming and the time for performance has not yet expired, the seller may seasonably notify the buyer of his intention to cure and may then within the contract time make a conforming delivery.

(2) Where the buyer rejects a non-conforming tender which the seller had reasonable grounds to believe would be acceptable with or without money allowance the seller may if he seasonably notifies the buyer have a further reasonable time to substitute a conforming tender.

"BATTLE OF THE FORMS"
<u>APPLICABLE UNIFORM COMMERCIAL CODE</u>

§ 2-207.   Additional Terms in Acceptance or Confirmation.

(1) A definite and seasonable expression of acceptance or a written confirmation which is sent within a reasonable time operates as an acceptance even though it states terms additional to or different from those offered or agreed upon, unless acceptance is expressly made conditional on assent to the additional or different terms.

(2) The additional terms are to be construed as proposals for addition to the contract. Between merchants such terms become part of the contract unless:

> (a) the offer expressly limits acceptance to the terms of the offer;

> (b) they materially alter it; or

> (c) notification of objection to them has already been given or is given within a reasonable time after notice of them is received.

(3) Conduct by both parties which recognizes the existence of a contract is sufficient to establish a contract for sale although the writings of the parties do not otherwise establish a contract. In such case the terms of the particular contract consist of those terms on which the writings of the parties agree, together with any supplementary terms incorporated under any other provisions of this Act.

STATUTE OF FRAUDS
<u>APPLICABLE UNIFORM COMMERCIAL CODE</u>

§ 2-201.   Formal Requirements; Statute of Frauds.

* * *

Official Comment

* * *

Purposes of Changes: The changed phraseology of this section is intended to make it clear that:

1. The required writing need not contain all the material terms of the contract and such material terms as are stated need not be precisely stated. All that is required is that the writing afford a basis for believing that the offered oral evidence rests on a real transaction. It may be written in lead pencil on a scratch pad. It need not indicate which party is the buyer and which the seller. The only term which must appear is the quantity term which need not be accurately stated but recovery is limited to the amount stated. The price, time and place of payment or delivery, the general quality of the goods, or any particular warranties may all be omitted.

* * *

Only three definite and invariable requirements as to the memorandum are made by this subsection. First, it must evidence a contract for the sale of goods; second, it must be "signed," a word which includes any authentication which identifies the party to be charged; and third, it must specify a quantity.

* * *

§ 2-104.   Definitions: "Merchant"; "Between Merchants"; "Financing Agency".

(1) "Merchant" means a person who deals in goods of the kind or otherwise by his occupation holds himself out as having knowledge or skill peculiar to the practices or goods involved in the transaction or to whom such knowledge or skill may be attributed by his employment of an agent or broker or other intermediary who by his occupation holds himself out as having such knowledge or skill.

* * *

(3) "Between merchants" means in any transaction with respect to which both parties are chargeable with the knowledge or skill of merchants.

§ 2-201. Formal Requirements; Statute of Frauds.

(1) Except as otherwise provided in this section a contract for the sale of goods for the price of $500 or more is not enforceable by way of action or defense unless there is some writing sufficient to indicate that a contract for sale has been made between the parties and signed by the party against whom enforcement is sought or by his authorized agent or broker. A writing is not insufficient because it omits or incorrectly states a term agreed upon but the contract is not enforceable under this paragraph beyond the quantity of goods shown in such writing.

(2) Between merchants if within a reasonable time a writing in confirmation of the contract and sufficient against the sender is received and the party receiving it has reason to know its contents, it satisfies the requirements of subsection (1) against such party unless written notice of objection to its contents is given within 10 days after it is received.

(3) A contract which does not satisfy the requirements of subsection (1) but which is valid in other respects is enforceable

> (a) if the goods are to be specially manufactured for the buyer and are not suitable for sale to others in the ordinary course of the seller's business and the seller, before notice of repudiation is received and under circumstances which reasonably indicate that the goods are for the buyer, has made either a substantial beginning of their manufacture or commitments for their procurement; or

> (b) if the party against whom enforcement is sought admits in his pleading, testimony or otherwise in court that a contract for sale was made, but the contract is not enforceable under this provision beyond the quantity of goods admitted; or

> (c) with respect to goods for which payment has been made and accepted or which have been received and accepted.

ACCORD AND SATISFACTION
APPLICABLE UNIFORM COMMERCIAL CODE

§ 3-311. Accord and Satisfaction by Use of Instrument.

(a) If a person against whom a claim is asserted proves that (i) that person in good faith tendered an instrument to the claimant as full satisfaction of the claim, (ii) the amount of the claim was unliquidated or subject to a bona fide dispute, and (iii) the claimant obtained payment of the instrument, the following subsections apply:

(b) Unless subsection (c) applies, the claim is discharged if the person against whom the claim is asserted proves that the instrument or an accompanying written communication contained a conspicuous statement to the effect that the instrument was tendered as full satisfaction of the claim.

(c) Subject to subsection (d), a claim is not discharged under subsection (b) if either of the following applies:

(1) The claimant, if an organization, proves that (i) within a reasonable time before the tender, the claimant sent a conspicuous statement to the person against whom the claim is asserted that communications concerning disputed debts, including an instrument tendered as full satisfaction of the debt, are to be sent to a designated person, office, or place, and (ii) the instrument or accompanying communication was not received by that designated person, office, or place.

(2) The claimant, whether or not an organization, proves that within 90 days after payment of the instrument, the claimant tendered repayment of the amount of the instrument to the person against whom the claim is asserted. This paragraph does not apply if that claimant is an organization that sent a statement complying with paragraph (1)(i).

(d) A claim is discharged if the person against whom the claim is asserted proves that within a reasonable time before collection of the instrument was initiated, the claimant, or an agent of the claimant having direct responsibility with respect to the disputed obligation, knew that the instrument was tendered in full satisfaction of the claim.

FRAUD & MISREPRESENTATION
APPLICABLE RESTATEMENT (SECOND) OF CONTRACTS

§ 159. Misrepresentation Defined

A misrepresentation is an assertion that is not in accord with the facts.

§ 160. When Action Is Equivalent to an Assertion (Concealment)

Action intended or known to be likely to prevent another from learning a fact is equivalent to an assertion that the fact does not exist.

§ 161. When Non-Disclosure Is Equivalent to an Assertion

A person's non-disclosure of a fact known to him is equivalent to an assertion that the fact does not exist in the following cases only:

(a) where he knows that disclosure of the fact is necessary to prevent some previous assertion from being a misrepresentation or from being fraudulent or material.

(b) where he knows that disclosure of the fact would correct a mistake of the other party as to a basic assumption on which that party is making the contract and if non-disclosure of the fact amounts to a failure to act in good faith and in accordance with reasonable standards of fair dealing.

(c) where he knows that disclosure of the fact would correct a mistake of the other party as to the contents or effect of a writing, evidencing or embodying an agreement in whole or in part.

(d) where the other person is entitled to know the fact because of a relation of trust and confidence between them.

§ 162.   When a Misrepresentation Is Fraudulent or Material

(1) A misrepresentation is fraudulent if the maker intends his assertion to induce a party to manifest his assent and the maker

    (a) knows or believes that the assertion is not in accord with the facts, or

    (b) does not have the confidence that he states or implies in the truth of the assertion, or

    (c) knows that he does not have the basis that he states or implies for the assertion.

(2) A misrepresentation is material if it would be likely to induce a reasonable person to manifest his assent, or if the maker knows that it would be likely to induce the recipient to do so.

* * *

§ 168.   Reliance on Assertions of Opinion

(1) An assertion is one of opinion if it expresses only a belief, without certainty, as to the existence of a fact or expresses only a judgment as to quality, value, authenticity, or similar matters.

(2) If it is reasonable to do so, the recipient of an assertion of a person's opinion as to facts not disclosed and not otherwise known to the recipient may properly interpret it as an assertion

    (a) that the facts known to that person are not incompatible with this opinion, or

    (b) that he knows facts sufficient to justify him in forming it.

PAROL EVIDENCE
APPLICABLE UNIFORM COMMERCIAL CODE

§ 2-202.   Final Written Expression: Parol or Extrinsic Evidence.

Terms with respect to which the confirmatory memoranda of the parties agree or which are otherwise set forth in a writing intended by the parties as a final expression of their agreement with respect to such terms as are included therein may not be contradicted by evidence of any prior agreement or of a contemporaneous oral agreement but may be explained or supplemented

(a) by course of performance, course of dealing, or usage of trade (Section 1-303); and

(b) by evidence of consistent additional terms unless the court finds the writing to have been intended also as a complete and exclusive statement of the terms of the agreement.

Official Comment

* * *

Purposes:

* * *

3. Under paragraph (b) consistent additional terms, not reduced to writing, may be proved unless the court finds that the writing was intended by both parties as a complete and exclusive statement of all the terms. If the additional terms are such that, if agreed upon, they would certainly have been included in the document in the view of the court, then evidence of their alleged making must be kept from the trier of fact.

MODIFICATION
APPLICABLE UNIFORM COMMERCIAL CODE

§ 2-209.   Modification, Rescission and Waiver.

(1) An agreement modifying a contract within this Article needs no consideration to be binding.

(2) A signed agreement which excludes modification or rescission except by a signed writing cannot be otherwise modified or rescinded, but except as between merchants such a requirement on a form supplied by the merchant must be separately signed by the other party.

(3) The requirements of the statute of frauds section of this Article (Section 2-201) must be satisfied if the contract as modified is within its provisions.

(4) Although an attempt at modification or rescission does not satisfy the requirements of subsection (2) or (3) it can operate as a waiver.

(5) A party who has made a waiver affecting an executory portion of the contract may retract the waiver by reasonable notification received by the other party that strict performance will be required of any term waived, unless the retraction would be unjust in view of a material change of position in reliance on the waiver.

§ 2-712.   "Cover"; Buyer's Procurement of Substitute Goods.

(1) After a breach within the preceding section the buyer may "cover" by making in good faith and without unreasonable delay any reasonable purchase of or contract to purchase goods in substitution for those due from the seller.

(2) The buyer may recover from the seller as damages the difference between the cost of cover and the contract price together with any incidental or consequential damages as hereinafter defined (Section 2-715), but less expenses saved in consequence of the seller's breach.

(3) Failure of the buyer to effect cover within this section does not bar him from any other remedy.

§ 2-713.   Buyer's Damages for Non-delivery or Repudiation.

(1) Subject to the provisions of this Article with respect to proof of market price (Section 2-723), the measure of damages for non-delivery or repudiation by the seller is the difference between the market price at the time when the buyer learned of the breach and the contract price together with any incidental and consequential damages provided in this Article (Section 2-715), but less expenses saved in consequence of the seller's breach.

(2) Market price is to be determined as of the place for tender or, in cases of rejection after arrival or revocation of acceptance, as of the place of arrival.

* * *

§ 2-715.   Buyer's Incidental and Consequential Damages.

(1) Incidental damages resulting from the seller's breach include expenses reasonably incurred in inspection, receipt, transportation and care and custody of goods rightfully rejected, any commercially reasonable charges, expenses or commissions in connection with effecting cover and any other reasonable expense incident to the delay or other breach.

(2) Consequential damages resulting from the seller's breach include

(a) any loss resulting from general or particular requirements and needs of which the seller at the time of contracting had reason to know and which could not reasonably be prevented by cover or otherwise; and

(b) injury to person or property proximately resulting from any breach of warranty.

SELLER'S REMEDIES
APPLICABLE UNIFORM COMMERCIAL CODE

§ 2-704.   Seller's Right to Identify Goods to the Contract Notwithstanding Breach
or to Salvage Unfinished Goods.

(1) An aggrieved seller under the preceding section may

(a) identify to the contract conforming goods not already identified if at the time
he learned of the breach they are in his possession or control;

(b) treat as the subject of resale goods which have demonstrably been
intended for the particular contract even though those goods are
unfinished.

(2) Where the goods are unfinished an aggrieved seller may in the exercise of
reasonable commercial judgment for the purposes of avoiding loss and of effective
realization either complete the manufacture and wholly identify the goods to the contract
or cease manufacture and resell for scrap or salvage value or proceed in any other
reasonable manner.

* * *

§ 2-706.   Seller's Resale Including Contract for Resale.

(1) Under the conditions stated in Section 2-703 on seller's remedies, the seller may
resell the goods concerned or the undelivered balance thereof. Where the resale is made
in good faith and in a commercially reasonable manner the seller may recover the
difference between the resale price and the contract price together with any incidental
damages allowed under the provisions of this Article (Section 2-710), but less expenses
saved in consequence of the buyer's breach.

(2) Except as otherwise provided in subsection (3) or unless otherwise agreed resale
may be at public or private sale including sale by way of one or more contracts to sell or
of identification to an existing contract of the seller. Sale may be as a unit or in parcels
and at any time and place and on any terms but every aspect of the sale including the
method, manner, time, place and terms must be commercially reasonable. The resale
must be reasonably identified as referring to the broken contract, but it is not necessary
that the goods be in existence or that any or all of them have been identified to the
contract before the breach.

(3) Where the resale is at private sale the seller must give the buyer reasonable
notification of his intention to resell.

* * *

(6) The seller is not accountable to the buyer for any profit made on any resale. A person in the position of a seller (Section 2-707) or a buyer who has rightfully rejected or justifiably revoked acceptance must account for any excess over the amount of his security interest, as hereinafter defined (subsection (3) of Section 2-711).

* * *

§ 2-708.   Seller's Damages for Non-acceptance or Repudiation.

(1) Subject to subsection (2) and to the provisions of this Article with respect to proof of market price (Section 2-723), the measure of damages for non-acceptance or repudiation by the buyer is the difference between the market price at the time and place for tender and the unpaid contract price together with any incidental damages provided in this Article (Section 2-710), but less expenses saved in consequence of the buyer's breach.

(2) If the measure of damages provided in subsection (1) is inadequate to put the seller in as good a position as performance would have done then the measure of damages is the profit (including reasonable overhead) which the seller would have made from full performance by the buyer, together with any incidental damages provided in this Article (Section 2-710), due allowance for costs reasonably incurred and due credit for payments or proceeds of resale.

§ 2-709.   Action for the Price.

(1) When the buyer fails to pay the price as it becomes due the seller may recover, together with any incidental damages under the next section, the price

  (a) of goods accepted or of conforming goods lost or damaged within a commercially reasonable time after risk of their loss has passed to the buyer; and

  (b) of goods identified to the contract if the seller is unable after reasonable effort to resell them at a reasonable price or the circumstances reasonably indicate that such effort will be unavailing.

(2) Where the seller sues for the price he must hold for the buyer any goods which have been identified to the contract and are still in his control except that if resale becomes possible he may resell them at any time prior to the collection of the judgment. The net proceeds of any such resale must be credited to the buyer and payment of the judgment entitles him to any goods not resold.

(3) After the buyer has wrongfully rejected or revoked acceptance of the goods or has failed to make a payment due or has repudiated (Section 2-610), a seller who is held not entitled to the price under this section shall nevertheless be awarded damages for non-acceptance under the preceding section.

MISTAKE
<u>APPLICABLE RESTATEMENT (SECOND) OF CONTRACTS</u>

§ 151.   Mistake Defined

A mistake is a belief that is not in accord with the facts.

§ 152.   When Mistake of Both Parties Makes a Contract Voidable

(1) Where a mistake of both parties at the time a contract was made as to a basic assumption on which the contract was made has a material effect on the agreed exchange of performances, the contract is voidable by the adversely affected party unless he bears the risk of the mistake under the rule stated in § 154.

(2) In determining whether the mistake has a material effect on the agreed exchange of performances, account is taken of any relief by way of reformation, restitution, or otherwise.

§ 153.   When Mistake of One Party Makes a Contract Voidable

Where a mistake of one party at the time a contract was made as to a basic assumption on which he made the contract has a material effect on the agreed exchange of performances that is adverse to him, the contract is voidable by him if he does not bear the risk of the mistake under the rule stated in § 154, and

(a) the effect of the mistake is such that enforcement of the contract would be unconscionable, or

(b) the other party had reason to know of the mistake or his fault caused the mistake.

§ 154.   When a Party Bears the Risk of a Mistake

A party bears the risk of a mistake when

(a) the risk is allocated to him by agreement of the parties, or

(b) he is aware, at the time the contract is made, that he has only limited knowledge with respect to the facts to which the mistake relates but treats his limited knowledge as sufficient, or

(c) the risk is allocated to him by the court on the ground that it is reasonable in the circumstances to do so.

TABLE OF CONTENTS -- SELECTED REPORTED CASES

Case 1:   **Objective Theory Applied**

Leonard v. Pepsico, Inc.
United States District Court, S.D. New York, 1999
88 F.Supp.2d 116

KIMBA M. WOOD, District Judge

Plaintiff brought this action seeking, among other things, specific performance of an alleged offer of a Harrier Jet, featured in a television advertisement for defendant's "Pepsi Stuff" promotion. Defendant has moved for summary judgment pursuant to Federal Rule of Civil Procedure 56. For the reasons stated below, defendant's motion is granted.

I. Background

This case arises out of a promotional campaign conducted by defendant, the producer and distributor of the soft drinks Pepsi and Diet Pepsi. The promotion, entitled "Pepsi Stuff," encouraged consumers to collect "Pepsi Points" from specially marked packages of Pepsi or Diet Pepsi and redeem these points for merchandise featuring the Pepsi logo. Before introducing the promotion nationally, defendant conducted a test of the promotion in the Pacific Northwest from October 1995 to March 1996. A Pepsi Stuff catalog was distributed to consumers in the test market, including Washington State. Plaintiff is a resident of Seattle, Washington. While living in Seattle, plaintiff saw the Pepsi Stuff commercial that he contends constituted an offer of a Harrier Jet.

A. *The Alleged Offer*

Because whether the television commercial constituted an offer is the central question in this case, the Court will describe the commercial in detail. The commercial opens upon an idyllic, suburban morning, where the chirping of birds in sun-dappled trees welcomes a paperboy on his morning route. As the newspaper hits the stoop of a conventional two-story house, the tattoo of a military drum introduces the subtitle, "MONDAY 7:58 AM." The stirring strains of a martial air mark the appearance of a well-coiffed teenager preparing to leave for school, dressed in a shirt emblazoned with the Pepsi logo, a red-white-and-blue ball. While the teenager confidently preens, the military drumroll again sounds as the subtitle "T-SHIRT 75 PEPSI POINTS" scrolls across the screen. Bursting from his room, the teenager strides down the hallway wearing a leather jacket. The drumroll sounds again, as the subtitle "LEATHER JACKET 1450 PEPSI POINTS" appears. The teenager opens the door of his house and, unfazed by the glare of the early morning sunshine, puts on a pair of sunglasses. The drumroll then accompanies the subtitle "SHADES 175 PEPSI POINTS." A voiceover then intones, "Introducing the new Pepsi Stuff catalog," as the camera focuses on the cover of the catalog.[1]

The scene then shifts to three young boys sitting in front of a high school building. The boy in the middle is intent on his Pepsi Stuff Catalog, while the boys on either side are each drinking Pepsi. The three boys gaze in awe at an object rushing overhead, as the military march builds to a crescendo. The Harrier Jet is not yet visible, but the observer senses the presence of a mighty plane as the extreme winds generated by its flight create a paper maelstrom in a classroom devoted to an otherwise dull physics lesson. Finally, the Harrier Jet swings into view and lands by the side of the school building, next to a bicycle rack. Several students run for cover, and the velocity of the wind strips one hapless faculty member down to his underwear. While the faculty member is being deprived of his dignity, the voiceover announces: "Now the more Pepsi you drink, the more great stuff you're gonna get."

The teenager opens the cockpit of the fighter and can be seen, helmetless, holding a Pepsi. "[L]ooking very pleased with himself," the teenager exclaims, "Sure beats the bus," and chortles. The military drumroll sounds a final time, as the following words appear: "HARRIER FIGHTER 7,000,000 PEPSI POINTS." A few seconds later, the following appears in more stylized script: "Drink Pepsi—Get Stuff." With that message, the music and the commercial end with a triumphant flourish.

Inspired by this commercial, plaintiff set out to obtain a Harrier Jet. Plaintiff explains that he is "typical of the 'Pepsi Generation' . . . he is young, has an adventurous spirit, and the notion of obtaining a Harrier Jet appealed to him enormously." Plaintiff consulted the Pepsi Stuff Catalog. The Catalog features youths dressed in Pepsi Stuff regalia or enjoying Pepsi Stuff accessories, such as "Blue Shades" ("As if you need another reason to look forward to sunny days."), "Pepsi Tees" ("Live in 'em. Laugh in 'em. Get in 'em."), "Bag of Balls" ("Three balls. One bag. No rules."), and "Pepsi Phone Card" ("Call your mom!"). The Catalog specifies the number of Pepsi Points required to obtain promotional merchandise. (*See* Catalog, at rear foldout pages.) The Catalog includes an Order Form which lists, on one side, fifty-three items of Pepsi Stuff merchandise redeemable for Pepsi Points. Conspicuously absent from the Order Form is any entry or description of a Harrier Jet. The amount of Pepsi Points required to obtain the listed merchandise ranges from 15 (for a "Jacket Tattoo" ("Sew 'em on your jacket, not your arm.")) to 3300 (for a "Fila Mountain Bike" ("Rugged. All-terrain. Exclusively for Pepsi.")). It should be noted that plaintiff objects to the implication that because an item was not shown in the Catalog, it was unavailable.

The rear foldout pages of the Catalog contain directions for redeeming Pepsi Points for merchandise. These directions note that merchandise may be ordered "only" with the original Order Form. The Catalog notes that in the event that a consumer lacks enough Pepsi Points to

---

[1] At this point, the following message appears at the bottom of the screen: "Offer not available in all areas. See details on specially marked packages."

obtain a desired item, additional Pepsi Points may be purchased for ten cents each; however, at least fifteen original Pepsi Points must accompany each order.

Although plaintiff initially set out to collect 7,000,000 Pepsi Points by consuming Pepsi products, it soon became clear to him that he "would not be able to buy (let alone drink) enough Pepsi to collect the necessary Pepsi Points fast enough." Reevaluating his strategy, plaintiff "focused for the first time on the packaging materials in the Pepsi Stuff promotion," (*id.*) and realized that buying Pepsi Points would be a more promising option. Through acquaintances, plaintiff ultimately raised about $700,000.

B. *Plaintiff's Efforts to Redeem the Alleged Offer*

On or about March 27, 1996, plaintiff submitted an Order Form, fifteen original Pepsi Points, and a check for $700,008.50. Plaintiff appears to have been represented by counsel at the time he mailed his check; the check is drawn on an account of plaintiff's first set of attorneys. At the bottom of the Order Form, plaintiff wrote in "1 Harrier Jet" in the "Item" column and "7,000,000" in the "Total Points" column. In a letter accompanying his submission, plaintiff stated that the check was to purchase additional Pepsi Points "expressly for obtaining a new Harrier jet as advertised in your Pepsi Stuff commercial."

On or about May 7, 1996, defendant's fulfillment house rejected plaintiff's submission and returned the check, explaining that:

> The item that you have requested is not part of the Pepsi Stuff collection. It is not included in the catalogue or on the order form, and only catalogue merchandise can be redeemed under this program.

> The Harrier jet in the Pepsi commercial is fanciful and is simply included to create a humorous and entertaining ad. We apologize for any misunderstanding or confusion that you may have experienced and are enclosing some free product coupons for your use.

Plaintiff's previous counsel responded on or about May 14, 1996, as follows:

> Your letter of May 7, 1996 is totally unacceptable. We have reviewed the video tape of the Pepsi Stuff commercial . . . and it clearly offers the new Harrier jet for 7,000,000 Pepsi Points. Our client followed your rules explicitly. . . .

> This is a formal demand that you honor your commitment and make immediate arrangements to transfer the new Harrier jet to our client. If we do not receive transfer instructions within ten (10) business days of the date of this letter you will leave us no choice but to file an appropriate action against Pepsi . . . .

This letter was apparently sent onward to the advertising company responsible for the actual commercial, BBDO New York ("BBDO"). In a letter dated May 30, 1996, BBDO Vice President Raymond E. McGovern, Jr., explained to plaintiff that:

> I find it hard to believe that you are of the opinion that the Pepsi Stuff commercial ("Commercial") really offers a new Harrier Jet. The use of the Jet was clearly a joke that was meant to make the Commercial more humorous and entertaining. In my opinion, no reasonable person would agree with your analysis of the Commercial.

On or about June 17, 1996, plaintiff mailed a similar demand letter to defendant.

   *   *   *   *   *   *

II. Discussion

   *   *   *   *   *   *

C. *An Objective, Reasonable Person Would Not Have Considered the Commercial an Offer*

Plaintiff's understanding of the commercial as an offer must also be rejected because the Court finds that no objective person could reasonably have concluded that the commercial actually offered consumers a Harrier Jet.

1. *Objective Reasonable Person Standard*

In evaluating the commercial, the Court must not consider defendant's subjective intent in making the commercial, or plaintiff's subjective view of what the commercial offered, but what an objective, reasonable person would have understood the commercial to convey. *See Kay-R Elec. Corp. v. Stone & Weber Constr. Co.*, 23 F.3d 55, 57 (2d Cir.1994) ("We are not concerned with what was going through the heads of the parties at the time [of the alleged contract]. Rather, we are talking about the objective principles of contract law."); *Mesaros*, 845 F.2d at 1581 ("A basic rule of contracts holds that whether an offer has been made depends on the objective reasonableness of the alleged offeree's belief that the advertisement or solicitation was intended as an offer."); Farnsworth, *supra*, § 3.10, at 237; Williston, *supra*, § 4:7 at 296-97.

If it is clear that an offer was not serious, then no offer has been made:

> What kind of act creates a power of acceptance and is therefore an offer? It must be an expression of will or intention. It must be an act that leads the offeree reasonably to conclude that a power to create a contract is conferred. This applies to the content of the power as well as to the fact of its existence. It is on this

ground that we must exclude invitations to deal or acts of mere preliminary negotiation, and acts evidently done in jest or without intent to create legal relations.

Corbin on Contracts, § 1.11 at 30 (emphasis added). An obvious joke, of course, would not give rise to a contract. *See, e.g., Graves v. Northern N.Y. Pub. Co.*, 260 A.D. 900, 22 N.Y.S.2d 537 (1940) (dismissing claim to offer of $1000, which appeared in the "joke column" of the newspaper, to any person who could provide a commonly available phone number). On the other hand, if there is no indication that the offer is "evidently in jest," and that an objective, reasonable person would find that the offer was serious, then there may be a valid offer. *See Barnes*, 549 P.2d at 1155 ("[I]f the jest is not apparent and a reasonable hearer would believe that an offer was being made, then the speaker risks the formation of a contract which was not intended."); *see also Lucy v. Zehmer*, 196 Va. 493, 84 S.E.2d 516, 518, 520 (1954) (ordering specific performance of a contract to purchase a farm despite defendant's protestation that the transaction was done in jest as "'just a bunch of two doggoned drunks bluffing'").

*   *   *   *   *   *

3. *Whether the Commercial Was "Evidently Done In Jest"*

Plaintiff's insistence that the commercial appears to be a serious offer requires the Court to explain why the commercial is funny. Explaining why a joke is funny is a daunting task; as the essayist E.B. White has remarked, "Humor can be dissected, as a frog can, but the thing dies in the process . . . ." The commercial is the embodiment of what defendant appropriately characterizes as "zany humor."

First, the commercial suggests, as commercials often do, that use of the advertised product will transform what, for most youth, can be a fairly routine and ordinary experience. The military tattoo and stirring martial music, as well as the use of subtitles in a Courier font that scroll terse messages across the screen, such as "MONDAY 7:58 AM," evoke military and espionage thrillers. The implication of the commercial is that Pepsi Stuff merchandise will inject drama and moment into hitherto unexceptional lives. The commercial in this case thus makes the exaggerated claims similar to those of many television advertisements: that by consuming the featured clothing, car, beer, or potato chips, one will become attractive, stylish, desirable, and admired by all. A reasonable viewer would understand such advertisements as mere puffery, not as statements of fact, *see, e.g., Hubbard v. General Motors Corp.*, 95 Civ. 4362(AGS), 1996 WL 274018, at *6 (S.D.N.Y. May 22, 1996) (advertisement describing automobile as "Like a Rock," was mere puffery, not a warranty of quality); *Lovett*, 207 N.Y.S. at 756; and refrain from interpreting the promises of the commercial as being literally true.

Second, the callow youth featured in the commercial is a highly improbable pilot, one who could barely be trusted with the keys to his parents' car, much less the prize aircraft of the United States Marine Corps. Rather than checking the fuel gauges on his aircraft, the teenager spends his precious preflight minutes preening. The youth's concern for his coiffure appears to extend to his flying without a helmet. Finally, the teenager's comment that flying a Harrier Jet to school "sure beats the bus" evinces an improbably insouciant attitude toward the relative difficulty and danger of piloting a fighter plane in a residential area, as opposed to taking public transportation.

Third, the notion of traveling to school in a Harrier Jet is an exaggerated adolescent fantasy. In this commercial, the fantasy is underscored by how the teenager's schoolmates gape in admiration, ignoring their physics lesson. The force of the wind generated by the Harrier Jet blows off one teacher's clothes, literally defrocking an authority figure. As if to emphasize the fantastic quality of having a Harrier Jet arrive at school, the Jet lands next to a plebeian bike rack. This fantasy is, of course, extremely unrealistic. No school would provide landing space for a student's fighter jet, or condone the disruption the jet's use would cause.

Fourth, the primary mission of a Harrier Jet, according to the United States Marine Corps, is to "attack and destroy surface targets under day and night visual conditions." United States Marine Corps, Factfile: AV-8B Harrier II (last modified Dec. 5, 1995) <http://www.hqmc. usmc.mil/factfile.nsf>. Manufactured by McDonnell Douglas, the Harrier Jet played a significant role in the air offensive of Operation Desert Storm in 1991. *See id.* The jet is designed to carry a considerable armament load, including Sidewinder and Maverick missiles. *See id.* As one news report has noted, "Fully loaded, the Harrier can float like a butterfly and sting like a bee—albeit a roaring 14-ton butterfly and a bee with 9,200 pounds of bombs and missiles." Jerry Allegood, *Marines Rely on Harrier Jet, Despite Critics*, News & Observer (Raleigh), Nov. 4, 1990, at C1. In light of the Harrier Jet's well-documented function in attacking and destroying surface and air targets, armed reconnaissance and air interdiction, and offensive and defensive anti-aircraft warfare, depiction of such a jet as a way to get to school in the morning is clearly not serious even if, as plaintiff contends, the jet is capable of being acquired "in a form that eliminates [its] potential for military use."

Fifth, the number of Pepsi Points the commercial mentions as required to "purchase" the jet is 7,000,000. To amass that number of points, one would have to drink 7,000,000 Pepsis (or roughly 190 Pepsis a day for the next hundred years—an unlikely possibility), or one would have to purchase approximately $700,000 worth of Pepsi Points. The cost of a Harrier Jet is roughly $23 million dollars, a fact of which plaintiff was aware when he set out to gather the amount he believed necessary to accept the alleged offer. Even if an objective, reasonable person were not aware of this fact, he would conclude that purchasing a fighter plane for $700,000 is a deal too good to be true.

Plaintiff argues that a reasonable, objective person would have understood the commercial to make a serious offer of a Harrier Jet because there was "absolutely no distinction in the manner" in which the items in the commercial were presented. Plaintiff also relies upon a press release highlighting the promotional campaign, issued by defendant, in which "no mention is made by [defendant] of humor, or anything of the sort." These arguments suggest merely that the humor of the promotional campaign was tongue in cheek. Humor is not limited to what Justice Cardozo called "the rough and boisterous joke . . . [that] evokes its own guffaws." *Murphy v. Steeplechase Amusement Co.*, 250 N.Y. 479, 483, 166 N.E. 173, 174 (1929). In light of the obvious absurdity of the commercial, the Court rejects plaintiff's argument that the commercial was not clearly in jest.

4. *Plaintiff's Demands for Additional Discovery*

In his Memorandum of Law, and in letters to the Court, plaintiff argues that additional discovery is necessary on the issues of whether and how defendant reacted to plaintiff's "acceptance" of their "offer"; how defendant and its employees understood the commercial would be viewed, based on test-marketing the commercial or on their own opinions; and how other individuals actually responded to the commercial when it was aired

Plaintiff argues that additional discovery is necessary as to how defendant reacted to his "acceptance," suggesting that it is significant that defendant twice changed the commercial, the first time to increase the number of Pepsi Points required to purchase a Harrier Jet to 700,000,000, and then again to amend the commercial to state the 700,000,000 amount and add "(Just Kidding)." Plaintiff concludes that, "Obviously, if PepsiCo truly believed that no one could take seriously the offer contained in the original ad that I saw, this change would have been totally unnecessary and superfluous." The record does not suggest that the change in the amount of points is probative of the seriousness of the offer. The increase in the number of points needed to acquire a Harrier Jet may have been prompted less by the fear that reasonable people would demand Harrier Jets and more by the concern that unreasonable people would threaten frivolous litigation. Further discovery is unnecessary on the question of when and how the commercials changed because the question before the Court is whether the commercial that plaintiff saw and relied upon was an offer, not that any other commercial constituted an offer.

Plaintiff's demands for discovery relating to how defendant itself understood the offer are also unavailing. Such discovery would serve only to cast light on defendant's subjective intent in making the alleged offer, which is irrelevant to the question of whether an objective, reasonable person would have understood the commercial to be an offer. *See Kay-R Elec. Corp.*, 23 F.3d at 57 ("We are not concerned with what was going through the heads of the parties at the time [of the alleged contract]."); *Mesaros*, 845 F.2d at 1581; *Corbin on Contracts*, § 1.11 at 30. Indeed, plaintiff repeatedly argues that defendant's subjective intent is irrelevant.

Finally, plaintiff's assertion that he should be afforded an opportunity to determine whether other individuals also tried to accumulate enough Pepsi Points to "purchase" a Harrier Jet is unavailing. The possibility that there were other people who interpreted the commercial as an "offer" of a Harrier Jet does not render that belief any more or less reasonable. The alleged offer must be evaluated on its own terms. Having made the evaluation, the Court concludes that summary judgment is appropriate on the ground that no reasonable, objective person would have understood the commercial to be an offer.

*   *   *   *   *   *

III. *Conclusion*

In sum, there are three reasons why plaintiff's demand cannot prevail as a matter of law. First, the commercial was merely an advertisement, not a unilateral offer. Second, the tongue-in-cheek attitude of the commercial would not cause a reasonable person to conclude that a soft drink company would be giving away fighter planes as part of a promotion. Third, there is no writing between the parties sufficient to satisfy the Statute of Frauds.

For the reasons stated above, the Court grants defendant's motion for summary judgment. The Clerk of Court is instructed to close these cases. Any pending motions are moot.

Case 2:   **Advertisement as an Offer**
                Statute of Frauds
                Unilateral Mistake

Donovan v. RRL Corp.
Supreme Court of California, 2001
26 Cal. 4th 261

GEORGE, C. J.

Defendant RRL Corporation is an automobile dealer doing business under the name Lexus of Westminster. Because of typographical and proofreading errors made by a local newspaper, defendant's advertisement listed a price for a used automobile that was significantly less than the intended sales price. Plaintiff Brian J. Donovan read the advertisement and, after examining the vehicle, attempted to purchase it by tendering the advertised price. Defendant refused to sell the automobile to plaintiff at that price, and plaintiff brought this action against defendant for breach of contract. The municipal court entered judgment for defendant on the ground that the mistake in the advertisement precluded the existence of a contract. The appellate department of the superior court and the Court of Appeal reversed, relying in part upon Vehicle Code section 11713.1, subdivision (e), which makes it unlawful for an automobile dealer not to sell a motor vehicle at the advertised price while the vehicle remains unsold and before the advertisement expires.

We conclude that a contract satisfying the statute of frauds arose from defendant's advertisement and plaintiff's tender of the advertised price, but that defendant's unilateral mistake of fact provides a basis for rescinding the contract. Although Vehicle Code section 11713.1, subdivision (e), justifies a reasonable expectation on the part of consumers that an automobile dealer intends that such an advertisement constitute an offer, and that the offer can be accepted by paying the advertised price, this statute does not supplant governing common law principles authorizing rescission of a contract on the ground of mistake. As we shall explain, rescission is warranted here because the evidence establishes that defendant's unilateral mistake of fact was made in good faith, defendant did not bear the risk of the mistake, and enforcement of the contract with the erroneous price would be unconscionable. Accordingly, we shall reverse the judgment of the Court of Appeal.

I

While reading the April 26, 1997, edition of the Costa Mesa Daily Pilot, a local newspaper, plaintiff noticed a full-page advertisement placed by defendant. The advertisement promoted a "PRE-OWNED COUP-A-RAMA SALE!/2-DAY PRE-OWNED SALES EVENT" and listed, along with 15 other used automobiles, a 1995 Jaguar XJ6 Vanden Plas. The advertisement described the color of this automobile as sapphire blue, included a vehicle identification number, and stated a price of $25,995. The name Lexus of Westminster was displayed prominently in three separate locations in the advertisement, which included defendant's address along with a small map showing the location of the dealership. The following statements appeared in small print at the bottom of the advertisement: "All cars plus tax, lic., doc., smog & bank fees. On approved credit. Ad expires 4/27/97[.]"

Also on April 26, 1997, plaintiff visited a Jaguar dealership that offered other 1995 Jaguars for sale at $8,000 to $10,000 more than the price specified in defendant's advertisement. The following day, plaintiff and his spouse drove to Lexus of Westminster and observed a blue Jaguar displayed on an elevated ramp. After verifying that the identification number on the sticker was the same as that listed in defendant's April 26 Daily Pilot advertisement, they asked a salesperson whether they could test drive the Jaguar. Plaintiff mentioned that he had seen the advertisement and that the price "looked really good." The salesperson responded that, as a Lexus dealer, defendant might offer better prices for a Jaguar automobile than would a Jaguar dealer. At that point, however, neither plaintiff nor the salesperson mentioned the specific advertised price.

After the test drive, plaintiff and his spouse discussed several negative characteristics of the automobile, including high mileage, an apparent rust problem, and worn tires. In addition, it was not as clean as the other Jaguars they had inspected. Despite these problems, they believed that the advertised price was a very good price and decided to purchase the vehicle. Plaintiff told the salesperson, "Okay. We will take it at your price, $26,000." When the salesperson did not respond, plaintiff showed him the advertisement. The salesperson immediately stated, "That's a mistake."

After plaintiff asked to speak with an individual in charge, defendant's sales manager also told plaintiff that the price listed in the advertisement was a mistake. The sales manager apologized and offered to pay for plaintiff's fuel, time, and effort expended in traveling to the dealership to examine the automobile. Plaintiff declined this offer and expressed his belief that there had been no mistake. Plaintiff stated that he could write a check for the full purchase price as advertised. The sales manager responded that he would not sell the vehicle at the advertised price. Plaintiff then requested the sales price. After performing some calculations, and based upon defendant's $35,000 investment in the automobile, the sales manager stated that he would sell it to plaintiff for $37,016. Plaintiff responded, "No, I want to buy it at your advertised price, and I will write you a check right now." The sales manager again stated that he would not sell the vehicle at the advertised price, and plaintiff and his spouse left the dealership.

Plaintiff subsequently filed this action against defendant for breach of contract, fraud, and negligence. In addition to testimony consistent with the facts set forth above, the following evidence was presented to the municipal court, which acted as the trier of fact.

Defendant's advertising manager compiles information for placement in advertisements in several local newspapers, including the Costa Mesa Daily Pilot. Defendant's advertisement published in the Saturday, April 19, 1997, edition of the Daily Pilot listed a 1995 Jaguar XJ6 Vanden Plas but did not specify a price for that automobile; instead, the word "Save" appeared in the space where a price ordinarily would have appeared. The following Thursday afternoon, defendant's sales manager instructed the advertising manager to delete the 1995 Jaguar from all advertisements and to substitute a 1994 Jaguar XJ6 with a price of $25,995. The advertising manager conveyed the new information to a representative of the Daily Pilot that same afternoon.

Because of typographical and proofreading errors made by employees of the Daily Pilot, however, the newspaper did not replace the description of the 1995 Jaguar with the description of the 1994 Jaguar, but did replace the word "Save" with the price of $25,995. Thus, the Saturday, April 26, edition of the Daily Pilot erroneously advertised the 1995 Jaguar XJ6 Vanden Plas at a price of $25,995. The Daily Pilot acknowledged its error in a letter of retraction sent to defendant on April 28. No employee of defendant reviewed a proof sheet of the revised Daily Pilot advertisement before it was published, and defendant was unaware of the mistake until plaintiff attempted to purchase the automobile.

Except for the 1995 Jaguar XJ6 Vanden Plas, defendant intended to sell each vehicle appearing in the April 26, 1997, Daily Pilot advertisement at the advertised price. Defendant's advertisements in the April 26 editions of several other newspapers correctly listed the *1994* Jaguar XJ6 with a price of $25,995. In May 1997, defendant's advertisements in several newspapers listed the 1995 Jaguar XJ6 Vanden Plas for sale at $ 37,995. Defendant subsequently sold the automobile for $38,399.

The municipal court entered judgment for defendant. During the trial, the court ruled that plaintiff had not stated a cause of action for negligence, and it precluded plaintiff from presenting evidence in support of such a claim. After the close of evidence and presentation of argument, the municipal court concluded as a matter of law that a newspaper advertisement for an automobile generally constitutes a valid contractual offer that a customer may accept by tendering payment of the advertised price. The court also determined that such an advertisement satisfies the requirements of the statute of frauds when the dealer's name appears in the advertisement. Nevertheless, the municipal court held that in the present case there was no valid offer because defendant's unilateral mistake of fact vitiated or negated contractual intent. The court made factual findings that defendant's mistake regarding the advertisement was made in good faith and was not intended to deceive the public. The municipal court also found that plaintiff was unaware of the mistake before it was disclosed to him by defendant's representatives.

Plaintiff appealed from the judgment to the appellate department of the superior court (Cal. Rules of Court, rule 121), limiting his contentions to the breach of contract claim. The appellate department reversed the judgment for defendant and directed the municipal court to calculate plaintiff's damages. Relying upon the public policies underlying Vehicle Code section 11713.1, subdivision (e), the appellate department concluded that the advertisement constituted an offer capable of acceptance by tender of the advertised price. Section 11713.1, subdivision (e), provides that it is a violation of the Vehicle Code for a dealer to "[f]ail to sell a vehicle to any person at the advertised total price . . . while the vehicle remains unsold, unless the advertisement states the advertised total price is good only for a specified time and the time has elapsed." The appellate department further concluded that defendant bore the risk of the mistaken transmission of its offer, because plaintiff was unaware of the mistake.

The appellate department of the superior court certified the appeal to the Court of Appeal, which ordered the case transferred to it for hearing and decision. (Cal. Rules of Court, rules 62(a), 63(a).) Like the appellate department, the Court of Appeal reversed the judgment of the municipal court and held that defendant's advertisement constituted a contractual offer that invited acceptance by the act of tendering the advertised price, which plaintiff performed. Acknowledging that the question was close, however, the Court of Appeal reasoned that Vehicle Code section 11713.1, subdivision (e), "tips the scale in favor of . . . construing the advertisement as an offer . . . ." The court disagreed with the municipal court's conclusion that defendant's unilateral mistake of fact, unknown to plaintiff at the time he tendered the purchase price, precluded the existence of a valid offer. With regard to the contention that defendant should not bear the risk of an error resulting solely from the negligence of the newspaper, the Court of Appeal made a factual finding based upon the appellate record (Code Civ. Proc., § 909) that defendant's failure to review a proof sheet for the Daily Pilot advertisement constituted negligence that contributed to the placement of the erroneous advertisement.

We granted defendant's petition for review and requested that the parties include in their briefing a discussion of the effect, if any, of California Uniform Commercial Code division 2, chapter 2, sections 2201-2210, upon the present case.

II

An essential element of any contract is the consent of the parties, or mutual assent. (Civ. Code, § 1550 , subd. 2, 1565, subd. 2.) Mutual assent usually is manifested by an offer communicated to the offeree and an acceptance communicated to the offeror. (1 Witkin, Summary of Cal. Law (9th ed. 1987) Contracts, § 128, p. 153 (hereafter Witkin).) " ' "An offer is the manifestation of willingness to enter into a bargain, so made as to justify another person in understanding that his assent to that bargain is invited and will conclude it." ' [Citations.]" (*City of Moorpark v. Moorpark Unified School Dist.* (1991) 54 Cal. 3d 921, 930 [1 Cal. Rptr. 2d 896, 819 P.2d 854] (*Moorpark*).) The determination of whether a particular communication constitutes an operative offer, rather than an inoperative step in the preliminary negotiation of a contract, depends upon all the surrounding circumstances. (1 Corbin, Contracts (rev. ed. 1993) § 2.2, p. 105.) The objective manifestation of the party's assent ordinarily controls, and the pertinent inquiry is whether the individual to whom the communication was made had reason to

82

believe that it was intended as an offer. (1 Witkin, *supra*, Contracts, § 119, p. 144; 1 Farnsworth, Contracts (2d ed. 1998) § 3.10, p. 237.)

In the present case, the municipal court ruled that newspaper advertisements for automobiles generally constitute offers that can be accepted by a customer's tender of the purchase price. Its conclusion that defendant's advertisement for the 1995 Jaguar did not constitute an offer was based solely upon the court's factual determination that the erroneous price in the advertisement was the result of a good faith mistake.

Because the existence of an offer depends upon an objective interpretation of defendant's assent as reflected in the advertisement, however, the mistaken price (not reasonably known to plaintiff to be a mistake) is irrelevant in determining the threshold question whether the advertisement constituted an offer. In this situation, mistake instead properly would be considered in deciding whether a contract resulted from the acceptance of an offer containing mistaken terms, or whether any such contract could be voided or rescinded. (See *Chakmak v. H. J. Lucas Masonry, Inc.* (1976) 55 Cal. App. 3d 124, 129 [127 Cal. Rptr. 404]; Rest.2d Contracts, § 153; 1 Corbin, Contracts, *supra*, § 4.11, pp. 623-627; 2 Williston, Contracts (4th ed. 1991) § 6:57, pp. 682-695.) Thus, the municipal court did not make any factual findings relevant to the issue whether defendant's advertisement constituted an offer, and we shall review the question de novo. (*Richards v. Flower* (1961) 193 Cal. App. 2d 233, 235 [14 Cal. Rptr. 228].)

Some courts have stated that an advertisement or other notice disseminated to the public at large generally does not constitute an offer, but rather is presumed to be an invitation to consider, examine, and negotiate. (E.g., *Harris v. Time, Inc.* (1987) 191 Cal. App. 3d 449, 455 [237 Cal. Rptr. 584]; see Rest.2d Contracts, § 26, com. b, p. 76; 1 Corbin, Contracts, *supra*, § 2.4, p. 116; 1 Farnsworth, Contracts, *supra*, § 3.10, p. 242; 1 Williston, Contracts (4th ed. 1990) § 4:7, pp. 285-287, 294.) Nevertheless, certain advertisements have been held to constitute offers where they invite the performance of a specific act without further communication and leave nothing for negotiation. Advertisements for rewards typically fall within this category, because performing the requested act (e.g., returning a lost article or supplying particular information) generally is all that is necessary to accept the offer and conclude the bargain. (1 Witkin, *supra*, Contracts, § 188, p. 200; Rest.2d Contracts, § 29, com. b, illus. 1, p. 84; 1 Corbin, Contracts, *supra*, § 2.4, p. 119.)

Various advertisements involving transactions in goods also have been held to constitute offers where they invite particular action. For example, a merchant's advertisement that listed particular goods at a specific price and included the phrase "First Come First Served" was deemed to be an offer, because it constituted a promise to sell to a customer at that price in exchange for the customer's act of arriving at the store at a particular time. (*Lefkowitz v. Great Minneapolis Surplus Store* (1957) 251 Minn. 188 [86 N.W. 2d 689, 691]; Rest.2d Contracts, § 26, com. b, illus. 1, p. 76.) Similarly, external wording on the envelope of an item of bulk rate mail promising to give the recipient a watch "just for opening the envelope" before a certain date was held to constitute an operative offer accepted by performance of the act of opening the envelope. (*Harris v. Time, Inc., supra,* 191 Cal. App. 3d 449, 455-456.) In addition, an advertisement stating that anyone who purchased a 1954 automobile from a dealer could exchange it for a 1955 model at no additional cost constituted an offer that was accepted when the plaintiff purchased the 1954 vehicle. (*Johnson v. Capital City Ford Co.* (La.Ct.App. 1955) 85 So.2d 75, 79-80; see also *Cobaugh v. Klick-Lewis* (1989) 385 Pa.Super. 587 [561 A.2d 1248, 1249-1250] [sign at golf course stated "hole-in-one wins" an automobile at a specified price].) In such cases, courts have considered whether the advertiser, in clear and positive terms, promised to render performance in exchange for something requested by the advertiser, and whether the recipient of the advertisement reasonably might have concluded that by acting in accordance with the request a contract would be formed. (1 Williston, Contracts, *supra,* § 4:7, pp. 296-297; 1 Corbin, Contracts, *supra,* § 2.4, pp. 116-117; see, e.g., *Chang v. First Colonial Sav. Bank* (1991) 242 Va. 388, 410 S.E.2d 928, 929-930 [bank's newspaper advertisement stating "Deposit $14,000 and receive . . . $20,136.12 upon maturity in 3 1/2 years" constituted an offer that was accepted by the plaintiffs' deposit of that sum for the specified period].)

Relying upon these decisions, defendant contends that its advertisement for the 1995 Jaguar XJ6 Vanden Plas did not constitute an offer, because the advertisement did not request the performance of a specific act that would conclude the bargain. According to defendant, plaintiff's assertion that the advertisement was an offer conflicts with the generally accepted "black-letter" rule that an advertisement that simply identifies goods and specifies a price is an invitation to negotiate.

This court has not previously applied the common law rules upon which defendant relies, including the rule that advertisements generally constitute invitations to negotiate rather than offers. Plaintiff observes that such rules governing the construction of advertisements have been criticized on the ground that they are inconsistent with the reasonable expectations of consumers and lead to haphazard results. (See Eisenberg, *Expression Rules in Contract Law and Problems of Offer and Acceptance* (1994) 82 Cal. L.Rev. 1127, 1166-1172.) Plaintiff urges this court to reject the black-letter advertising rule.

In the present case, however, we need not consider the viability of the black-letter rule regarding the interpretation of advertisements *in general.* Like the Court of Appeal, we conclude that a licensed automobile dealer's advertisement for the sale of a particular vehicle at a specific price—when construed in light of Vehicle Code section 11713.1, subdivision (e)—reasonably justifies a consumer's understanding that the dealer intends the advertisement to constitute an offer and that the consumer's assent to the bargain is invited and will conclude it.

Vehicle Code section 11713.1 sets forth comprehensive requirements governing a licensed automobile dealer's advertisements for motor vehicles. This statute requires, among other things, that an advertisement for a specific automobile identify the vehicle by its identification number or license number (*id.,* subd. (a)), disclose the type of charges that will be added to the advertised price at the time of sale (*id.,* subd. (b)), and refrain from containing various types of misleading information (*id.,* subds. (i), (*l*), (o), (p), (r)).

In addition, Vehicle Code section 11713.1, subdivision (e) (hereafter section 11713.1(e)), states that it is a violation of the Vehicle Code for the holder of any dealer's license to "[f]ail to sell a vehicle to any person at the advertised total price, exclusive of [specified charges such as taxes and registration fees], while the vehicle remains unsold, unless the advertisement states the advertised total price is good only for a specified time and the time has elapsed."

The administrative regulation implementing section 11713.1(e) states in relevant part: "A specific vehicle advertised by a dealer . . . shall be willingly shown and sold at the advertised price and terms while such vehicle remains unsold . . ., unless the advertisement states that the advertised price and terms are good only for a specific time and such time has elapsed. Advertised vehicles must be sold at or below the advertised price irrespective of whether or not the advertised price has been communicated to the purchaser." (Cal. Code Regs., tit. 13, § 260.04, subd. (b).)

Plaintiff asserts that because a dealer is prohibited by section 11713.1(e) from failing to sell a particular vehicle at the advertised price, an advertisement for such a vehicle cannot be a mere request for offers from consumers or an invitation to negotiate, but instead must be deemed an operative offer that is accepted when a consumer tenders the full advertised price. We agree that, in light of the foregoing regulatory scheme, a licensed automobile dealer's advertisement for a particular vehicle at a specific price constitutes an offer.

As one commentator has observed, legislation can affect consumer expectations and cause reasonable individuals to regard certain retail advertisements for the sale of goods as offers to complete a bargain. (1 Corbin, Contracts, *supra*, § 2.4, p. 118.) By authorizing disciplinary action against a licensed automobile dealer that fails to sell a vehicle at the advertised price, section 11713.1(e) creates a reasonable expectation on the part of consumers that the dealer intends to make an offer to sell at that price, and that the consumer can accept the offer by paying the price specified in the advertisement. Interpreted in light of the regulatory obligations imposed upon dealers, an advertisement for a particular automobile at a specific price constitutes an objective manifestation of the dealer's willingness to enter into a bargain on the stated terms, and justifies the consumer's understanding that his or her assent to the bargain is invited and will conclude it. Such an advertisement therefore constitutes an offer that is accepted when a consumer tenders the advertised price.[1]

Defendant and its supporting amici curiae contend that section 11713.1(e) was not intended to modify the common law of contracts, and that therefore the statute should not be considered in determining whether a contract arose from defendant's advertisement and plaintiff's tender of the advertised price. As we shall explain (pt. IV, *post*), we agree that section 11713.1(e) does not reflect a legislative intent to supplant the common law governing contracts for the sale

---

[1] Of course, the consumer's tender of payment must be in a form that is commercially acceptable (see Cal. U. Com. Code, § 2511), and other legal requirements necessary to complete the transaction must be satisfied, such as execution of a formal written agreement containing the required statutory disclosures, and proper delivery of the certificate of ownership and registration (see Veh. Code, § 5600).

85

of motor vehicles by licensed dealers. Nevertheless, the statute does govern the conduct of dealers and thus creates an objective expectation that dealers intend to sell vehicles at the advertised price. Therefore, even though section 11713.1(e) does not alter the applicable common law regarding contractual offers, consumer expectations arising from the statute are relevant in determining whether defendant's advertisement constituted an offer pursuant to governing principles of contract law.

Amicus curiae California Motor Car Dealers Association further asserts that an advertisement for the sale of a vehicle does not constitute an offer because consumers have reason to believe that an automobile dealer does not intend to conclude the bargain until agreement is reached with regard to numerous terms other than price and until the contract is reduced to writing. (See Rest.2d Contracts, §§ 26, 27; 1 Witkin, *supra*, Contracts, § 142, pp. 166-167.) For example, a written contract for the sale of an automobile by a dealer typically includes terms such as the form of payment, warranties, insurance, title, registration, delivery, taxes, documentation fees, and, if applicable, financing. (See *Twaite v. Allstate Ins. Co.* (1989) 216 Cal. App. 3d 239, 243 [264 Cal. Rptr. 598]; *O'Keefe v. Lee Calan Imports, Inc.* (1970) 128 Ill.App.2d 410 [262 N.E.2d 758, 760, 43 A.L.R.3d 1097]; see also Civ. Code, § 2981 et seq. [requirements for conditional contracts for the sale of motor vehicles].) In addition, specific written disclosures, required by statute, must appear in the contract. (E.g., Veh. Code, § 11713.1, subds. (v) [retail automobile sales contract clearly and conspicuously must disclose whether the vehicle is being sold as used or new], (x) [dealer must disclose on the face of the contract whether the transaction is or is not subject to a fee received by an "autobroker" as defined in the Vehicle Code].)

Plaintiff, on the other hand, contends that the existence of a contract is not defeated by the circumstance that he and defendant might have included additional terms in their ultimate written agreement, or that acceptance of defendant's offer might have been communicated by means other than tender of the purchase price, for example by signing a written contract. Plaintiff relies upon the following principle: "Manifestations of assent that are in themselves sufficient to conclude a contract will not be prevented from so operating by the fact that the parties also manifest an intention to prepare and adopt a written memorial thereof; but the circumstances may show that the agreements are preliminary negotiations." (Rest.2d Contracts, § 27.) Plaintiff also observes that "[a]n offer to make a contract shall be construed as inviting acceptance in any manner and by any medium reasonable in the circumstances," unless otherwise indicated. (Cal. U. Com. Code, § 2206, subd. (1)(a).)

Although dealers are required by statute to prepare a written contract when selling an automobile, and such a contract contains terms other than the price of the vehicle, we agree with plaintiff that a dealer's advertisement specifying a price for a particular vehicle constitutes a sufficient manifestation of the dealer's assent to give rise to a contract. As we have explained, in light of section 11713.1(e) such an advertisement objectively reflects the dealer's intention to sell the vehicle to a member of the public who tenders the full advertised price while the vehicle remains unsold and before the advertisement expires. The price almost always is the most important term of the bargain, and the dealer's intention to include other terms in a written contract does not preclude the existence of mutual assent sufficient to conclude a contract.

In sum, because section 11713.1(e) makes it unlawful for a dealer not to sell a particular vehicle at the advertised price while the vehicle remains unsold and before the advertisement expires, plaintiff reasonably could believe that defendant intended the advertisement to be an offer. Therefore, we conclude that defendant's advertisement constituted an offer that was accepted by plaintiff's tender of the advertised price.

III

Defendant contends that even if its advertisement constituted an offer that was accepted by plaintiff's tender of the purchase price, plaintiff is not authorized by law to enforce the resulting contract, because there was no signed writing that satisfied the requirements of the statute of frauds for the sale of goods. Plaintiff, on the other hand, maintains that defendant's name, as it appeared in the newspaper advertisement for the sale of the vehicle, constituted a signature within the meaning of the statute.

The applicable statute of frauds states in relevant part: "Except as otherwise provided in this section a contract for the sale of goods for the price of five hundred dollars ($ 500) or more is not enforceable by way of action or defense unless there is some writing sufficient to indicate that a contract for sale has been made between the parties and *signed by the party against whom enforcement is sought or by his or her authorized agent or broker*. A writing is not insufficient because it omits or incorrectly states a term agreed upon[,] but the contract is not enforceable under this paragraph beyond the quantity of goods shown in the writing." (Cal. U. Com. Code, § 2201, subd. (1), italics added.)

The California Uniform Commercial Code defines the term "signed" as including "any symbol executed or adopted by a party with present intention to authenticate a writing." (Cal. U. Com. Code, § 1201, subd. (38).) The comment regarding the corresponding provision of the Uniform Commercial Code states: "The inclusion of authentication in the definition of 'signed' is to make clear that as the term is used in [the code] a complete signature is not necessary. Authentication may be printed, stamped, or written; it may be by initials or by thumbprint. It may be on any part of the document and in appropriate cases may be found in a billhead or letterhead. No catalog of possible authentications can be complete and the court must use common sense and commercial experience in passing upon these matters. The question always is whether the symbol was executed or adopted by the party with present intention to authenticate the writing." (U. Com. Code com., reprinted at 23A West's Ann. Cal. U. Com. Code (1964 ed.) foll. § 1201, p. 65; see 1 Witkin, *supra*, Contracts, § 281, p. 273 [citing California decisions generally consistent with this comment]; Rest.2d Contracts, § 134.)

Some decisions have relaxed the signature requirement considerably to accommodate various forms of electronic communication. For example, a party's printed or typewritten name in a telegram has been held to satisfy the statute of frauds. (E.g., *Hessenthaler v. Farzin* (1989) 388 Pa.Super. 37 [564 A.2d 990, 993-994]; *Hillstrom v. Gosnay* (1980) 188 Mont. 388 [614 P.2d 466, 470].) Even a tape recording identifying the parties has been determined to meet the signature requirement of the Uniform Commercial Code. (*Ellis Canning Company v. Bernstein* (D.Colo. 1972) 348 F. Supp. 1212, 1228.)

When an advertisement constitutes an offer, the printed name of the merchant is intended to authenticate the advertisement as that of the merchant. (See Rest.2d Contracts, § 131, com. d, illus. 2, p. 335 [newspaper advertisement constituting an offer to purchase certain goods, with offeror's name printed therein, satisfies the requirements of the statute of frauds].) In other words, where the advertisement reasonably justifies the recipient's understanding that the communication was intended as an offer, the offeror's intent to authenticate his or her name as a signature can be established from the face of the advertisement.

In the present case, the parties presented no evidence with regard to whether defendant intended that its name in the advertisement constitute a signature. Therefore, the issue whether the appearance of defendant's name supports a determination that the writing was "signed" is closely related to the question whether the advertisement constituted an offer. Those characteristics of the advertisement justifying plaintiff's belief that defendant intended it to be an offer also support a finding that defendant intended that its name serve as an authentication.

As established above, defendant's advertisement reflected an objective manifestation of its intention to make an offer for the sale of the vehicle at the stated price. Defendant's printed name in the advertisement similarly evidenced an intention to authenticate the advertisement as an offer and therefore constituted a signature satisfying the statute of frauds.

IV

Having concluded that defendant's advertisement for the sale of the Jaguar automobile constituted an offer that was accepted by plaintiff's tender of the advertised price, and that the resulting contract satisfied the statute of frauds, we next consider whether defendant can avoid enforcement of the contract on the ground of mistake.

A party may rescind a contract if his or her consent was given by mistake. (Civ. Code, § 1689, subd. (b)(1).) A factual mistake by one party to a contract, or unilateral mistake, affords a ground for rescission in some circumstances. Civil Code section 1577 states in relevant part: "Mistake of fact is a mistake, not caused by the neglect of a legal duty on the part of the person making the mistake, and consisting in: [¶] 1. An unconscious ignorance or forgetfulness of a fact past or present, material to the contract . . . ."

The Court of Appeal determined that defendant's error did not constitute a mistake of fact within the meaning of Civil Code section 1577. In support of this determination, the court relied upon the following principle: "[A] unilateral misinterpretation of contractual terms, without knowledge by the other party at the time of contract, does not constitute a mistake under either Civil Code section 1577 [mistake of fact] or 1578 [mistake of law]." (*Hedging Concepts, Inc. v. First Alliance Mortgage Co.* (1996) 41 Cal. App. 4th 1410, 1422 [49 Cal. Rptr. 2d 191] (*Hedging Concepts*).)

The foregoing principle has no application to the present case. In *Hedging Concepts*, the plaintiff believed that he would fulfill his contractual obligations by introducing potential business prospects to the defendant. The contract, however, required the plaintiff to procure a completed business arrangement. The Court of Appeal held that the plaintiff's subjective misinterpretation of the terms of the contract constituted, at most, a mistake of law. Because the defendant was unaware of the plaintiff's misunderstanding at the time of the contract, the court held that rescission was not a proper remedy. (*Hedging Concepts, supra*, 41 Cal. App. 4th at pp. 1418-1422, citing 1 Witkin, *supra*, Contracts, § 379, pp. 345-346 [relief for unilateral mistake of law is authorized only where one party knows of, does not correct, and takes advantage or enjoys the benefit of another party's mistake].) Defendant's mistake in the present case, in contrast, did not consist of a subjective misinterpretation of a contract term, but rather resulted from an unconscious ignorance that the Daily Pilot advertisement set forth an incorrect price for the automobile. Defendant's lack of knowledge regarding the typographical error in the advertised price of the vehicle cannot be considered a mistake of law. Defendant's error constituted a mistake of fact, and the Court of Appeal erred in concluding otherwise. As we shall explain, the Court of Appeal also erred to the extent it suggested that a unilateral mistake of fact affords a ground for rescission only where the other party is aware of the mistake.

Under the first Restatement of Contracts, unilateral mistake did not render a contract voidable unless the other party knew of or caused the mistake. (1 Witkin, *supra*, Contracts, § 370, p. 337; see Rest., Contracts, § 503.) In *Germain etc. Co. v. Western Union etc. Co.* (1902) 137 Cal. 598, 602 [70 P. 658], this court endorsed a rule similar to that of the first Restatement. Our opinion indicated that a seller's price quotation erroneously transcribed and delivered by a telegraph company contractually could bind the seller to the incorrect price, unless the buyer knew or had reason to suspect that a mistake had been made. Some decisions of the Court of Appeal have adhered to the approach of the original Restatement. (See, e.g., *Conservatorship of O'Connor* (1996) 48 Cal. App. 4th 1076, 1097-1098 [56 Cal. Rptr. 2d 386], and cases cited therein.) Plaintiff also advocates this approach and contends that rescission is unavailable to defendant, because plaintiff was unaware of the mistaken price in defendant's advertisement when he accepted the offer.

The Court of Appeal decisions reciting the traditional rule do not recognize that in *M. F. Kemper Const. Co. v. City of L. A.* (1951) 37 Cal. 2d 696, 701 [235 P.2d 7] (*Kemper*), we acknowledged but rejected a strict application of the foregoing Restatement rule regarding unilateral mistake of fact. The plaintiff in *Kemper* inadvertently omitted a $301,769 item from its bid for the defendant city's public works project—approximately one-third of the total contract price. After discovering the mistake several hours later, the plaintiff immediately notified the city and subsequently withdrew its bid. Nevertheless, the city accepted the erroneous bid, contending that rescission of the offer was unavailable for the plaintiff's unilateral mistake.

Our decision in *Kemper* recognized that the bid, when opened and announced, resulted in an irrevocable option contract conferring upon the city a right to accept the bid, and that the plaintiff could not withdraw its bid unless the requirements for rescission of this option contract were satisfied. (*Kemper, supra*, 37 Cal. 2d at pp. 700, 704.) We stated: "Rescission may be had for mistake of fact if the mistake is material to the contract and was not the result of neglect of a legal duty, if enforcement of the contract as made would be unconscionable, and if the other party can be placed in statu quo. [Citations.]" (*Id.* at p. 701.) Although the city knew of the plaintiff's mistake before it accepted the bid, and this circumstance was relevant to our determination that requiring the plaintiff to perform at the mistaken bid price would be unconscionable (*id.* at pp. 702-703), we authorized rescission of the city's option contract even though the city had not known of or contributed to the mistake before it opened the bid.

Similarly, in *Elsinore Union etc. Sch. Dist. v. Kastorff* (1960) 54 Cal. 2d 380 [6 Cal. Rptr. 1, 353 P.2d 713] (*Elsinore*), we authorized the rescission of an erroneous bid even where the contractor had assured the public agency, after the agency inquired, that his figures were accurate, and where the agency already had accepted the bid before it was aware of the mistake. In this situation, the other party clearly had no reason to know of the contractor's mistake before it accepted the bid.

The decisions in *Kemper* and *Elsinore* establish that California law does not adhere to the original Restatement's requirements for rescission based upon unilateral mistake of fact—i.e., only in circumstances where the other party knew of the mistake or caused the mistake. Consistent with the decisions in *Kemper* and *Elsinore*, the Restatement Second of Contracts authorizes rescission for a unilateral mistake of fact where "the effect of the mistake is such that enforcement of the contract would be unconscionable." (Rest.2d Contracts, § 153, subd. (a).)[2] The comment following this section recognizes "a growing willingness to allow avoidance where the consequences of the mistake are so grave that enforcement of the contract would be unconscionable." (*Id.*, com. a, p. 394.) Indeed, two of the illustrations recognizing this additional ground for rescission in the Restatement Second of Contracts are based in part upon this court's decisions in *Kemper* and *Elsinore*. (Rest.2d Contracts, § 153, com. c, illus. 1, 3, pp. 395, 396, and Reporter's Note, pp. 400-401; see also *Schultz v. County of Contra Costa* (1984) 157 Cal. App. 3d 242, 249-250 [203 Cal. Rptr. 760] [applying section 153, subdivision (a), of the Restatement Second of Contracts], disagreed with on another ground in *Van Petten v. County of San Diego* (1995) 38 Cal. App. 4th 43, 50-51 [44 Cal. Rptr. 2d 816]; 1 Witkin, *supra*, Contracts,

---

[2] Section 153 of the Restatement Second of Contracts states: "Where a mistake of one party at the time a contract was made as to a basic assumption on which he made the contract has a material effect on the agreed exchange of performances that is adverse to him, the contract is voidable by him if he does not bear the risk of the mistake under the rule stated in § 154, and [¶] (a) the effect of the mistake is such that enforcement of the contract would be unconscionable, or [¶] (b) the other party had reason to know of the mistake or his fault caused the mistake."

§ 370, p. 337 [reciting the rule of the same Restatement provision].) Although the most common types of mistakes falling within this category occur in bids on construction contracts, section 153 of the Restatement Second of Contracts is not limited to such cases. (Rest.2d Contracts, § 153, com. b, p. 395.)

Because the rule in section 153, subdivision (a), of the Restatement Second of Contracts, authorizing rescission for unilateral mistake of fact where enforcement would be unconscionable, is consistent with our previous decisions, we adopt the rule as California law. As the author of one treatise recognized more than 40 years ago, the decisions that are inconsistent with the traditional rule "are too numerous and too appealing to the sense of justice to be disregarded." (3 Corbin, Contracts (1960) § 608, p. 675, fn. omitted.) We reject plaintiff's contention and the Court of Appeal's conclusion that, because plaintiff was unaware of defendant's unilateral mistake, the mistake does not provide a ground to avoid enforcement of the contract.

Having concluded that a contract properly may be rescinded on the ground of unilateral mistake of fact as set forth in section 153, subdivision (a), of the Restatement Second of Contracts, we next consider whether the requirements of that provision, construed in light of our previous decisions, are satisfied in the present case. Where the plaintiff has no reason to know of and does not cause the defendant's unilateral mistake of fact, the defendant must establish the following facts to obtain rescission of the contract: (1) the defendant made a mistake regarding a basic assumption upon which the defendant made the contract; (2) the mistake has a material effect upon the agreed exchange of performances that is adverse to the defendant; (3) the defendant does not bear the risk of the mistake; and (4) the effect of the mistake is such that enforcement of the contract would be unconscionable. We shall consider each of these requirements below.

A significant error in the price term of a contract constitutes a mistake regarding a basic assumption upon which the contract is made, and such a mistake ordinarily has a material effect adverse to the mistaken party. (See, e.g., *Elsinore, supra,* 54 Cal. 2d at p. 389 [7 percent error in contract price]; *Lemoge Electric v. County of San Mateo* (1956) 46 Cal. 2d 659, 661-662 [297 P.2d 638] [6 percent error]; *Kemper, supra,* 37 Cal. 2d at p. 702 [28 percent error]; *Brunzell Const. Co. v. G. J. Weisbrod, Inc.* (1955) 134 Cal. App. 2d 278, 286 [285 P.2d 989] [20 percent error]; Rest.2d Contracts, § 152, com. b, illus. 3, p. 387 [27 percent error].) In establishing a material mistake regarding a basic assumption of the contract, the defendant must show that the resulting imbalance in the agreed exchange is so severe that it would be unfair to require the defendant to perform. (Rest.2d Contracts, § 152, com. c, p. 388.) Ordinarily, a defendant can satisfy this requirement by showing that the exchange not only is less desirable for the defendant, but also is more advantageous to the other party. (*Ibid.*)

Measured against this standard, defendant's mistake in the contract for the sale of the Jaguar automobile constitutes a material mistake regarding a basic assumption upon which it made the contract. Enforcing the contract with the mistaken price of $25,995 would require defendant to sell the vehicle to plaintiff for $12,000 less than the intended advertised price of

$37,995—an error amounting to 32 percent of the price defendant intended. The exchange of performances would be substantially less desirable for defendant and more desirable for plaintiff. Plaintiff implicitly concedes that defendant's mistake was material.

The parties and amici curiae vigorously dispute, however, whether defendant should bear the risk of its mistake. Section 154 of the Restatement Second of Contracts states: "A party bears the risk of a mistake when [¶] (a) the risk is allocated to him by agreement of the parties, or [¶] (b) he is aware, at the time the contract is made, that he has only limited knowledge with respect to the facts to which the mistake relates but treats his limited knowledge as sufficient, or [¶] (c) the risk is allocated to him by the court on the ground that it is reasonable in the circumstances to do so." Neither of the first two factors applies here. Thus, we must determine whether it is reasonable under the circumstances to allocate to defendant the risk of the mistake in the advertisement.

Civil Code section 1577, as well as our prior decisions, instructs that the risk of a mistake must be allocated to a party where the mistake results from that party's neglect of a legal duty. (*Kemper, supra,* 37 Cal. 2d at p. 701.) It is well established, however, that ordinary negligence does not constitute neglect of a legal duty within the meaning of Civil Code section 1577. (*Kemper, supra,* 37 Cal. 2d at p. 702.) For example, we have described a careless but significant mistake in the computation of the contract price as the type of error that sometimes will occur in the conduct of reasonable and cautious businesspersons, and such an error does not necessarily amount to neglect of legal duty that would bar equitable relief. (*Ibid.*; see also *Sun 'n Sand, Inc. v. United California Bank* (1978) 21 Cal. 3d 671, 700-70 [148 Cal. Rptr. 329, 582 P.2d 920] (plur. opn. of Mosk, J.); *Elsinore, supra,* 54 Cal. 2d at pp. 388-389.)

A concept similar to neglect of a legal duty is described in section 157 of the Restatement Second of Contracts, which addresses situations in which a party's fault precludes relief for mistake. Only where the mistake results from "a failure to act in good faith and in accordance with reasonable standards of fair dealing" is rescission unavailable. (Rest.2d Contracts, § 157.) This section, consistent with the California decisions cited in the preceding paragraph, provides that a mistaken party's failure to exercise due care does not necessarily bar rescission under the rule set forth in section 153.

"The mere fact that a mistaken party could have avoided the mistake by the exercise of reasonable care does not preclude . . . avoidance . . . [on the ground of mistake]. Indeed, since a party can often avoid a mistake by the exercise of such care, the availability of relief would be severely circumscribed if he were to be barred by his negligence. Nevertheless, in *extreme cases* the mistaken party's fault is a proper ground for denying him relief for a mistake that he otherwise could have avoided. . . . [T]he rule is stated in terms of good faith and fair dealing. . . . [A] failure to act in good faith and in accordance with reasonable standards of fair dealing during pre-contractual negotiations does not amount to a breach. Nevertheless, under the rule stated in this Section, the failure bars a mistaken party from relief based on a mistake that otherwise would not have been made. During the negotiation stage each party is held to a degree of responsibility appropriate to the justifiable expectations of the other. The terms 'good faith' and 'fair dealing' are used, in this context, in much the same sense as in . . . Uniform Commercial Code § 1-203." (Rest.2d Contracts, § 157, com. a, pp. 416-417, italics added.) Section 1201, subdivision (19), of the California Uniform Commercial Code defines "good faith," as used in section 1203 of that code, as "honesty in fact in the conduct or transaction concerned."

Because of its erroneous conclusion that defendant's error was not a mistake of fact, the Court of Appeal did not reach the question whether the mistake resulted from defendant's neglect of a legal duty. The Court of Appeal did make an independent finding of fact on appeal that, in light of the statutory duties imposed upon automobile dealers, defendant's failure to review the proof sheet for the advertisement constituted *negligence*. This finding, however, was relevant only to the Court of Appeal's determination that defendant's concurrent negligence rendered it unnecessary for the court to consider the application of *Germain etc. Co. v. Western Union etc. Co.*, *supra*, 137 Cal. 598, to the present case, because *Germain* involved a mistaken offer resulting solely from the negligence of an intermediary. In any event, as established above, ordinary negligence does not constitute the neglect of a legal duty within the meaning of Civil Code section 1577 and the governing decisions. (See also 3 Corbin, Contracts, *supra*, § 606, pp. 649-656 [negligence is no bar to relief from unilateral mistake if other party can be placed in status quo].) Accordingly, we shall consider in the first instance whether defendant's mistake resulted from its neglect of a legal duty, barring the remedy of rescission.

Plaintiff contends that section 11713.1(e) imposes a legal duty upon licensed automobile dealers to ensure that their advertisements containing sale prices are accurate. As established above, section 11713.1(e) provides that it is a violation of the Vehicle Code for a dealer to "[f]ail to sell a vehicle to any person at the advertised total price . . . while the vehicle remains unsold, unless the advertisement states the advertised total price is good only for a specified time and the time has elapsed." Plaintiff also relies upon Vehicle Code section 11713, subdivision (a), which provides that a licensed dealer shall not "[m]ake or disseminate . . . in any newspaper . . . any statement which is untrue or misleading and which is known, or which by the exercise of reasonable care should be known, to be untrue or misleading . . . ." According to plaintiff, defendant's alleged violation of the duties arising from these statutes also constitutes the neglect of a legal duty within the meaning of Civil Code section 1577.

Even if we were to conclude that the foregoing statutes impose a duty of care upon automobile dealers to ensure that prices in an advertisement are accurate, a violation of such a duty would not necessarily preclude the availability of equitable relief. Our prior decisions instruct that the circumstance that a statute imposes a duty of care does not establish that the violation of such a duty constitutes "the neglect of a legal duty" (Civ. Code, § 1577) that would preclude rescission for a unilateral mistake of fact.

In *Sun 'n Sand, Inc. v. United California Bank*, *supra*, 21 Cal. 3d 671, for example, a bank contended that a customer's violation of its statutory duty to examine bank statements and returned checks for alterations or forgeries (Cal. U. Com. Code, § 4406) constituted the neglect of a legal duty within the meaning of Civil Code section 1577, thus barring relief for the customer's mistake of fact. We rejected the bank's defense: "It does not follow . . . that breach of this duty by failure to exercise reasonable care in discharging it constitutes the 'neglect of a legal duty' such that a cause of action for mistake of fact must be barred. . . . We have . . . recognized on a number of occasions that 'ordinary negligence does not constitute the neglect of a legal duty as that term is used in section 1577 of the Civil Code.' [Citations] The rule developed in these cases reflects a determination that the 'neglect of a legal duty' qualification derives content from equitable considerations and principles, and that it would be inequitable to bar relief for mistake because of the breach of a duty of care when the [other] party . . . suffers no loss. That [the plaintiff] may have failed to exercise care in examining its bank statements is thus not a sufficient basis for denying it equitable relief for mistake." (*Sun 'n Sand, Inc. v. United California Bank, supra*, 21 Cal. 3d at pp. 700-701 (plur. opn. of Mosk, J.); see *id*. at p. 709 (conc. & dis. opn. of Sullivan, J.) [agreeing with conclusion of plur. opn. on this claim].)

Plaintiff also seeks to preclude relief for defendant's mistake on the ground that defendant's alleged violation of Vehicle Code section 11713.1(e) constitutes negligence per se pursuant to Evidence Code section 669, which provides that an individual's violation of a statute can lead to a presumption that he or she failed to exercise due care. As we have seen, however, a failure to exercise due care, by itself, does not constitute the neglect of a legal duty. Without evidence of bad faith on the part of defendant, its alleged violation of any duty of care arising from section 11713.1(e) constitutes, at most, ordinary negligence. Accordingly, a negligent violation of any duty imposed by section 11713.1(e) does not constitute the neglect of a legal duty or a sufficient basis for denying defendant equitable relief for its good faith mistake.

In a related claim, plaintiff contends that section 11713.1(e) imposes upon automobile dealers an absolute obligation to sell a vehicle at the advertised price—notwithstanding any mistake regarding the price, or the circumstances under which the mistake was made—and that this statute therefore supplants the common law regarding rescission of contracts and eliminates the defense of mistake. Allowing automobile dealers to avoid contracts because of carelessness in proofreading advertisements, plaintiff asserts, would undermine the legislative intent and public policy favoring the protection of consumers and ensuring accuracy in advertisements.

Plaintiff's contention regarding the effect of section 11713.1(e) upon the common law is inconsistent with our prior decisions. In *Moorpark, supra*, 54 Cal. 3d 921, we held that a statute supplying the parameters for the price term of a contract, and requiring one party to perform certain acts as part of the process of making the contract, "does not remove the contract-making process from the purview of the common law unless the Legislature intends to occupy the field." (*Id*. at p. 929.) Our decision in *Moorpark* indicated that where a statutory scheme neither explicitly defines an offer nor, by the breadth of its regulation, implicitly supplants the common law of contracts, general common law principles govern the question whether an effective legal offer has been made. (*Id*. at p. 930)

Section 11713.1(e) does not eliminate mistake as a ground for rescission of the contract, as plaintiff contends. The statute is part of a regulatory scheme that subjects licensed dealers to potential discipline for a violation of the duties set forth therein. As in *Moorpark, supra*, 54 Cal. 3d 921, nothing in section 11713.1(e) or the regulatory scheme reflects a legislative intent completely to remove the contract-making process from the purview of the common law. At most, section 11713.1(e) reflects an intent to *supplement* contract law by establishing a ceiling for the price term of a contract for the sale of an advertised vehicle. Therefore, the common law, including the law governing mistake, remains applicable.

In *Kemper, supra*, 37 Cal. 2d 696, we rejected a contention similar to that advanced by plaintiff. Relying upon a charter provision that "no bid shall be withdrawn" after being opened and declared, the city maintained that the public interest precluded the contractor from having the right to rescind its bid for mistake. Our decision stated that the offer remained subject to rescission upon proper equitable grounds, and that prior cases did not recognize any distinction between public and private contracts with regard to the right of equitable relief. (*Id.* at p. 704.) In support of this statement, we quoted from *Moffett, Hodgkins &c. Co. v. Rochester* (1900) 178 U.S. 373, 386 [20 S. Ct. 957, 961, 44 L. Ed. 1108], which had rejected a similar argument, as follows: " 'If the [city is] correct in [its] contention[,] there is absolutely no redress for a bidder for public work, no matter how aggravated or palpable his blunder. The moment his proposal is opened by the executive board he is held as in a grasp of steel. There is no remedy, no escape. If, through an error of his clerk, he has agreed to do work worth a million dollars for ten dollars, he must be held to the strict letter of his contract, while equity stands by with folded hands and sees him driven to bankruptcy. The [city's] position admits of no compromise, no exception, no middle ground.' " (*Kemper, supra*, 37 Cal. 2d at p. 704.)

In *Kemper* we further rejected the city's contention that a statement in the official bid form that bidders "'will not be released on account of errors' "(*Kemper, supra*, 37 Cal. 2d at p. 703) required all contractors to waive the right to seek relief for mistake. Our decision recognized a distinction between mere mechanical or clerical errors in tabulating or transcribing figures, on the one hand, and errors of judgment, on the other. "Where a person is denied relief because of an error in judgment, the agreement which is enforced is the one he intended to make, whereas if he is denied relief from a clerical error, he is forced to perform an agreement he had no intention of making. . . . If we were to give the language the sweeping construction contended for by the city, it would mean holding that the contractor intended to assume the risk of a clerical error no matter in what circumstances it might occur or how serious it might be. Such interpretation is contrary to common sense and ordinary business understanding and would result in the loss of heretofore well-established equitable rights to relief from certain types of mistake." (*Id.* at pp. 703-704.)

As in the foregoing cases, if we were to accept plaintiff's position that section 11713.1(e), by requiring a dealer to sell a vehicle at the advertised price, necessarily precludes relief for mistake, and that the dealer always must be held to the strict terms of a contract arising from an advertisement, we would be holding that the dealer intended to assume the risk of all typographical errors in advertisements, no matter how serious the error and regardless of the circumstances in which the error was made. For example, if an automobile dealer proofread an advertisement but, through carelessness, failed to detect a typographical error listing a $75,000 automobile for sale at $75, the defense of mistake would be unavailable to the dealer.

The trial court expressed a similar concern when it posed the following hypothetical to plaintiff. "The perennial mistakes in ads are infinite. You can move the decimal point over two, three places, so you are selling a $1,000,000 item for $100, any ridiculous example you can think of. [¶] If your theory is correct, that a printout would constitute an unconditional offer to sell, would that same result be attained if we had one of these mistakes, where some printer, instead of printing a million, left off some of the zeros, put in a thousand, and you are selling a million dollar yacht, and it came out to a thousand dollars, would a person be entitled, under your theory of the law, to say here's my thousand bucks, and I would like to sail away?" Consistent with his contention that the violation of section 11713.1(e) constitutes the neglect of a legal duty, plaintiff responded that the answer to the court's hypothetical is "yes." Plaintiff reiterated his position in this regard at oral argument in this court.[3]

Giving such an effect to section 11713.1(e), however, "is contrary to common sense and ordinary business understanding and would result in the loss of heretofore well-established equitable rights to relief from certain types of mistake." (*Kemper, supra,* 37 Cal. 2d at p. 704.) Although this statute obviously reflects an important public policy of protecting consumers from injury caused by unscrupulous dealers who publish deceptive advertisements (see *Ford Dealers Assn. v. Department of Motor Vehicles* (1982) 32 Cal. 3d 347, 356 [185 Cal. Rptr. 453, 650 P.2d 328]), and establishes that automobile dealers that violate the statute can suffer the suspension or revocation of their licenses, there is no indication in the statutory scheme that the Legislature intended to impose such an absolute *contractual* obligation upon automobile dealers who make an honest mistake. Therefore, absent evidence of bad faith, the violation of any obligation imposed by this statute does not constitute the neglect of a legal duty that precludes rescission for unilateral mistake of fact.

The municipal court made an express finding of fact that "the mistake on the part of [defendant] was made in good faith[;] it was an honest mistake, not intended to deceive the public . . . ." The Court of Appeal correctly recognized that "[w]e must, of course, accept the trial

---

[3] In addition, if we were to accept plaintiff's position that Vehicle Code section 11713.1(e) imposes an absolute contractual obligation upon dealers to sell a vehicle at the advertised price to any person notwithstanding any legal justification for refusing to do so a dealer would be required to enter into a sales contract with an individual who obviously lacks the mental capacity to contract. (See Civ. Code, §§ 38, 1556, 1557.) And, under plaintiff's view of the statute, a dealer would be required to sell a vehicle at an erroneous price mistakenly broadcast by a radio announcer, even though the dealer would have had no opportunity to correct the announcer's error before it was made. Pursuant to analogous consumer protection legislation, an unintentional publication of a false or misleading advertisement does not result in statutory liability. (See Civ. Code, § 1784 [no damages may be awarded for unintentionally false advertising resulting from bona fide error]; Bus. & Prof. Code, § 17502 [newspaper protected from liability for unknowingly publishing false advertising].)

court's finding that there was a 'good faith' mistake that caused the error in the advertisement." The evidence presented at trial compellingly supports this finding.

Defendant regularly advertises in five local newspapers. Defendant's advertising manager, Crystal Wadsworth, testified that ordinarily she meets with Kristen Berman, a representative of the Daily Pilot, on Tuesdays, Wednesdays, and Thursdays to review proof sheets of the advertisement that will appear in the newspaper the following weekend. When Wadsworth met with Berman on Wednesday, April 23, 1997, defendant's proposed advertisement listed a 1995 Jaguar XJ6 Vanden Plas without specifying a price, as it had the preceding week. On Thursday, April 24, a sales manager instructed Wadsworth to substitute a 1994 Jaguar XJ6 with a price of $25,995. The same day, Wadsworth met with Berman and conveyed to her this new information. Wadsworth did not expect to see another proof sheet reflecting this change, however, because she does not work on Friday, and the Daily Pilot goes to press on Friday and the edition in question came out on Saturday, April 26.

Berman testified that the revised advertisement was prepared by the composing department of the Daily Pilot. Berman proofread the advertisement, as she does all advertisements for which she is responsible, but Berman did not notice that it listed the 1995 Jaguar XJ6 Vanden Plas for sale at $25,995, instead of listing the 1994 Jaguar at that price. Both Berman and Wadsworth first learned of the mistake on Monday, April 28, 1997. Defendant's sales manager first became aware of the mistake after plaintiff attempted to purchase the automobile on Sunday, April 27. Berman confirmed in a letter of retraction that Berman's proofreading error had led to the mistake in the advertisement.

Defendant's erroneous advertisement in the Daily Pilot listed 16 used automobiles for sale. Each of the advertisements prepared for several newspapers in late April 1997, except for the one in the Daily Pilot, correctly identified the 1994 Jaguar XJ6 for sale at a price of $25,995. In May 1997, defendant's advertisements in several newspapers listed the 1995 Jaguar XJ6 Vanden Plas for sale at $37,995, and defendant subsequently sold the automobile for $38,399. Defendant had paid $35,000 for the vehicle.

Evidence at trial established that defendant adheres to the following procedures when an incorrect advertisement is discovered. Defendant immediately contacts the newspaper and requests a letter of retraction. Copies of any erroneous advertisements are provided to the sales staff, the error is explained to them, and the mistake is circled in red and posted on a bulletin board at the dealership. The sales staff informs customers of any advertising errors of which they are aware.

No evidence presented at trial suggested that defendant knew of the mistake before plaintiff attempted to purchase the automobile, that defendant intended to mislead customers, or that it had adopted a practice of deliberate indifference regarding errors in advertisements.[4]

---

[4] Plaintiff attempted to establish at trial that defendant continued to advertise the 1995 Jaguar at an erroneous price. He introduced into evidence defendant's advertisements in the May 31, 1997, edition of two newspapers. One listed a price of $37,995 for the automobile; the other stated a price of $35,995. Wadsworth, however, offered a reasonable explanation for the discrepancy. After consistently advertising the vehicle for $37,995

Wadsworth regularly reviews proof sheets for the numerous advertisements placed by defendant, and representatives of the newspapers, including the Daily Pilot, also proofread defendant's advertisements to ensure they are accurate. Defendant follows procedures for notifying its sales staff and customers of errors of which it becomes aware. The uncontradicted evidence established that the Daily Pilot made the proofreading error resulting in defendant's mistake.

Defendant's fault consisted of failing to review a proof sheet reflecting the change made on Thursday, April 24, 1997, and/or the actual advertisement appearing in the April 26 edition of the Daily Pilot—choosing instead to rely upon the Daily Pilot's advertising staff to proofread the revised version. Although, as the Court of Appeal found, such an omission might constitute negligence, it does not involve a breach of defendant's duty of good faith and fair dealing that should preclude equitable relief for mistake. In these circumstances, it would not be reasonable for this court to allocate the risk of the mistake to defendant.

As indicated above, the Restatement Second of Contracts provides that during the negotiation stage of a contract "each party is held to a degree of responsibility appropriate to the justifiable expectations of the other." (Rest.2d Contracts, § 157, com. a, p. 417.) No consumer reasonably can expect 100 percent accuracy in each and every price appearing in countless automobile advertisements listing numerous vehicles for sale. The degree of responsibility plaintiff asks this court to impose upon automobile dealers would amount to strict contract liability for any typographical error in the price of an advertised automobile, no matter how serious the error or how blameless the dealer. We are unaware of any other situation in which an individual or business is held to such a standard under the law of contracts. Defendant's good faith, isolated mistake does not constitute the type of extreme case in which its fault constitutes the neglect of a legal duty that bars equitable relief. Therefore, whether or not defendant's failure to sell the automobile to plaintiff could amount to a violation of section 11713.1(e) an issue that is not before us defendant's conduct in the present case does not preclude rescission.

The final factor defendant must establish before obtaining rescission based upon mistake is that enforcement of the contract for the sale of the 1995 Jaguar XJ6 Vanden Plas at $25,995 would be unconscionable. Although the standards of unconscionability warranting rescission for mistake are similar to those for unconscionability justifying a court's refusal to enforce a contract or term, the general rule governing the latter situation (Civ. Code, § 1670.5) is inapplicable here, because unconscionability resulting from mistake does not appear at the time the contract is made. (Rest.2d Contracts, § 153, com. c, p. 395; 1 Witkin, *supra*, Contracts, § 370, pp. 337-338.)

An unconscionable contract ordinarily involves both a procedural and a substantive element: (1) oppression or surprise due to unequal bargaining power, and (2) overly harsh or one-sided results. (*Armendariz v. Foundation Health Psychcare Services, Inc.* (2000) 24 Cal. 4th 83, 114 [99 Cal. Rptr. 2d 745, 6 P.3d 669].) Nevertheless, " 'a sliding scale is invoked which disregards the regularity of the procedural process of the contract formation, that creates the

---

in several newspapers throughout the month of May, defendant reduced the price by $2,000 at the end of the month, and the two newspapers had gone to press on different dates. The trial court's findings establish that the court found this testimony to be credible.

terms, in proportion to the greater harshness or unreasonableness of the substantive terms themselves.' [Citations.]" (*Ibid.*) For example, the Restatement Second of Contracts states that "[i]nadequacy of consideration does not of itself invalidate a bargain, but gross disparity in the values exchanged may be an important factor in a determination that a contract is unconscionable and may be sufficient ground, without more, for denying specific performance." (Rest.2d Contracts, § 208, com. c, p. 108.) In ascertaining whether rescission is warranted for a unilateral mistake of fact, substantive unconscionability often will constitute the determinative factor, because the oppression and surprise ordinarily results from the mistake—not from inequality in bargaining power. Accordingly, even though defendant is not the weaker party to the contract and its mistake did not result from unequal bargaining power, defendant was surprised by the mistake, and in these circumstances overly harsh or one-sided results are sufficient to establish unconscionability entitling defendant to rescission.

Our previous cases support this approach. In *Kemper, supra,* 37 Cal. 2d 696, we held that enforcement of the city's option to accept a construction company's bid, which was 28 percent less than the intended bid, would be unconscionable. Our decision reasoned that (1) the plaintiff gave prompt notice upon discovering the facts entitling it to rescind, (2) the city therefore was aware of the clerical error before it exercised the option, (3) the city already had awarded the contract to the next lowest bidder, (4) the company had received nothing of value it was required to restore to the city, and (5) "the city will not be heard to complain that it cannot be placed in statu quo because it will not have the benefit of an inequitable bargain." (*Id.* at p. 703.) Therefore, "under all the circumstances, it appears that it would be unjust and unfair to permit the city to take advantage of the company's mistake." (*Id.* at pp. 702-703.) Nothing in our decision in *Kemper* suggested that the mistake resulted from surprise related to inequality in the bargaining process. (Accord, *Farmers Sav. Bank, Joice v. Gerhart* (Iowa 1985) 372 N.W.2d 238, 243-245 [holding unconscionable the enforcement of sheriff's sale against bank that overbid because of a mistake caused by negligence of its own attorney].) Similarly, in *Elsinore, supra,* 54 Cal. 2d 380, we authorized rescission of a bid based upon a clerical error, without suggesting any procedural unconscionability, even where the other party afforded the contractor an opportunity to verify the accuracy of the bid before it was accepted.

In the present case, enforcing the contract with the mistaken price of $25,995 would require defendant to sell the vehicle to plaintiff for $12,000 less than the intended advertised price of $37,995—an error amounting to 32 percent of the price defendant intended. Defendant subsequently sold the automobile for slightly more than the intended advertised price, suggesting that that price reflected its actual market value. Defendant had paid $35,000 for the 1995 Jaguar and incurred costs in advertising, preparing, displaying, and attempting to sell the vehicle. Therefore, defendant would lose more than $9,000 of its original investment in the automobile. Plaintiff, on the other hand, would obtain a $12,000 windfall if the contract were enforced, simply because he traveled to the dealership and stated that he was prepared to pay the advertised price.

These circumstances are comparable to those in our prior decisions authorizing rescission on the ground that enforcing a contract with a mistaken price term would be unconscionable. Defendant's 32 percent error in the price exceeds the amount of the errors in cases such as

Kemper and *Elsinore*. For example, in *Elsinore*, *supra*, 54 Cal. 2d at page 389, we authorized rescission for a $6,500 error in a bid that was intended to be $96,494—a mistake of approximately 7 percent in the intended contract price. As in the foregoing cases, plaintiff was informed of the mistake as soon as defendant discovered it. Defendant's sales manager, when he first learned of the mistake in the advertisement, explained the error to plaintiff, apologized, and offered to pay for plaintiff's fuel, time, and effort expended in traveling to the dealership to examine the automobile. Plaintiff refused this offer to be restored to the status quo. Like the public agencies in *Kemper* and *Elsinore*, plaintiff should not be permitted to take advantage of defendant's honest mistake that resulted in an unfair, one-sided contract. (Cf. *Drennan v. Star Paving Co.* (1958) 51 Cal. 2d 409, 415-416 [333 P.2d 757] [no rescission of mistaken bid where other party detrimentally altered his position in reasonable reliance upon the bid and could not be restored to the status quo].)

The circumstance that section 11713.1(e) makes it unlawful for a dealer not to sell a vehicle at the advertised price does not preclude a finding that enforcing an automobile sales contract containing a mistaken price would be unconscionable. Just as the statute does not eliminate the defense of mistake, as established above, the statute also does not dictate that enforcing a contract with an erroneous advertised price necessarily must be considered equitable and fair for purposes of deciding whether the dealer is entitled to rescission on the ground of mistake. In *Kemper*, *supra*, 37 Cal. 2d 696, we concluded that it would be unconscionable to bar rescission of a bid pursuant to a city charter provision prohibiting the withdrawal of bids, where "it appear[ed] that it would be unjust and unfair to permit the city to take advantage of the company's mistake." (*Id.* at p. 703.) Thus, notwithstanding the public interest underlying the charter provision, our decision in *Kemper* precluded the city from relying upon that provision to impose absolute contractual liability upon the contractor. (*Id.* at p. 704.)

Accordingly, section 11713.1(e) does not undermine our determination that, under the circumstances, enforcement of the contract for the sale of the 1995 Jaguar XJ6 Vanden Plas at the $25,995 mistaken price would be unconscionable. The other requirements for rescission on the ground of unilateral mistake have been established. Defendant entered into the contract because of its mistake regarding a basic assumption, the price. The $12,000 loss that would result from enforcement of the contract has a material effect upon the agreed exchange of performances that is adverse to defendant. Furthermore, defendant did not neglect any legal duty within the meaning of Civil Code section 1577 or breach any duty of good faith and fair dealing in the steps leading to the formation of the contract. Plaintiff refused defendant's offer to compensate him for his actual losses in responding to the advertisement. "The law does not penalize for negligence beyond requiring compensation for the loss it has caused." (3 Corbin, Contracts, *supra*, § 609, p. 684.) In this situation, it would not be reasonable for this court to allocate the risk of the mistake to defendant.

Having determined that defendant satisfied the requirements for rescission of the contract on the ground of unilateral mistake of fact, we conclude that the municipal court correctly entered judgment in defendant's favor.

V

The judgment of the Court of Appeal is reversed.

*   *   *   *   *   *

Case 3:   **Option to Purchase**

Steiner v. Thexton
Supreme Court of California, 2010
48 Cal. 4th 411

MORENO, J.

    Plaintiff Martin A. Steiner * * * seek[s] specific performance of a sales agreement with defendant property owner Paul Thexton. Based on language granting Steiner " absolute and sole discretion" to terminate the transaction, the Court of Appeal construed the agreement as an option and further concluded the option was revocable because it was unsupported by consideration. The Court of Appeal also rejected plaintiffs' claim that promissory estoppel required the agreement's enforcement. The court therefore upheld the trial court's refusal to order specific performance of the agreement.

    We agree the agreement was an option; however, we conclude sufficient consideration existed to render the option irrevocable. We accordingly reverse the Court of Appeal's judgment and remand the action for further proceedings. In light of our conclusion, we need not reach the promissory estoppel issue.

I. FACTUAL AND PROCEDURAL BACKGROUND

    In 2003, Steiner, a real estate developer, was interested in purchasing and developing several residences on a 10–acre portion of Thexton's 12.29–acre parcel of land.[1] County approvals for a parcel split and development permits were required. Thexton had previously rejected an offer from a different party for $750,000 because that party wanted Thexton to obtain the required approval and permits. The written agreement between Steiner and Thexton, prepared by Steiner, provided for Thexton to sell the 10–acre parcel for $500,000 by September 2006 if Steiner decided to purchase the property after pursuing, at his own expense, the county approvals and permits. Paragraph 7 of the "Contingencies" section of the agreement provided Steiner was not obliged to do anything and could cancel the transaction at any time at his "absolute and sole discretion...." (footnote omitted.)

    After Steiner and Thexton signed the agreement on September 4, 2003,[3] Steiner began pursuing the necessary county approvals and * * * ultimately spent thousands of dollars.[4] In May and August 2004, Thexton cooperated with Steiner's efforts by signing, among other things, an application to the county planning department for a tentative parcel map. In October 2004, however, Thexton asked the title company to cancel escrow and told Steiner he no longer wanted to sell the property. Steiner nevertheless proceeded with the final hearing of the parcel review

---

[1] The factual and procedural history is largely taken from the Court of Appeal's opinion.

[3] In January 2004, the parties executed an addendum allowing Steiner to purchase up to 10.17 (instead of 10) acres and eliminating several requirements the original agreement had imposed on Steiner.

[4] Plaintiffs alleged (and the Court of Appeal assumed without deciding) that they had spent $60,000 on efforts to obtain the parcel split.

committee and apparently obtained approval for a tentative map. Steiner opposed cancelling escrow and filed suit seeking specific performance of the agreement. In his answer, Thexton asserted various defenses, including that the agreement constituted an option unsupported by consideration. (footnote omitted.)

Following a bench trial, the trial court entered judgment in favor of Thexton. It concluded the agreement was unenforceable against Thexton "because it is, in effect, an option that is not supported by any consideration." First, it pointed out that the agreement bound Thexton to sell the property to Steiner for $500,000 for a period of up to three years while Steiner retained " 'absolute and sole discretion' " to cancel the transaction. "The unilateral nature of this agreement," the trial court explained, "is the classic feature of an option."

Second, in concluding, "[b]ased on the evidence and the language of the contract itself, ... that the option was not supported by consideration," the trial court noted no money was paid to Thexton for his grant of the option to purchase the property, nor did he receive any other benefit or thing of value in exchange for the option.[6] The trial court rejected plaintiffs' claim that the agreement obligated them to expeditiously proceed with the parcel split and that their work and expenses constituted sufficient consideration for the option. The trial court reasoned that the adequacy of consideration is measured as of the time a contract is entered into and pointed out the agreement did not bind plaintiffs to do anything; rather, it gave them the power to terminate the transaction at any time. Finally, the trial court rejected plaintiffs' claim that, in the absence of consideration for the option, their efforts merited applying the doctrine of promissory estoppel. The Court of Appeal affirmed for the reasons given by the trial court and we granted review.

II. DISCUSSION

We consider whether the agreement was an option and, if so, whether the option was irrevocable because it was supported by sufficient consideration. We conclude, for the following reasons, that the agreement is an irrevocable option.[7]

A. The Sales Agreement Constitutes an Option

Plaintiffs contend the Court of Appeal erred when it concluded the sales agreement constituted an option. We disagree. We begin by briefly setting forth the established law concerning what constitutes an option.

As this court explained long ago, "When by the terms of an agreement the owner of property binds himself to sell on specified terms, and leaves it discretionary with the other party to the contract whether he will or will not buy, it constitutes simply an optional contract."

---

[6] The agreement required Steiner to pay $1,000 into an escrow account, but the trial court concluded the payment did not constitute consideration.

[7] The interpretation of the agreement is subject to de novo review. (*Parsons v. Bristol Development Co.* (1965) 62 Cal.2d 861, 865–866, 44 Cal.Rptr. 767, 402 P.2d 839.) We review the trial court's conclusion that no consideration supported the option under the substantial evidence test. (*Bard v. Kent* (1942) 19 Cal.2d 449, 452, 122 P.2d 8; see *Crocker National Bank v. City and County of San Francisco* (1989) 49 Cal.3d 881, 888, 264 Cal.Rptr. 139, 782 P.2d 278.)

(*Johnson v. Clark* (1917) 174 Cal. 582, 586, 163 P. 1004.) Thus, an option to purchase property is "a unilateral agreement. The optionor offers to sell the subject property at a specified price or upon specified terms and agrees, in view of the payment received, that he will hold the offer open for the fixed time. Upon the lapse of that time the matter is completely ended and the offer is withdrawn. If the offer be accepted upon the terms and in the time specified, then a bilateral contract arises which may become the subject of a suit to compel specific performance, if performance by either party thereafter be refused." (*Auslen v. Johnson* (1953) 118 Cal.App.2d 319, 321–322, 257 P.2d 664.)

In the present case, although the agreement was titled "REAL ESTATE PURCHASE CONTRACT," the label is not dispositive. Rather, we look through the agreement's form to its substance. (*Mahoney v. San Francisco* (1927) 201 Cal. 248, 258, 257 P. 49.) Viewing the substance, we conclude, as did the trial court, that the agreement between Steiner and Thexton contained "the classic feature[s] of an option." First, the agreement obliged Thexton to hold open an offer to sell the parcel at a fixed price for three years. (*Ante,* 106 Cal.Rptr.3d at p. 256, fn. 2, 226 P.3d at pp. 362–363, fn. 2 [close of escrow provisions].) Second, Steiner had the power to accept the offer by satisfying or waiving the contingencies and paying the balance of the purchase price; however, because of the escape clause, Steiner was not obligated to do anything. The relevant term provided "It is expressly understood that [Steiner] may, at [his] *absolute and sole discretion* during this period, elect not to continue in this transaction and this purchase contract will become null and void." (*Ibid.* [contingencies provision 7], italics added.)

Moreover, it appears that the term's broad and express language permitted Steiner to terminate the agreement *even if* all contingencies had been satisfied—indeed, Steiner testified at trial that the term gave him the power to terminate the agreement at any time for any reason, including if he had found a better deal. For that reason we reject the notion, advanced by Steiner and various amici curiae, that the agreement should instead be construed as a bilateral contract subject to a contingency. It is true, as amicus curiae California Association of Realtors explains, that a common form of real estate contract binds both parties at the outset (rendering the transaction a bilateral contract) while including a contingency, such as a loan or inspection contingency, that allows one or both parties to withdraw should the contingency fail. However, withdrawal from such a contract is permitted *only* if the contingency fails. By contrast, the agreement here placed no such constraint on Steiner. Rather, it limited *Thexton's* ability to withdraw, but explicitly allowed *Steiner* to terminate at any time for any reason.[8] Even had the agreement obligated Steiner, as he contends, to move expeditiously to remove the contingencies, we would nonetheless conclude that the "absolute and sole" right to withdraw he enjoyed means the agreement is an option.

We briefly address a number of plaintiffs' other arguments, finding none persuasive. First, plaintiffs argue that in the event of ambiguity, California law presumes a contract to be bilateral rather than an option. (*Patty v. Berryman* (1949) 95 Cal.App.2d 159, 212 P.2d 937.) But no ambiguity exists here. The agreement plainly gave him "absolute and sole discretion" to cancel the transaction. Second, in contending the agreement did not unilaterally bind Thexton,

_____

[8] Thus, bilateral contracts subject to a contingency, which are widely used in real estate transactions, are not affected by our holding.

plaintiffs assert "nothing in the Contract required Thexton to keep his Property off the market for any defined period of time." Not so. The agreement explicitly obligated Thexton to hold open the offer for up to three years.[9]

Third, plaintiffs contend the agreement obliged them to act expeditiously. Even if true, it is irrelevant to whether the agreement constituted an option. Steiner's unfettered power to withdraw at any time for any reason overrode any other obligations. Fourth, plaintiffs argue the Court of Appeal should have applied the implied covenant of good faith and fair dealing to narrow the escape clause to give Steiner only a limited power to terminate the agreement. We disagree. While this court has held that all contracts impose a duty of good faith and fair dealing and that the covenant particularly applies when "one party is invested with a discretionary power affecting the rights of another" (*Carma Developers (Cal.), Inc. v. Marathon Development California, Inc.* (1992) 2 Cal.4th 342, 372, 6 Cal.Rptr.2d 467, 826 P.2d 710), it has also noted the *implied* covenant does not trump an agreement's *express* language (*id.* at p. 374, 6 Cal.Rptr.2d 467, 826 P.2d 710). " 'The general rule [regarding the covenant of good faith] is plainly subject to the exception that the parties may, by express provisions of the contract, grant the right to engage in the very acts and conduct which would otherwise have been forbidden by an implied covenant of good faith and fair dealing.' " (*Ibid.*) Given the broad and express language of the escape clause, Steiner's power to withdraw was not constrained by the implied covenant of good faith and fair dealing.

In light of the foregoing reasons, we conclude the Court of Appeal correctly construed the so called "purchase contract" as an option. We next consider whether the option was irrevocable.

B. Sufficient Consideration Rendered the Option Irrevocable

"An option is transformed into a contract of purchase and sale when there is an unconditional, unqualified acceptance by the optionee of the offer in harmony with the terms of the option and within the time span of the option contract. [Citation.]" (*Erich v. Granoff* (1980) 109 Cal.App.3d 920, 928, 167 Cal.Rptr. 538.) At the time Thexton terminated the agreement, plaintiffs had not unconditionally accepted the offer within the terms of the option. Plaintiffs had not satisfied or waived all of the contingencies and deposited the balance of the purchase price into the escrow account. Therefore, the option never ripened into a purchase contract. However, even if an option has not yet ripened into a purchase contract, it may nonetheless be irrevocable for the negotiated period of time if sufficient bargained-for consideration is present.

"[A]n option based on consideration contemplates two separate [contracts], i.e., the option contract itself, which for something of value gives to the optionee the irrevocable right to buy under specified terms and conditions, and the mutually enforceable agreement to buy and sell into which the option ripens after it is exercised. Manifestly, then, an irrevocable option based on consideration is a contract...." (*Torlai v. Lee* (1969) 270 Cal.App.2d 854, 858, 76 Cal.Rptr. 239.) Conversely, an option without consideration is not binding on either party until

---

[9] Indeed, plaintiffs contradict themselves, later arguing "nothing in the Contract suggests that Thexton reserved the right to revoke, withdraw, or terminate his promise to sell the Property to Steiner...."

exercised (*id.* at pp. 858–859, 76 Cal.Rptr. 239); until then, the option " 'is simply a continuing offer which may be revoked at any time.' [Citation.]" (*Thomas v. Birch* (1918) 178 Cal. 483, 489, 173 P. 1102.)

Civil Code section 1605 defines consideration as "Any benefit conferred, or agreed to be conferred, upon the promisor, by any other person, to which the promisor is not lawfully entitled, or any prejudice suffered, or agreed to be suffered, by such person, other than such as he is at the time of consent lawfully bound to suffer, as an inducement to the promisor...." Thus, there are two requirements in order to find consideration. The promisee must confer (or agree to confer) a benefit or must suffer (or agree to suffer) prejudice. We emphasize either alone is sufficient to constitute consideration; "it is not necessary to the existence of a good consideration that a benefit should be conferred upon the promisor. It is enough that a 'prejudice be suffered or agreed to be suffered' by the promisee. [Citation.]" (*Bacon v. Grosse* (1913) 165 Cal. 481, 490–491, 132 P. 1027.)

It is not enough, however, to confer a benefit or suffer prejudice for there to be consideration. As we held in *Bard v. Kent, supra,* 19 Cal.2d at page 452, 122 P.2d 8, the second requirement is that the benefit or prejudice " 'must actually be bargained for as the exchange for the promise.' " Put another way, the benefit or prejudice must have induced the promisor's promise. In *Bard,* the property owner indicated she was willing to grant an extension of a lease for four years if the lessee's sublessee undertook $10,000 of improvements to the property. The owner suggested that the lessee have an architect draw sketches to get a cost estimate. The owner then granted an option to extend the lease in return for consideration of $10; however, the $10 was never paid to the owner and she died before the option was exercised. (*Id.* at p. 451, 122 P.2d 8.) The lessee nonetheless argued the money he spent for the architect's drawing was sufficient consideration to make the option irrevocable. The trial court disagreed, concluding the owner agreed to be bound in exchange for the unpaid $10, not for the lessee engaging the architect. (*Id.* at pp. 452–453, 122 P.2d 8.) We affirmed, quoting the Restatement of Contracts, section 75: " 'The fact that the promisee relies on the promise to his injury, or the promisor gains some advantage therefrom, does not establish consideration without the element of bargain or agreed exchange.' " (*Bard,* at p. 452, 122 P.2d 8.) In sum, in determining here whether sufficient consideration rendered the option to purchase the 10–acre parcel irrevocable, we consider whether Steiner conferred or agreed to confer a benefit or suffered or agreed to suffer prejudice that was bargained for in exchange for the option.

The lower courts concluded no such consideration supported the option. They reasoned no money was paid for the grant of the option nor did the work performed and expenses incurred by plaintiffs in pursuit of a parcel split benefit Thexton. Citing *O'Connell v. Lampe* (1929) 206 Cal. 282, 285, 274 P. 336, and *Drullinger v. Erskine* (1945) 71 Cal.App.2d 492, 495, 163 P.2d 48, the lower courts explained that the "adequacy of consideration" must be measured at the time an agreement was entered into. The lower courts concluded that, at the time Steiner and Thexton struck their bargain, the promise to seek the parcel split was unenforceable because the escape clause gave plaintiffs the power to terminate the transaction at any time for any reason. Thus, the lower courts held, Steiner's promise was illusory and did not constitute valid consideration. The courts found it immaterial that plaintiffs had begun to perform because plaintiffs were under no actual obligation to do so. To the contrary, we conclude as a matter of law that plaintiffs' part performance of the bargained-for promise to seek a parcel split created sufficient consideration to render the option irrevocable.

It is true that Steiner's promise to undertake the burden and expense of seeking a parcel split may have been illusory at the time the agreement was entered into, given the language of the escape clause. However, there can be no dispute that plaintiffs subsequently undertook substantial steps toward obtaining the parcel split and incurred significant expenses doing so.[10] Among other things, plaintiffs paid for the required civil engineering and surveying for the parcel and spent a number of months applying to the county planning department for a tentative parcel map, proceeding with the final hearing of the parcel review committee, and obtaining approval of the tentative map. On this record, the only possible conclusion is that Steiner both conferred a bargained-for benefit on Thexton and suffered bargained-for prejudice unaffected by his power to cancel, making up for the initially illusory nature of his promise.

It is undisputed that a parcel split of the 12.29 acres was necessary for Thexton to be able to sell a portion of his land to anyone while still retaining a two-acre parcel for himself to live on. There is also no dispute that Thexton did not want to have to go through the process of obtaining the parcel split himself. Indeed, he had previously rejected an offer of $750,000 for the 10 acres ($250,000 more than Steiner was to pay for the parcel) because that buyer wanted Thexton to obtain the required approval. It is clear then that a critical part of Thexton's willingness to sell was that Steiner would bear the expense, risk, and burden of seeking the parcel split. Indeed, there is evidence that Thexton told Steiner it was important to him that any interested buyer undertake the process of obtaining the parcel split. Thus, both elements of consideration were present. First, the effort to obtain the parcel split clearly conferred a benefit on Thexton *and* constituted prejudice suffered by plaintiffs.[11] Second, the promise to pursue the split was plainly bargained-for and induced Thexton to grant the option. Accordingly, plaintiffs' part performance cured the illusory nature of their promise.[12]

Two cases illustrate the point. In *Burgermeister Brewing Corp. v. Bowman* (1964) 227 Cal.App.2d 274, 38 Cal.Rptr. 597, a brewery entered into an oral contract with a distributor whereby the distributor would sell the brewer's product. (*Id.* at p. 278, 38 Cal.Rptr. 597.) The brewer agreed to give the distributor all the beer the distributor could sell using its best efforts.

---

[10] Plaintiffs completed 75 to 90 percent of the work needed to obtain the parcel split and county approvals and alleged they collectively spent $60,000 in doing so. We have no occasion to consider whether any act, no matter how small, would be sufficient part performance to make an option irrevocable.

[11] As Steiner's counsel acknowledged at oral argument, the outcome may have been different had plaintiffs' efforts been exclusively in their own interest, such as only securing county approvals to develop the 10-acre parcel.

[12] Although our conclusion is based upon plaintiffs' part performance of the promise to obtain a parcel split, we also note the agreement required Steiner to deposit $1,000 into escrow, which he did. The trial court concluded the payment did not constitute consideration because Steiner would recover the money if he terminated the agreement; thus, the money did not confer a benefit on Thexton. However, even assuming the trial court's interpretation of the agreement is accurate, it is not clear its ultimate conclusion is correct. As previously discussed, for consideration to exist it is sufficient that a promisee suffers bargained-for prejudice. By placing the money in escrow, Steiner gave up use of the money for as much as three years. This arguably constituted prejudice to Steiner even if he ultimately got the money back. In light of our conclusion regarding plaintiffs' part performance, we need not resolve the effect of the escrow payment.

Nineteen years later, after the distributor had spent significant time and resources selling the beer, the brewer cancelled the agreement. (*Id.* at pp. 278–280, 38 Cal.Rptr. 597.) When sued, the brewer argued the contract was illusory, lacking mutuality; it bound the brewer to provide the beer but did not bind the distributor to use its best efforts. (*Id.* at p. 280, 38 Cal.Rptr. 597.) In ruling for the distributor, the Court of Appeal explained that, even if the distributor had not promised to use its best efforts, its subsequent performance gave the brewery consideration not affected by the distributor's power to cancel and thereby made up for any defects in the original consideration. (*Ibid.,* citing 1A Corbin on Contracts, § 163, p. 76.)

In *Kowal v. Day* (1971) 20 Cal.App.3d 720, 98 Cal.Rptr. 118, the plaintiff entered into an agreement to purchase real property from the defendant. (*Id.* at p. 722, 98 Cal.Rptr. 118.) The escrow instructions required the plaintiff to give the defendant an automobile for the defendant's use and permitted the plaintiff to terminate the sale within 45 days after the close of escrow. The plaintiff subsequently gave the defendant the automobile, however, the defendant ultimately refused to convey the property to the plaintiff. In the resultant action, the trial court ruled in favor of the defendant, because of the plaintiff's unconditional and unilateral right to terminate the transaction. (*Id.* at pp. 722–723, 98 Cal.Rptr. 118.) The Court of Appeal reversed, explaining that although consideration is typically lacking when an exchange of promises does not impose mutual obligations, the plaintiff's part performance in the form of transferring possession of the car created sufficient consideration transforming the agreement's termination clause into an enforceable option, even though the plaintiff was entitled to return of the car upon disaffirmation of the transaction. (*Id.* at pp. 724, 726, 98 Cal.Rptr. 118.)

In sum, it is true that, where consideration for an agreement consists of an exchange of promises, that one party's promise is illusory generally means there is no consideration. (*Mattei v. Hopper* (1958) 51 Cal.2d 119, 122, 330 P.2d 625.) "A corollary to that rule exists, however. An agreement that is otherwise illusory may be enforced where the promisor has rendered at least part performance. [Citations.]" (*Money Store Investment Corp. v. Southern Cal. Bank* (2002) 98 Cal.App.4th 722, 728–729, 120 Cal.Rptr.2d 58.) Moreover, as this court explained in *Drennan v. Star Paving Co.* (1958) 51 Cal.2d 409, 414, 333 P.2d 757, when an offer for a unilateral contract is made (as in the case of an option) " 'and *part of the consideration requested in the offer is given or tendered by the offeree in response thereto,* the offeror is bound by a contract, the duty of immediate performance of which is conditional on the full consideration being given or tendered within the time stated in the offer....' "[13] (Italics added.) Applied here, plaintiffs' substantial efforts and expenditures to perform the bargained-for promise to seek a parcel split cured the initially illusory nature of the promise and rendered the option irrevocable.

We address two final points. First, as noted above, the lower courts concluded that the adequacy of consideration is to be determined at the time an agreement is entered into. However, the two cases relied upon are inapplicable here. In both cases, the parties had entered into option contracts for the purchase of real property. (*O'Connell v. Lampe, supra,* 206 Cal. at p. 282, 274 P. 336; *Drullinger v. Erskine, supra,* 71 Cal.App.2d at p. 494, 163 P.2d 48.) The parties agreed

---

[13] Thus, we reject the contention made by Thexton's counsel at oral argument that part performance can never constitute consideration for an option. (See also *Kowal v. Day, supra,* 20 Cal.App.3d at p. 726, 98 Cal.Rptr. 118.)

upon a price for the properties when they entered into the option contracts; however, at the time the buyers exercised their options, the sellers refused to perform, contending the agreed-upon consideration was inadequate due to a subsequent increase in the properties' value. (*O'Connell,* at p. 283, 274 P. 336; *Drullinger,* at pp. 494–495, 163 P.2d 48.) It was in this context that the courts ruled in favor of the buyers, explaining that the *adequacy* of consideration is determined at the time of the agreement. (*O'Connell,* at p. 285, 274 P. 336; *Drullinger,* at p. 495, 163 P.2d 48.) Here, by contrast, we consider not whether the agreed-upon consideration for the purchase was adequate, but whether consideration existed at all to support the option.

Second, we acknowledge that *Prather v. Vasquez* (1958) 162 Cal.App.2d 198, 327 P.2d 963 reached a seemingly different result. The case involved an agreement for the sale of property. The escrow instructions called for the buyer to deposit money and a trust deed. At the buyer's request, the agreement also required he pay all escrow costs in the event he withdrew; he explained he did not wish to buy the land if it could not be subdivided and he wanted to be protected from suit in that event. The buyer then sought to obtain development approval, but the owners cancelled the agreement before the buyer deposited money into escrow. The buyer argued the option was irrevocable because it was supported by valid consideration. (*Id.* at pp. 200, 202, 204, 327 P.2d 963.) In rejecting that argument, the Court of Appeal concluded the buyer's effort to seek development approval did not constitute consideration as it was not a bargained-for inducement for the offer of an option; nor did the buyer's obligation to pay costs if he cancelled the agreement provide consideration because it did not benefit the seller. (*Id.* at pp. 204–205, 327 P.2d 963.) Even if *Prather* were correct, it is factually distinguishable. There can be no dispute that Steiner's promise to seek the parcel split induced Thexton's offer of the option. Moreover, the parcel split itself, unlike the development approval sought in *Prather,* was necessary to Thexton's ability to sell the property because he wanted to retain two acres of the parcel.

In conclusion, we hold plaintiffs' part performance of their bargained-for promise to seek a parcel split cured the initially illusory nature of the promise and thereby constituted sufficient consideration to render the option irrevocable.

III. DISPOSITION

The judgment of the Court of Appeal is reversed and the case is remanded for further proceedings.[14]

WE CONCUR: GEORGE, C.J., KENNARD, BAXTER, WERDEGAR, CHIN, and CORRIGAN, JJ.

---

[14] Thexton raised a number of affirmative defenses in addition to the ones considered here. Among them were that plaintiffs' claims are barred by various equitable doctrines and that their claims are barred by the applicable statute of limitations. On remand, the lower courts can consider whether plaintiffs' claims survive Thexton's other defenses and, if so, what the appropriate remedy might be. Because the remedy of specific performance is equitable in nature (see, e.g., 13 Witkin, Summary of Cal. Law (10th ed. 2005) Equity, § 24, pp. 312–314), the lower courts can consider whether ordering specific performance is warranted or whether other relief might suffice.

Case 4:   Predominant Purpose Test
UCC 2-207

C 9 Ventures v. SVC–W., L.P.
California Court of Appeal, Fourth District, 2012
202 Cal.App.4th 1483

FYBEL, J.

INTRODUCTION

This case could serve as a question on a law school final examination for a course on the Uniform Commercial Code. As in a law school examination, the facts are undisputed. On July 3, 2007, SVC–West, L.P. (SVC), telephoned C9 Ventures (C9) and placed a rush order for eight helium-filled tanks used to inflate festive balloons. C9 accepted the order and later that day delivered the tanks without obtaining a signature on an invoice for them. On the reverse of the invoice was an indemnification provision requiring SVC to indemnify C9 for any loss arising out of the use or possession of the helium-filled tanks. C9 later picked up the tanks, and, weeks later, SVC paid the invoice. SVC had obtained helium-filled tanks from C9 on prior occasions.

After the tanks were delivered on July 3, a boy was injured when one of the helium-filled tanks fell on him. SVC and C9 each paid the boy's family to settle a lawsuit brought to recover for his injuries. C9 filed a cross-complaint against SVC to enforce the indemnification provision on the back of the unsigned invoice.

The question: Is the indemnification provision on the back of the unsigned invoice enforceable against SVC?

The trial court answered the question yes, finding under California Uniform Commercial Code[1] section 2207, the indemnification provision did not materially alter the contract and therefore became an added term. The trial court accordingly granted judgment in favor of C9 and awarded it attorney fees.

We answer the question differently and hold the indemnification provision is not binding on SVC. Our complete answer to the question is parts II. and III. of the Discussion section; the summary of our answer is the following. SVC and C9 entered into an oral contract when C9 accepted SVC's telephone order for eight helium-filled tanks. The oral lease was sufficiently definite, although it left open various terms. Under section 2207, on which the trial court relied, additional terms proposed in an acceptance or confirmation may become terms of the contract in certain situations. Section 2207 is part of division 2 of the California Uniform Commercial Code, and division 2 governs transactions in goods. The oral contract between SVC and C9, however,

---

[1] Further code citations are to the California Uniform Commercial Code.

110

was a *lease* of personal property (the helium-filled tanks), and personal property leases are governed by division 10, not division 2, of the California Uniform Commercial Code.

Division 10 of the California Uniform Commercial Code, which governs the oral contract between SVC and C9, does not have an analog to section 2207. The terms on the back of the unsigned invoice would have become part of the parties' oral contract only if SVC manifested assent to those terms. SVC did not manifest such assent by course of dealing or course of performance, or under basic contract law. SVC did not sign the invoice or otherwise expressly agree to its terms. An unsigned invoice itself is not a contract, and repeated delivery of a particular form does not make the form part of the parties' agreement. Payment of the invoice merely constituted SVC's performance of the obligation under the oral contract to pay for the rental of the helium-filled tanks.

To cover all bases (as one should when answering a law school examination question), we also construe the oral contract between SVC and C9 as if it were a transaction in goods governed by division 2 of the California Uniform Commercial Code and address whether the indemnification provision would have become an additional term under section 2207, as the trial court found. We conclude it would not. If SVC is not a merchant, the terms of the invoice are considered to be mere proposals for additional terms, which SVC did not accept. If SVC is a merchant, the indemnification provision would not have become part of the contract if the provision materially altered the contract. Because an indemnification provision is deemed a material alteration to an agreement as a matter of law, the indemnification provision on the back of the invoice would not, under section 2207, become part of the contract between SVC and C9.

We therefore reverse the judgment and remand with directions to enter judgment in SVC's favor. Because we reverse the judgment on which attorney fees were awarded, we also reverse the order awarding attorney fees. (*Metropolitan Water Dist. v. Imperial Irrigation Dist.* (2000) 80 Cal.App.4th 1403, 1436, 96 Cal.Rptr.2d 314.)

FACTS

*   *   *   *   *   *

SVC was in the business of selling time-shares, and had begun using C9 as a provider of event supplies, including helium-filled tanks and balloons, in November 2006. SVC typically placed an order by telephone, and C9 would deliver the supplies with a standard form invoice, which C9 would ask an SVC employee to sign.

The invoice was on a single piece of paper, on the reverse side of which was a section entitled "INDEMNITY/HOLD HARMLESS" (boldface omitted), which stated in part: "Customer agrees to indemnify[,] defend and hold harmless C9 ... from and against any and all liability, claims, judgments, attorneys fees and cost of ... every[ ] kind and nature, including, but not limited to injuries or death to persons and damage to property, arising out of the use, maintenance, instruction, operation, possession, ownership or Rental & Decor of the items rented, however cause[d], except claims or litigation arising through the solo [*sic*] gross negligence or willful misconduct of C9...." * * *

The accident underlying the cross-claim at issue took place on July 3, 2007. Before then, C9 had presented the same or similar invoice to SVC 10 times, but had received the signature of an SVC employee only six times. SVC never attempted to substitute its own form agreement for C9's form.

On July 3, SVC had time-share presentations scheduled for 3:30 p.m. and 5:30 p.m. on the mezzanine of the Crowne Plaza Resort in Garden Grove. In the late morning, Veronica Pasco, an employee of SVC, called C9 for a rush order of eight helium-filled tanks. C9 typically delivered the tanks in the morning when no SVC guests were present, but on July 3, C9's employee, Ernesto Roque, did not arrive at the SVC premises to make the delivery until about 5:00 p.m. Pasco had gone home, so Roque asked another SVC employee, Zayra Renteria, where to place the eight helium-filled tanks.

Renteria, who was expecting the delivery during her shift, instructed Roque to bring the tanks up to the mezzanine level of the resort, at which point she would inform him where to place them. Roque stacked five to seven tanks against the walls next to the service elevator. He was in the process of bringing up another tank when a young boy, whose parents were attending the time-share presentation, ran up to the tanks and hugged one of them, pulling it over. The tank, which was about five feet tall and weighed 130 pounds, fell on the boy's hand. He was hospitalized and underwent surgery for his injuries.

C9 did not obtain a signature from an SVC employee on the invoice for this delivery. Roque wrote the following note on the invoice: "[N]obody would sign [¶] all running around in lobby [¶] nobody knew who.... [¶] After accident nobody got signatures."

The invoice for the helium-filled tanks delivered on July 3 was invoice number 493, which was submitted for payment by SVC employee Angela Pringle, approved by an SVC manager, and paid by SVC on August 23, 2007. The invoice asked that the top portion, which referred to the invoice number, be returned with payment.

PROCEDURAL HISTORY

In January 2008, the injured boy and his parents sued SVC and C9 for injuries resulting from the accident. SVC and C9 paid $350,000 each to settle the case. C9 filed a cross-complaint for express indemnity against SVC, claiming the indemnification provision on the back of the July 3 invoice bound SVC to indemnify it for the sum paid to the injured boy's family and for attorney fees. C9 asserted section 2207, which allows merchants to add additional terms through acceptance of an offer or written confirmation, was applicable. SVC argued the terms of the invoice were not binding because it was never signed.

The trial court granted judgment in favor of C9 and explained its reasoning in a minute order stating: "The indemnity provision was contained on the reverse side of an unsigned invoice from C9 delivered with the helium tanks to SVC. [¶] The accident happened on July 3, 2007. During the year before the accident C9 had provided helium tanks and other product[s] to SVC on about 10 occasions. Each time, C9 would provide an invoice with the identical indemnity

112

language. On about half the prior occasions employees of SVC would sign the invoices and on the other occasions the invoices were not signed. SVC never objected to the indemnity language and accepted the product as it did on the day of the accident. C9 and SVC continued to do business in this manner after the accident as well. [¶] SVC's primary argument is that it never agreed to the indemnity language because the invoice was never signed. However, the Commercial Code has modified traditional concepts of offer and acceptance when the dealings are between merchants. SVC offered to purchase helium tanks for an agreed price. When C9 accepted the offer, it delivered the tanks with an invoice that contained indemnity language. The parties had followed this precise course of conduct multiple times in the past. Com.Code § 2207 provides that an offeree may add additional terms to an offer and those terms are deemed part of the agreement unless the offer expressly limits acceptance to the terms of the offer (which did not occur here) or the new terms materially alter the agreement. [¶] The court finds that the indemnity provision did not materially alter the terms of the agreement. SVC never objected to the language in their prior dealings and it is highly unlikely the helium tanks would have been rejected because the invoice added an indemnity clause. By accepting the goods on this and prior occasions SVC accepted the indemnity clause. Com.Code § 2206 provides that an acceptance can be made in any manner and by any medium reasonable in the circumstances."

* * * SVC timely appealed from the judgment.

DISCUSSION

*　　　　*　　　　*　　　　*　　　　*　　　　*

II.

The Indemnification Provision on the Invoice Was Not Part of the July 3, 2007 Oral Contract Between SVC and C9 for the Lease of the Helium-filled Tanks.

A. *SVC and C9 Entered into an Oral Contract on July 3, 2007.*

We begin our analysis by addressing whether a contract existed between SVC and C9 for the helium-filled tanks delivered to SVC on July 3, 2007. A contract for the sale of goods may be made "in any manner sufficient to show agreement, including conduct by both parties which recognizes the existence of such a contract." (§ 2204, subd. (1).) Likewise, a personal property lease may be made "in any manner sufficient to show agreement, including conduct by both parties which recognizes the existence of a lease contract." (§ 10204, subd. (a).) In the case of either a contract for the sale of goods or a personal property lease, the offer must be construed as "inviting acceptance in any manner and by any medium reasonable in the circumstances." (§§ 2206, subd. (1)(a), 10206, subd. (a).)

On July 3, 2007, SVC called C9 to request that it provide eight helium-filled tanks. This constituted an offer to make a contract. C9 orally accepted the offer by agreeing to provide the tanks and delivered them. An SVC employee, who was expecting the delivery, told C9's employee where to place the tanks. Under these facts, an oral contract was formed. SVC's telephone offer and C9's oral acceptance were sufficient to show agreement, and C9's acceptance was reasonable in both manner and medium under the circumstances. As in previous transactions with SVC, C9 delivered the helium-filled tanks with a standard form invoice. That invoice was generated after the contract had been formed and was not signed by SVC. Whether the invoice added terms to the oral contract is addressed in parts II.E., II.F., and III of the Discussion section.

This oral contract was sufficiently definite although it left open various terms. Although one or more terms are left open, neither a contract for the sale of goods nor a personal property lease fails for indefiniteness if the parties intended to make a contract and there is a reasonably certain basis for providing an appropriate remedy. (§§ 2204, subd. (3), 10204, subd. (c).) Here, SVC and C9 undoubtedly intended to make a contract by which SVC would pay C9 to provide helium-filled tanks on July 3, 2007. The property to be leased or purchased, the quantity, and the place of delivery were explicitly agreed upon. A reasonably certain basis for remedy would exist if one of the parties breached the agreement.

B. *The July 3, 2007 Oral Contract Between SVC and C9 Was for the Lease of Helium-filled Tanks.*

Having established there was an oral contract between SVC and C9, we next determine whether it was for the sale of goods or for the lease of personal property. This distinction is significant because sales of goods and leases of personal property are different kinds of transactions and are governed by different divisions of the California Uniform Commercial Code. Division 2, entitled "Sales," governs "transactions in goods." (§ 2102.) Division 10, entitled "Personal Property Leases," applies "to any transaction, regardless of form, that creates a lease." (§ 10102.)

C9 contends division 2 applies because the oral contract was essentially a sale of helium rather than a rental of tanks; that is, the tanks themselves were merely vessels for transporting the helium. SVC argues division 10 applies because "[t]his case did not concern the *sale* of goods; it concerned a *lease* of personal property."

The contract between SVC and C9 arguably involved both the sale of helium and the rental of the helium-filled tanks. A lease is defined as "a transfer of an interest in goods" and "does not include a sale." (Official Comments on U. Com.Code, 23C West's Ann. Cal. U. Com.Code (2002 ed.) foll. § 10102, p. 334.) A sale occurs when title passes from seller to buyer for a price. (§ 2106, subd. (1).) SVC had C9's permission to use as much of the helium in the tanks as was needed; C9 therefore relinquished "title" to the helium (to the extent someone can have title to a gas) either upon delivery to SVC or when SVC used the helium gas. But title to the tanks themselves never changed hands. The oral contract anticipated, as in previous transactions, that SVC would return the tanks to C9 when it next made a delivery.

We find no legal test to determine whether a *hybrid* transaction involving lease of a vessel *and* sale of its contents is a lease or transaction for the sale of goods. However, in deciding the somewhat analogous question whether a hybrid transaction for goods and services is predominantly a sale of goods governed by the Uniform Commercial Code, or predominantly a transaction for services governed by common law, courts have looked to the essence of the transaction. (*Filmservice Laboratories, Inc. v. Harvey Bernhard Enterprises, Inc.* (1989) 208 Cal.App.3d 1297, 1305, 256 Cal.Rptr. 735; *Bonebrake v. Cox* (8th Cir.1974) 499 F.2d 951, 960.) The court may compare the relative cost of the goods and services in the transaction and the purpose of the agreement in order to determine whether it is predominantly a sale of goods or transaction for services. (See *Pittsley v. Houser* (1994) 125 Idaho 820, 823, 875 P.2d 232, 235 [transaction for purchase and installation of carpet predominantly transaction for sale of goods].) "The test for inclusion or exclusion is not whether [goods and services] are mixed, but, granting that they are mixed, whether their predominant factor, their thrust, their purpose, reasonably stated, is the rendition of service, with goods incidentally involved (*e.g.,* contract with artist for painting) or is a transaction of sale, with labor incidentally involved (*e.g.,* installation of a water heater in a bathroom)." (*Bonebrake v. Cox, supra,* 499 F.2d at p. 960, fns. omitted.)

The predominant factor and purpose of the oral contract between SVC and C9 were the lease of helium-filled tanks to SVC. The July 3, 2007 invoice, and prior invoices, specified a flat fee of $65 for each tank provided, regardless of the amount of helium used by SVC to inflate balloons. At the end of the rental period, C9 retrieved the tanks and whatever helium was left in them. The invoice, and prior invoices, stated: "Title to the Rental & Decor items is and shall remain in ... C9" and if the "items are not returned and/or levied upon for any reason whatsoever, C9 ... may retake said items without f[u]rther notice or legal process and use whatever force is reasonably necessary to do so."

The injury out of which C9's claim for indemnification arose was caused by a helium-filled tank, which, without question, was being rented to SVC. The indemnification provision, which C9 seeks to enforce, applied by its terms only to rented items. The invoice itself stated, "[c]ustomer agrees to indemnify[,] defend and hold harmless C9 ... from and against any and all liability ... arising out of the use, maintenance, instruction, operation, possession, ownership or Rental & Decor of the *items rented.*" (Italics added.) The invoice did contain a separate section, entitled "TERMS AND CONDITIONS OF SALE" (boldface omitted), but it addressed only warranties.

C9 cannot have its cake and eat it too, demanding indemnification under a clause covering "items rented" while basing its legal arguments on a section of the code inapplicable to leased items. If the injury had been caused by the helium itself rather than the tank, the result might be less clear. The facts show the indemnification provision applied only to rented items, the helium-filled tank was rented, and the injury in question was caused by the tank. We therefore conclude the July 3, 2007 oral contract between SVC and C9 was for the lease of personal property and is governed by division 10 of the California Uniform Commercial Code.

C. *The Oral Contract for the Lease of Helium-filled Tanks Was Enforceable.*

Under division 10 of the California Uniform Commercial Code, a lease contract is enforceable only if there is a writing signed by the party against whom enforcement is sought or "[i]n a lease contract that is not a consumer lease, the total payments to be made under the lease contract ... are less than one thousand dollars ($1,000)." (§ 10201, subd. (a)(1), (2).) A consumer lease is one that "a lessor regularly engaged in the business of leasing or selling makes to a lessee who is an individual and who takes under the lease primarily for a personal, family, or household purpose." (§ 10103, subd. (a)(5).)

The oral contract between SVC and C9 was not a consumer lease because SVC did not rent the helium-filled tanks for a personal, family, or household purpose. Although the lease was not memorialized by a writing signed by SVC, the amount to be paid was less than $1,000 (the July 3 invoice is in the amount of $520). The oral lease contract therefore was enforceable despite the lack of a writing.

D. *Section 2207 Does Not Apply to a Personal Property Lease.*

The trial court relied on section 2207, part of division 2 of the California Uniform Commercial Code, as the basis for its finding the indemnification provision of the invoice bound SVC. Section 2207, which applies to transactions in goods between merchants, states, "[a] definite and seasonable expression of acceptance or a written confirmation which is sent within a reasonable time operates as an acceptance even though it states terms additional to or different from those offered or agreed upon, unless acceptance is expressly made conditional on assent to the additional or different terms." (§ 2207, subd. (1).) Section 2207 creates an exception to the traditional common law requirement that acceptance must mirror the terms of the offer in order to bind the offeror. (*Steiner v. Mobil Oil Corp.* (1977) 20 Cal.3d 90, 99, 141 Cal.Rptr. 157, 569 P.2d 751.) Division 10 of the California Uniform Commercial Code, which applies to personal property leases, has no provision similar in language or effect to section 2207.

Courts have generally declined to apply division 2 of the California Uniform Commercial Code, or its analogy as adopted in other jurisdictions, if the transaction in question is a lease rather than a sale of goods. (E.g., *Miley v. Harmony Mill Ltd. Partnership* (D.Del.1992) 803 F.Supp. 965, 968; *Technicon Instruments Corp. v. Pease* (Mo.Ct.App.1992) 829 S.W.2d 489, 490–491 ["Lease transactions are not governed by Article Two of the [Uniform Commercial] Code"]; *Prime Financial Group, Inc. v. Masters* (1996) 141 N.H. 33, 36, 676 A.2d 528, 531 ["we note that the provisions of article 2 of the [Uniform Commercial Code], dealing with sales of goods, do not apply to this case because the trial court specifically found that the contract at issue was a true lease and not a contract for the sale of goods"]; *Skinner v. Turner* (1986) 30 Ohio App.3d 232, 234, 507 N.E.2d 392, 394–395 ["Ohio's version of Article 2 of the Uniform Commercial Code ... is inapplicable to ... a lease agreement of limited duration where the lessor specifically retains title to the subject matter of the lease"].) Courts which have extended article 2 of the Uniform Commercial Code to leases have done so only when the lease was analogous to or the functional equivalent of a sale and only in the case of extending warranties for public policy reasons. (See *American Family Mut. Ins. Co. v. Jepson* (8th Cir.1998) 148 F.3d 954, 956 [installment purchase a sale despite contract labeled "lease"]; *Hornberger v. General Motors Corp.* (E.D.Pa.1996) 929 F.Supp. 884, 887 [five-year automobile lease analogous to a sale, so warranty provisions applicable to sales apply]; *W.E. Johnson Equipment Co. v. United Airlines, Inc.* (Fla.1970) 238 So.2d 98, 99–100 [extending warranty of fitness to cover leased goods]; *Cucchi v. Rollins Protective Services Co.* (1988) 377 Pa.Super. 9, 28, 546 A.2d 1131, 1140–1141 [express warranty provisions of article applied to leases of goods], revd. on other grounds (1990) 524 Pa. 514, 526, 574 A.2d 565, 571.)

In this case, the oral contract between SVC and C9 was not analogous to or the functional equivalent of a sale. Thus, division 2, including section 2207, of the California Uniform Commercial Code does not apply to that contract. Instead, we determine whether the indemnity provision is enforceable under division 10 of the California Uniform Commercial Code.

E. *The Indemnification Provision of the Unsigned Invoice Did Not Become Part of the Oral Contract to Lease the Helium-filled Tanks Under Course of Performance or Course of Dealing.*

The express terms of the July 3, 2007 oral contract between SVC and C9 for the lease of eight helium-filled tanks did not include an indemnification provision. The unsigned invoice, confirming the oral contract, included the indemnification provision C9 seeks to enforce. Did the terms of the invoice become part of the oral contract between SVC and C9 for the lease of the helium-filled tanks?

We hold the indemnification provision in the invoice did not become part of the contract. The terms of the invoice were not incorporated into the contract under a course of performance or course of dealing analysis for the following reasons.

The California Uniform Commercial Code provides that "[a] course of performance or course of dealing between the parties ... is relevant in ascertaining the meaning of the parties' agreement, may give particular meaning to specific terms of the agreement, and may supplement or qualify the terms of the agreement." (§ 1303, subd. (d).) A " 'course of performance' " exists when "the agreement of the parties with respect to the transaction involves repeated occasions for performance by a party." (§ 1303, subd. (a)(1).) A " 'course of dealing,' " on the other hand, requires "a sequence of conduct concerning previous transactions between the parties to a particular transaction that is fairly to be regarded as establishing a common basis of understanding for interpreting their expressions and other conduct." (§ 1303, subd. (b).)

1. Course of Performance

Course of performance is governed by the general provisions of the California Uniform Commercial Code contained in section 1303. Section 1303's course of performance analysis applies only where "the agreement of the parties with respect to the transaction involves repeated occasions for performance by a party." (§ 1303, subd. (a)(1).)

A course of performance did not exist in this case because the agreement in issue here—the July 3, 2007 oral contract for the eight helium-filled tanks—did not involve repeated occasions for performance. The oral contract was a single agreement created when C9 accepted SVC's offer to rent helium-filled tanks on that date. The tanks were delivered to SVC, retrieved by C9, and paid for by SVC at a later date. There were no other occasions for performance of the oral contract, and there were never in the course of the relationship between SVC and C9 any occasions for performance of the terms on the back of the invoices.

Each prior transaction in which SVC rented helium-filled tanks from C9 constituted a separate, individual contract that was created by a separate telephone offer and acceptance by C9 for which a separate invoice was generated. Each prior transaction cannot be said to be part performance of a long-term or master contract covering all of SVC's rentals of helium-filled tanks from C9, and there was no evidence of such a contract between SVC and C9. There was not, for example, a " 'requirements contract' " by which C9 agreed to " 'furnish all goods of a certain kind which the other party may *need* or require in a certain business for a definite period.' " (*Fisher v. Parsons* (1963) 213 Cal.App.2d 829, 834, 29 Cal.Rptr. 210.) Performance on prior occasions based on different agreements to rent helium-filled tanks did not establish a course of performance creating additional terms to the July 3, 2007 oral contract

2. Course of Dealing

As for course of dealing, SVC and C9 engaged in a sequence of conduct involving previous instances in which SVC rented helium-filled tanks. Before July 3, 2007, C9 and SVC entered into 10 such transactions in which C9 provided an invoice with identical terms, including the indemnification provision, on the back. On six of those 10 occasions, an SVC employee signed the invoice. That means, of course, on four of those 10 occasions, an SVC employee did not sign the invoice. The question is whether these facts establish, in the statute's words, "a common basis of understanding" with respect to the indemnification provision on the back of C9's July 3, 2007 invoice. (§ 1303, subd. (b).) "An inference of the parties' common knowledge or understanding that is based upon a prior course of dealing is a question of fact." (*In re CFLC, Inc.* (9th Cir.1999) 166 F.3d 1012, 1017 (*CFLC*).) We review findings of fact under a substantial evidence standard of review. (*Haraguchi v. Superior Court* (2008) 43 Cal.4th 706, 711, 76 Cal.Rptr.3d 250, 182 P.3d 579.) Here, the trial court's minute order stated judgment for C9 was based on section 2207, which we have concluded does not apply to the oral contract between SVC and C9. However, no party requested a statement of decision, and, absent a statement of decision, "[t]he doctrine of implied findings requires the appellate court to infer the trial court made all factual findings necessary to support the judgment." (*Fladeboe v. American Isuzu Motors Inc.* (2007) 150 Cal.App.4th 42, 58–59, 58 Cal.Rptr.3d 225.)

Thus, we infer the trial court made an implied finding SVC and C9 engaged in a course of dealing fairly to be regarded as establishing a common basis of understanding, and review that implied finding for substantial evidence. (*Fladeboe v. American Isuzu Motors Inc., supra,* 150 Cal.App.4th at pp. 59–60, 58 Cal.Rptr.3d 225.) We conclude substantial evidence supports a finding that SVC engaged in a course or pattern of conduct with each transaction, but substantial evidence does not support a finding such course or pattern of conduct established a course of dealing by which SVC and C9 commonly understood the indemnification provision on the back of the invoice would be part of their contract.

The evidence established only the common understanding that with each delivery of helium-filled tanks, C9 would present an invoice and request a signature. We may infer C9 requested a signature from SVC as a manifestation of its assent to the terms of the invoice. Six times SVC signed, four times it did not. Those facts do not support an inference that SVC understood the terms on the back of the invoice would be a common basis of understanding for every transaction with C9.

An analogous case is *CFLC, supra,* 166 F.3d 1012. In that case, the Ninth Circuit of the United States Court of Appeals concluded an invoice did not add terms to a contract under the California Uniform Commercial Code because "[c]ourse of dealing analysis is not proper in an instance where the only action taken has been the repeated delivery of a particular form by one of the parties." (*CFLC, supra,* at p. 1017.) Adopting the reasoning of the Third Circuit Court of Appeals in *Step–Saver Data Systems, Inc. v. Wyse Technology* (3d Cir.1991) 939 F.2d 91 (*Step–Saver*), the *CFLC* court refused to extend course of dealing analysis "to a situation where the parties had not previously taken any action with respect to the matters addressed by the disputed terms." (*CFLC, supra,* at p. 1017.) The court concluded, "the repeated exchange of forms merely indicated the seller's desire to have these terms included" because "[t]he failure to obtain the purchaser's express assent to those terms indicates the seller's agreement to do business on other terms—those expressly agreed upon by the parties." (*Ibid.*)

F. *The Indemnification Provision Did Not Become Part of the Oral Contract to Lease Helium-filled Tanks Under Principles of Contract Law.*

Division 10 of the California Uniform Commercial Code does not include a section similar to section 2207, permitting the addition of terms to a contract by means of an acceptance or written confirmation. Thus, unlike division 2 of the California Uniform Commercial Code, division 10 in itself provides no basis for incorporating the indemnification provision on the back of the invoice into the oral contract between SVC and C9 to rent helium-filled tanks.

Under common law principles, SVC could have assented to the terms on the back of the invoice by signing it or manifesting assent in some other way. SVC did not, however, sign the July 3 invoice. "[U]nder the common law, '[s]ilence in the face of an offer is not an acceptance, unless there is a relationship between the parties or a previous course of dealing pursuant to which silence would be understood as acceptance.' [Citation]." (*CFLC, supra,* 166 F.3d at p. 1018, quoting *Southern Cal. Acoustics Co. v. C.V. Holder, Inc.* (1969) 71 Cal.2d 719, 722, 79 Cal.Rptr. 319, 456 P.2d 975.) As discussed above, no course of dealing existed that would allow us to treat SVC's silence as acceptance. SVC did not sign the invoice on four of the 10 occasions before July 3, 2007, on which C9 presented an invoice to SVC.

SVC did pay the invoice. The stipulation of facts presented at trial included the fact that "invoice # 493, dated July 3, 2007, was submitted for payment by SVC employee, Angela Pringle, and approved by a manager. SVC paid the invoice on August 23, 2007. There was no discussion between SVC and [C]9 of the terms on the reverse side of the document before the [underlying] lawsuit was filed." Did approval and payment of the invoice constitute acceptance of the indemnification provision?

A provision on a form agreement signed by the party against whom enforcement is sought is binding even if the party was unaware of the provision. (*N.A.M.E.S. v. Singer* (1979) 90 Cal.App.3d 653, 656, 153 Cal.Rptr. 472.) "A party cannot avoid the terms of a contract on the ground that he or she failed to read it before signing. [Citations.]" (*Marin Storage & Trucking, Inc. v. Benco Contracting & Engineering, Inc.* (2001) 89 Cal.App.4th 1042, 1049, 107 Cal.Rptr.2d 645 (*Marin*).) Unsigned invoices, however, cannot on their own create a contract or add terms to a contract. "The prevailing rule is that an invoice, standing alone, is not a contract [citations]; and a buyer is ordinarily not bound by statements thereon which are not a part of the original agreement." (*India Paint & Lacquer Co. v. United Steel Prod. Corp.* (1954) 123 Cal.App.2d 597, 607, 267 P.2d 408.) "After the orders were placed the seller transmitted certain invoices on which it attempted to place certain additional covenants into the contract. Such additions were mere self-serving declarations on the part of the seller and were not binding on the purchasers." (*Kocher v. Cartman Tire Exchange* (1930) 108 Cal.App. 619, 620, 291 P. 856.) "An invoice, as such, is no contract." (*Tanenbaum Textile Co. v. Schlanger* (1942) 287 N.Y. 400, 404, 40 N.E.2d 225, 226.)

Payment of an invoice with terms different from those of the oral contract also does not constitute acceptance of additional terms. The Ninth Circuit Court of Appeals has concluded an invoice does not modify an oral contract even if the party against whom enforcement of those terms is being sought has repeatedly paid on the invoices. (*Chateau des Charmes Wines Ltd. v. Sabate USA Inc.* (9th Cir.2003) 328 F.3d 528 (*Chateau des Charmes*).) In *Chateau des Charmes,* the plaintiff, a winery, agreed by telephone with the defendant, a manufacturer of special wine corks, to purchase a certain number of corks at a specific price. (*Id.* at p. 529.) For each shipment of corks, the defendant sent an invoice stating (in French) the sole jurisdiction for " '[a]ny dispute arising under the present contract' " would be in France. (*Ibid.*) After the corks tainted the plaintiff's wine, the plaintiff sued the defendant in federal district court in California for breach of contract, among other things. (*Id.* at pp. 529–530.)

The district court dismissed the complaint based on the forum selection clause, finding it was part of the contract between the parties. (*Chateau des Charmes, supra,* 328 F.3d at p. 529.) The Ninth Circuit reversed. (*Ibid.*) It concluded mere acceptance and payment of the invoices containing the forum selection clause did not constitute assent to the clause as an additional term of the contract. (*Id.* at p. 531.) "There is no indication that [the plaintiff] conducted itself in a manner that evidenced any affirmative assent to the forum selection clauses in the invoices. Rather, [the plaintiff] merely performed its obligations under the oral contract." (*Ibid.*)

The contract in *Chateau des Charmes* was subject to the United Nations Convention on Contracts for the International Sale of Goods (CISG). The Ninth Circuit stated, "[n]othing in the [CISG] suggests that the failure to object to a party's unilateral attempt to alter materially the terms of an otherwise valid agreement is an 'agreement' within the terms of Article 29 [of the

CISG]." (*Chateau des Charmes, supra,* 328 F.3d at p. 531.) Division 10 of the California Uniform Commercial Code likewise does not include a provision suggesting failure to object to additional terms contained in an invoice may constitute acceptance of those terms. Section 2207 does address additional terms included in a written confirmation of acceptance, such as an invoice, but section 2207 applies only to transactions in goods, not leases of personal property, and, as we shall conclude, under section 2207, the indemnification provision did not become a term of the contract between SVC and C9.

*   *   *   *   *   *

III.

Under Section 2207, the Indemnification Provision Was Not Part of the Oral Contract Between SVC and C9.

The trial court relied on section 2207, subdivision (2) to reach the conclusion the indemnification provision on the back of the invoice was part of the contract between SVC and C9. We have concluded the contract between SVC and C9 was for the rental of helium-filled tanks. Section 2207 applies only to the sale of goods, and division 10 of the California Uniform Commercial Code, which governs personal property leases, does not have a provision similar to section 2207. Nonetheless, we address whether, even under section 2207, the indemnification provision would have become a term of the contract between SVC and C9.

Under section 2207, parties may conclude a contract for the sale of goods even when the forms they exchange to memorialize the agreement have different terms. Subdivisions (1) and (2) of section 2207 read: "(1) A definite and seasonable expression of acceptance or a written confirmation which is sent within a reasonable time operates as an acceptance even though it states terms additional to or different from those offered or agreed upon, unless acceptance is expressly made conditional on assent to the additional or different terms. [¶] (2) The additional terms are to be construed as proposals for addition to the contract. Between merchants such terms become part of the contract unless: [¶] (a) The offer expressly limits acceptance to the terms of the offer; [¶] (b) They materially alter it; or [¶] (c) Notification of objection to them has already been given or is given within a reasonable time after notice of them is received."

Section 2207 "establishes a legal rule that proceeding with a contract after receiving a writing that purports to define the terms of the parties'[ ] contract is not sufficient to establish the party's consent to the terms of the writing to the extent that the terms of the writing either add to, or differ from, the terms detailed in the parties'[ ] earlier writings or discussions. In the absence of a party's express assent to the additional or different terms of the writing, section 2–207 provides a default rule that the parties intended, as the terms of their agreement, those terms to which both parties have agreed, along with any terms implied by the provisions of the [Uniform Commercial Code]." (*Step–Saver, supra,* 939 F.2d at p. 99, fns. omitted.)

When both parties to the transaction are "merchants,"[2] the additional terms in the

_____

[2] " 'Merchant' means a person who deals in goods of the kind or otherwise by his occupation holds himself

acceptance or written confirmation automatically become part of the contract unless (1) the offer expressly limits acceptance to the terms of the offer, (2) the additional terms materially alter the contract, or (3) the other party has objected to the additional terms or objects to them within a reasonable time after receiving the acceptance or confirmation. (§ 2207, subd. (2).)

SVC and C9 made an oral contract for SVC to rent helium-filled tanks from C9 on July 3, 2007.[3] That contract became enforceable at the point when C9 delivered the helium-filled tanks and SVC had a reasonable time to inspect them. (§ 2201, subds.(1), (3)(c).) Even assuming the oral contract was for the sale of goods, such that section 2207 would apply, the invoice constituted a written confirmation of the agreement and made proposals for additional terms, including the indemnification provision, which differed from the parties' oral contract.

If SVC is not considered to be a merchant, those additional terms would be construed as proposals for additions to the contract and would become part of the agreement only if SVC expressly assented to them. (See Official Comments on U. Com.Code, 23A pt. 1 West's Ann. Cal. U. Com.Code (2002 ed.) foll. § 2207, p. 219 ["Under this Article a proposed deal which in commercial understanding has in fact been closed is recognized as a contract. Therefore, any additional matter contained in the confirmation ... falls within subsection (2) and must be regarded as a proposal for an added term unless the acceptance is made conditional on the acceptance of the additional or different terms"].)

Substantial evidence would not support a finding, express or implied, that SVC expressly assented to the additional terms proposed in the invoice. SVC did not sign the invoice four of the 10 times in which it ordered helium-filled tanks from C9 before July 3, 2007. SVC did not sign the invoice for the July 3, 2007 helium-filled tank order and did not otherwise communicate to C9 an assent to the additional terms proposed in the invoice. Payment of the invoice did not constitute assent to its proposed additional terms because payment is deemed to be performance of SVC's obligation under the oral contract to pay for the helium-filled tanks. (*Chateau des Charmes, supra,* 328 F.3d at p. 531.) C9's repeated use in the past of invoices with the same indemnification provision, without express objection from SVC, does not constitute a course of dealing or assent to the terms of the invoice. (*CFLC, supra,* 166 F.3d 1012, 1017 [sending preprinted invoices claiming a general lien for unpaid charges and expenses does not constitute a course of dealing]; *Step–Saver, supra,* 939 F.2d at pp. 103–104; *Diskin v. J.P. Stevens & Co., Inc.* (1st Cir.1987) 836 F.2d 47, 51 ["mere *use* of the same ineffective form of contract is not the functional equivalent of evidence which affirmatively establishes a party's prior consent" to the disputed provision]; *Maxon Corp. v. Tyler Pipe Industries, Inc.* (Ind.Ct.App.1986) 497 N.E.2d 570, 575–576 [repeated use of same forms does not imply parties' awareness or assent to terms]; see also 1 White & Summers, Uniform Commercial Code (5th ed.2006) § 3–3, p. 192 ["the mere sending of terms back and forth does not, without more, create a course of dealing"]; see also *Transwestern Pipeline Co. v. Monsanto Co.* (1996) 46 Cal.App.4th 502, 517–518, 53

---

out as having knowledge or skill peculiar to the practices or goods involved in the transaction or to whom such knowledge or skill may be attributed by his employment of an agent or broker or other intermediary who by his occupation holds himself out as having such knowledge or skill." (§ 2104, subd. (1).)

[3] "A contract for sale of goods may be made in any manner sufficient to show agreement, including conduct by both parties which recognizes the existence of such a contract." (§ 2204, subd. (1).)

Cal.Rptr.2d 887 [citing *Step–Saver* with approval].)

If SVC is considered to be a merchant, however, the additional terms of the invoice, including the indemnification provision, would become terms of the contract unless they materially altered the contract or SVC objected to them. (There is no dispute that the offer did not expressly limit acceptance to the terms of the offer.) There is no evidence SVC ever objected to the terms of the July 3, 2007 invoice within a reasonable time of receiving it, so the issue would be whether the indemnification provision materially altered the terms of the parties' oral contract.

A clause that would materially alter the contract is one which "result [s] in surprise or hardship if incorporated without express awareness by the other party." (Official Comments on U. Com.Code, 23A pt. 1 West's Ann. Cal. U. Com.Code, *supra,* foll. § 2207 at p. 219.)

In this case, the trial court found the indemnification provision on the reverse side of the invoice did not materially alter the terms of the agreement.[4] That finding is legally erroneous. An indemnification provision would constitute a material alteration, as a matter of law, to the oral contract between SVC and C9. In *Trans–Aire International, Inc. v. Northern Adhesive Co.* (7th Cir.1989) 882 F.2d 1254, 1256, 1260, the plaintiff placed 12 separate telephone orders to purchase an adhesive from the defendant and confirmed each order with a purchase order containing an indemnity clause. The plaintiff sued the defendant to enforce the indemnity clause after the adhesive damaged the interiors of the recreational vehicles in which it had been used. (*Id.* at pp. 1256–1257.) The district court, granting summary judgment in the defendant's favor, found as a matter of law the indemnity provision materially altered the terms of the parties' agreement. (*Id.* at p. 1261.) The Seventh Circuit Court of Appeals agreed, concluding "the indemnification clause clearly imposes an unreasonable hardship upon [the defendant] which should not be enforced without evidence of mutual assent to that term." (*Id.* at p. 1262.)

The Seventh Circuit reasoned an indemnity clause has the same effect as a provision disclaiming or excluding warranties, which is "regularly characterized as a material alteration as a matter of law." (*Trans–Aire International, Inc. v. Northern Adhesive Co., supra,* 882 F.2d at p. 1263.) The court explained: "An indemnification clause, like a warranty disclaimer, relieves a party of otherwise well-established legal duties and obligations. Clearly, a shift in legal liability which has the effect of relieving one party of the potential for significant economic hardship and placing this burden upon another party is an important term in any contract. Thus, it is not surprising that such a term, if it is to be included in a contract, is ordinarily the subject of active negotiation between parties. We therefore do not believe that a party charged with legal duties and obligations may reasonably rely upon a boilerplate clause in a boilerplate form and a corresponding operation of law to shift substantial economic burdens from itself to a nonassenting party when it had every opportunity to negotiate such a term if it desired." (*Ibid.*)

Other courts also have reached the conclusion an indemnity provision constitutes a material alteration of an agreement. (*Union Carbide Corp. v. Oscar Mayer Foods Corp.* (7th

---

[4] The trial court also found SVC was neither surprised by nor unaware of the indemnification provision because the same invoice had been used on 10 prior occasions. The test is not whether SVC was aware of the indemnification provision but whether it "materially alter[ed]" the parties' agreement. (§ 2207, subd. (2)(b).)

Cir.1991) 947 F.2d 1333, 1337–1338; *St. Charles Cable TV, Inc. v. Eagle Comtronics, Inc.* (S.D.N.Y.1988) 687 F.Supp. 820, 828; *Resch v. Greenlee Bros. & Co.* (1985) 128 Wis.2d 237, 381 N.W.2d 590; *Power Press Sales Co. v. MSI Battle Creek Stamping* (1999) 238 Mich.App. 173, 181, 604 N.W.2d 772, 776; see also *Palmer G. Lewis Co. v. ARCO Chemical Co.* (Alaska 1995) 904 P.2d 1221, 1230 ["we have found no case where an indemnity clause was held to be 'immaterial' under section 2–207" of the Uniform Commercial Code].) We agree with these opinions and conclude an indemnity provision constitutes a material alteration of an agreement.

*   *   *   *   *   *

Because the indemnification provision would have materially altered the terms of the oral contract between SVC and C9, the provision did not become part of their contract under section 2207. A party to an agreement can decide nonetheless to accept the additional term, even if it modifies the agreement. Such acceptance may be made expressly or "from silence, in the face of a course of dealings that makes it reasonable for the other party to infer consent from a failure to object." (*Union Carbide Corp. v. Oscar Mayer Foods Corp., supra,* 947 F.2d at p. 1336.) As we have explained, SVC did not expressly accept the additional terms on the back of the invoice, payment on the invoice did not constitute assent to its additional terms, and past use of the invoice did not constitute assent or a course of dealing from which assent can be inferred.

DISPOSITION

The judgment * * * is reversed and the matter is remanded with directions to enter judgment in SVC's favor. Appellant to recover costs incurred on appeal.

WE CONCUR: BEDSWORTH, Acting P.J., and O'LEARY, J.

Case 5:   **Fraud – Failure to Disclose a Material Fact**

Reed v. King
California Court of Appeals, Third District, 1983
145 Cal.App.3d 261

BLEASE, J.

In the sale of a house, must the seller disclose it was the site of a multiple murder?

Dorris Reed purchased a house from Robert King. Neither King nor his real estate agents (the other named defendants) told Reed that a woman and her four children were murdered there 10 years earlier. However, it seems "truth will come to light; murder cannot be hid long." (Shakespeare, Merchant of Venice, act II, scene II.) Reed learned of the gruesome episode from a neighbor after the sale. She sues seeking rescission and damages. King and the real estate agent defendants successfully demurred to her first amended complaint for failure to state a cause of action. Reed appeals the ensuing judgment of dismissal. We will reverse the judgment.

Facts

We take all issuable facts pled in Reed's complaint as true. (See 3 Witkin, Cal. Procedure (2d ed. 1971) Pleading, § 800.) King and his real estate agent knew about the murders and knew the event materially affected the market value of the house when they listed it for sale. They represented to Reed the premises were in good condition and fit for an "elderly lady" living alone. They did not disclose the fact of the murders. At some point King asked a neighbor not to inform Reed of that event. Nonetheless, after Reed moved in neighbors informed her no one was interested in purchasing the house because of the stigma. Reed paid $76,000, but the house is only worth $65,000 because of its past.

The trial court sustained the demurrers to the complaint on the ground it did not state a cause of action. The court concluded a cause of action could only be stated "if the subject property, by reason of the prior circumstances, were *presently* the object of community notoriety . . . ." (Original italics.) Reed declined the offer of leave to amend.

Discussion

Does Reed's pleading state a cause of action? Concealed within this question is the nettlesome problem of the duty of disclosure of blemishes on real property which are not physical defects or legal impairments to use.

Reed seeks to state a cause of action sounding in contract, i.e. rescission, or in tort, i.e., deceit. In either event her allegations must reveal a fraud. (See Civ. Code, §§ 1571- 1573, 1689,

1709- 1710.) "The elements of actual fraud, whether as the basis of the remedy in contract or tort, may be stated as follows: There must be (1) a *false representation* or concealment of a material fact (or, in some cases, an opinion) susceptible of knowledge, (2) made with *knowledge* of its falsity or without sufficient knowledge on the subject to warrant a representation, (3) with the *intent* to induce the person to whom it is made to act upon it; and such person must (4) act in *reliance* upon the representation (5) to his *damage*."[1] (Original italics. (1 Witkin, Summary of Cal. Law (8th ed. 1973) Contracts, § 315.)

The trial court perceived the defect in Reed's complaint to be a failure to allege concealment of a material fact. "Concealment" and "material" are legal conclusions concerning the effect of the issuable facts pled. As appears, the analytic pathways to these conclusions are intertwined.

Concealment is a term of art which includes mere nondisclosure when a party has a duty to disclose. (See, e.g., *Lingsch* v. *Savage* (1963) 213 Cal.App.2d 729, 738 [29 Cal.Rptr. 201, 8 A.L.R.3d 537]; Rest.2d Contracts, § 161; Rest.2d Torts, § 551; Rest., Restitution, § 8, esp. com. b.) Reed's complaint reveals only nondisclosure despite the allegation King asked a neighbor to hold his peace. There is no allegation the attempt at suppression was a cause in fact of Reed's ignorance.[2] (See Rest.2d Contracts, §§ 160, 162-164; Rest.2d Torts, § 550; Rest., Restitution, § 9.) Accordingly, the critical question is: does the seller have a duty to disclose here? Resolution of this question depends on the materiality of the fact of the murders.

In general, a seller of real property has a duty to disclose: "where the seller knows of facts *materially* affecting the value or desirability of the property which are known or accessible only to him and also knows that such facts are not known to, or within the reach of the diligent attention and observation of the buyer, the seller is under a duty to disclose them to the buyer.[3] [Italics added, citations omitted.]" (*Lingsch* v. *Savage, supra,* 213 Cal.App.2d at p. 735.) This broad statement of duty has led one commentator to conclude: "The ancient maxim *caveat emptor* ('let the buyer beware.') has little or no application to California real estate transactions." (1 Miller & Starr, Current Law of Cal. Real Estate (rev.ed. 1975) § 1:80.)

---

[1] Proof of damage, i.e. specific pecuniary loss, is not essential to obtain rescission alone. (See 1 Witkin, *op. cit. supra,* §§ 324-325; see also *Earl* v. *Saks & Co.* (1951) 36 Cal.2d 602 [226 P.2d 340].)

[2] Reed elsewhere in the complaint asserts defendants "actively concealed" the fact of the murders and this in part misled her. However, no connection is made or apparent between the legal conclusion of active concealment and any issuable fact pled by Reed. Accordingly, the assertion is insufficient. (See *Bacon* v. *Soule* (1912) 19 Cal.App. 428, 438 [126 P. 384].) Similarly we do not view the statement the house was fit for Reed to inhabit as transmuting her case from one of nondisclosure to one of false representation. To view the representation as patently false is to find "elderly ladies" uniformly susceptible to squeamishness. We decline to indulge this stereotypical assumption. To view the representation as misleading because it conflicts with a duty to disclose is to beg that question.

[3] The real estate agent or broker representing the seller is under the same duty of disclosure. (*Lingsch* v. *Savage, supra,* 213 Cal.App.2d at p. 736.)

Whether information "is of sufficient materiality to affect the value or desirability of the property . . . depends on the facts of the particular case." (Lingsch, *supra*, 213 Cal.App.2d at p. 737.) Materiality "is a question of law, and is part of the concept of right to rely or justifiable reliance." (3 Witkin, Cal. Procedure (2d ed. 1971) Pleading, § 578, p. 2217.) Accordingly, the term is essentially a label affixed to a normative conclusion. Three considerations bear on this legal conclusion: the gravity of the harm inflicted by nondisclosure; the fairness of imposing a duty of discovery on the buyer as an alternative to compelling disclosure, and the impact on the stability of contracts if rescission is permitted.

Numerous cases have found nondisclosure of physical defects and legal impediments to use of real property are material. (See 1 Miller & Starr, *supra*, § 181.)[4] However, to our knowledge, no prior real estate sale case has faced an issue of nondisclosure of the kind presented here. (Compare *Earl* v. *Saks & Co., supra*, 36 Cal.2d 602; *Kuhn* v. *Gottfried* (1951) 103 Cal.App.2d 80, 85-86 [229 P.2d 137].) Should this variety of ill-repute be required to be disclosed? Is this a circumstance where "non-disclosure of the fact amounts to a failure to act in good faith and in accordance with reasonable standards of fair dealing[?]" (Rest.2d Contracts, § 161, subd. (b).)

The paramount argument against an affirmative conclusion is it permits the camel's nose of unrestrained irrationality admission to the tent. If such an "irrational" consideration is permitted as a basis of rescission the stability of all conveyances will be seriously undermined. Any fact that might disquiet the enjoyment of some segment of the buying public may be seized upon by a disgruntled purchaser to void a bargain.[5] In our view, keeping this genie in the bottle is not as difficult a task as these arguments assume. We do not view a decision allowing Reed to survive a demurrer in these unusual circumstances as indorsing the materiality of facts predicating peripheral, insubstantial, or fancied harms.

The murder of innocents is highly unusual in its potential for so disturbing buyers they may be unable to reside in a home where it has occurred. This fact may foreseeably deprive a

---

[4] For example, the following have been held of sufficient materiality to require disclosure: the home sold was constructed on filled land (*Burkett* v. *J.A. Thompson & Son* (1957) 150 Cal.App.2d 523, 526 [310 P.2d 56]); improvements were added without a building permit and in violation of zoning regulations (*Barder* v. *McClung* (1949) 93 Cal.App.2d 692, 697 [209 P.2d 808]) or in violation of building codes (*Curran* v. *Heslop* (1953) 115 Cal.App.2d 476, 480-481 [252 P.2d 378]); the structure was condemned (*Katz* v. *Department of Real Estate* (1979) 96 Cal.App.3d 895, 900 [158 Cal.Rptr. 766]); the structure was termite-infested (*Godfrey* v. *Steinpress* (1982) 128 Cal.App.3d 154 [180 Cal.Rptr. 95]); there was water infiltration in the soil (*Barnhouse* v. *City of Pinole* (1982) 133 Cal.App.3d 171, 187-188 [183 Cal.Rptr. 881]); the amount of net income a piece of property would yield was overstated (*Ford* v. *Cournale* (1973) 36 Cal.App.3d 172, 179-180 [111 Cal.Rptr. 334, 81 A.L.R.3d 704].)

[5] Concern for the effects of an overly indulgent rescission policy on the stability of bargains is not new. Our Supreme Court early on quoted with approval the sentiment: "'The power to cancel a contract is a most extraordinary power. It is one which should be exercised with great caution,—nay, I may say, with great reluctance,—unless in a clear case. A too free use of this power would render all business uncertain, and, as has been said, make the length of a chancellor's foot the measure of individual rights. The greatest liberty of making contracts is essential to the business interests of the country. In general, the parties must look out for themselves.'" (*Colton* v. *Stanford* (1980) 82 Cal. 351, 398 [23 P. 16].)

buyer of the intended use of the purchase. Murder is not such a common occurrence that *buyers* should be charged with anticipating and discovering this disquieting possibility. Accordingly, the fact is not one for which a duty of inquiry and discovery can sensibly be imposed upon the buyer.

Reed alleges the fact of the murders has a quantifiable effect on the market value of the premises. We cannot say this allegation is inherently wrong and, in the pleading posture of the case, we assume it to be true. If information known or accessible only to the seller has a significant and measurable effect on market value and, as is alleged here, the seller is aware of this effect, we see no principled basis for making the duty to disclose turn upon the character of the information. Physical usefulness is not and never has been the sole criterion of valuation. Stamp collections and gold speculation would be insane activities if utilitarian considerations were the sole measure of value. (See also Civ. Code, § 3355 [deprivation of property of peculiar value to owner]; Annot. (1950) 12 A.L.R.2d 902 [Measure of Damages for Conversion or Loss of, or Damage to, Personal Property Having No Market Value].)

Reputation and history can have a significant effect on the value of realty. "George Washington slept here" is worth something, however physically inconsequential that consideration may be. Ill-repute or "bad will" conversely may depress the value of property. Failure to disclose such a negative fact where it will have a foreseeably depressing effect on income expected to be generated by a business is tortious. (See Rest.2d Torts, § 551, illus. 11.) Some cases have held that *unreasonable* fears of the potential buying public that a gas or oil pipeline may rupture may depress the market value of land and entitle the owner to incremental compensation in eminent domain. (See Annot., Eminent Domain: Elements and Measure of Compensation for Oil or Gas Pipeline Through Private Property (1954) 38 A.L.R.2d 788, 801-804.)

Whether Reed will be able to prove her allegation the decade-old multiple murder has a significant effect on market value we cannot determine.[6] If she is able to do so by competent evidence she is entitled to a favorable ruling on the issues of materiality and duty to disclose. Her demonstration of objective tangible harm would still the concern that permitting her to go forward will open the floodgates to rescission on subjective and idiosyncratic grounds.

A more troublesome question would arise if a buyer in similar circumstances were unable to plead or establish a significant and quantifiable effect on market value. However, this question is not presented in the posture of this case. Reed has not alleged the fact of the murders has

rendered the premises useless to her as a residence. As currently pled, the gravamen of her case is pecuniary harm. We decline to speculate on the abstract alternative.

The judgment is reversed.

---

[6] [In] determining what factors would motivate [buyers and sellers] in reaching an agreement as to price, and in weighing the effect of their motivation, [the trier of fact] may rely upon the opinion of experts in the field and also upon its knowledge and experience shared in common with people in general." (*South Bay Irr. Dist., supra*, 61 Cal.App.3d at p. 970; see also 3 Wigmore, Evidence (Chadbourn rev.ed. 1970) § 711 et seq.)

Case 6:   Unconscionability

America Software, Inc. v. Ali
California Court of Appeal, First District, 1996
46 Cal.App.4th 1386

KING, J.

The appellant, American Software, Inc., appeals from a decision of the trial court granting a former employee, respondent Melane Ali, unpaid commissions based upon software sales she generated while in American Software's employ but which were remitted by customers after she voluntarily severed her employment. The key issue in this appeal is whether a provision of Ali's employment contract which, generally speaking, terminates her right to receive commissions on payments received on her accounts 30 days after severance of her employment is unconscionable, and therefore, unenforceable. The trial court found that Ali was entitled to recover the disputed commissions because this contractual provision was unconscionable. We disagree and reverse.

Facts

Ali was an account executive for American Software from September 5, 1991, to March 2, 1994. The employment relationship commenced after Ali was approached by a professional recruiter on behalf of American Software and was terminated when Ali voluntarily resigned because she had a job offer from one of American Software's competitors. Ali was hired to sell and market licensing agreements for software products to large companies. These products are designed to the customer's specifications for the purpose of integrating the customer's accounting, manufacturing, sales and distribution processes.

In exchange for her services, American Software agreed to pay Ali a base monthly salary plus a draw. If products were sold during the month, any commissions paid were reduced by the amount of the draw. However, the draw portion of the salary was paid regardless of whether or not the salesperson earned commissions to cover the draw. Any negative amount would be carried over from month-to-month until such time as the commissions were large enough to cover the previous draws, or until such time as the employment relationship was severed. If the amount of draws exceeded commissions at the time of termination, American Software would suffer the loss. At the time of her resignation, Ali's annual guaranteed salary, exclusive of commissions, was $75,000. Her base monthly salary was $3,333 per month and her nonrefundable draw was $2,917.

The terms and conditions of Ali's employment were set out in a written contract which was prepared by American Software. Ali reviewed the contract, and had an attorney, who she described as a "buddy," review it prior to employment. Of pertinence to the instant controversy, the contract included the specific circumstances under which Ali was to receive commissions after termination of employment with American Software. The employment agreement first states that "[c]ommissions are considered earned when the payment is received by the Company." It goes on to provide: "In the event of termination, the right of all commissions which would normally be due and payable are forfeited 30 days following the date of termination in the case of voluntary termination and 90 days in the case of involuntary termination."

Based on her testimony at trial, there is no question that Ali was aware of this provision prior to her execution of the agreement and commencement of work at American Software. She testified she reviewed the two-and-one-half-page contract for one-half hour and caused certain handwritten deletions and revisions to be made to it, most notably deleting a provision requiring her to reimburse American Software $5,000 for the recruiter's fee in the event that she terminated her employment within a year. Ali testified that she signed the employment contract even though she believed certain provisions were unenforceable in California.

After Ali left American Software's employment, she sought additional commissions in connection with transactions with IBM and Kaiser Foundation Health Plan. American Software received payment from both companies more than 30 days after Ali's resignation.

After Ali's claim for unpaid commissions was denied by the Labor Commissioner, she sought de novo review in the superior court. (Lab. Code, § 98.2.) The trial court awarded Ali approximately $30,000 in unpaid commissions after finding that the contract provision regarding postemployment commissions was unconscionable and thus, unenforceable. The trial court found the evidence "overwhelming that the forfeiture provision inures to the benefit of the party with superior bargaining power without any indication of a reason for tying such benefit to the timing of a payment, rather than to the service actually provided in completing the sale." American Software timely appealed.

Discussion

In 1979, our Legislature enacted Civil Code section 1670.5, which codified the established doctrine that a court can refuse to enforce an unconscionable provision in a contract.[1] (For a review of the legislative history of Civ. Code, § 1670.5, see *IMO Development Corp. v. Dow Corning Corp.* (1982) 135 Cal. App. 3d 451, 459-460 [185 Cal. Rptr. 341].) While the term "unconscionability" is not defined by statute, the official comment explains the term as follows: "The basic test is whether, in the light of the general background and the needs of the particular case, the clauses involved are so one-sided as to be unconscionable under the circumstances existing at the time of the making of the contract. . . . The principle is one of the prevention of

---

[1] The statute provides in pertinent part: "If the court as a matter of law finds the contract or any clause of the contract to have been unconscionable at the time it was made the court may refuse to enforce the contract, or it may enforce the remainder of the contract without the unconscionable clause, or it may so limit the application of any unconscionable clause as to avoid any unconscionable result." (Civ. Code, § 1670.5, subd. (a).)

oppression and unfair surprise [citation] and not of disturbance of allocation of risks because of superior bargaining power." (Legis. committee com., Deering's Ann. Civ. Code (1994 ed.) § 1670.5, pp. 328-329.)

Most California cases analyze unconscionability as having two separate elements—procedural and substantive. (See, e.g., *Shaffer v. Superior Court* (1995) 33 Cal. App. 4th 993, 1000 [39 Cal. Rptr. 2d 506]; *Vance v. Villa Park Mobilehome Estates* (1995) 36 Cal. App. 4th 698, 709 [42 Cal. Rptr. 2d 723].) Substantive unconscionability focuses on the actual terms of the agreement, while procedural unconscionability focuses on the manner in which the contract was negotiated and the circumstances of the parties. California courts generally require a showing of both procedural and substantive unconscionability at the time the contract was made. (See *A & M Produce Co. v. FMC Corp.* (1982) 135 Cal. App. 3d 473, 487 [186 Cal. Rptr. 114, 38 A.L.R.4th 1].) Some courts have indicated that a sliding scale applies—for example, a contract with extraordinarily oppressive substantive terms will require less in the way of procedural unconscionability. (*Ilkhchooyi v. Best* (1995) 37 Cal. App. 4th 395, 410 [45 Cal. Rptr. 2d 766]; *Carboni v. Arrospide* (1991) 2 Cal. App. 4th 76, 83 [2 Cal. Rptr. 2d 845]; *Dean Witter Reynolds, Inc. v. Superior Court* (1989) 211 Cal. App. 3d 758, 768 [259 Cal. Rptr. 789].)

Indicia of procedural unconscionability include "oppression, arising from inequality of bargaining power and the absence of real negotiation or a meaningful choice" and "surprise, resulting from hiding the disputed term in a prolix document." (*Vance v. Villa Park Mobilehome Estates, supra,* 36 Cal. App. 4th at p. 709.) Substantive unconscionability is indicated by contract terms so one-sided as to "*shock the conscience.*" (*California Grocers Assn. v. Bank of America* (1994) 22 Cal. App. 4th 205, 214 [27 Cal. Rptr. 2d 396], italics in original.) A less stringent standard of "reasonableness" was applied in *A & M Produce Co. v. FMC Corp., supra,* 135 Cal. App. 3d at pages 486-487. This standard was expressly rejected by Division Two of this court in *California Grocers Assn.* as being inherently subjective. (*California Grocers Assn., supra,* at p. 214.) We agree. With a concept as nebulous as "unconscionability" it is important that courts not be thrust in the paternalistic role of intervening to change contractual terms that the parties have agreed to merely because the court believes the terms are unreasonable. The terms must shock the conscience.

The critical juncture for determining whether a contract is unconscionable is the moment when it is entered into by both parties—not whether it is unconscionable in light of subsequent events. (Civ. Code, § 1670.5.) Unconscionability is ultimately a question of law for the court. (*Ilkhchooyi v. Best, supra,* 37 Cal. App. 4th at p. 411; *Vance v. Villa Park Mobilehome Estates, supra,* 36 Cal. App. 4th at p. 709; *Patterson v. ITT Consumer Financial Corp.* (1993) 14 Cal. App. 4th 1659, 1663 [18 Cal. Rptr. 2d 563].)

In assessing procedural unconscionability, the evidence indicates that Ali was aware of her obligations under the contract and that she voluntarily agreed to assume them. In her business as a salesperson it is reasonable to assume she had become familiar with contracts and their importance. In fact, in Ali's testimony, she indicated that as part of her responsibilities for

American Software, she helped negotiate the terms of a contract with IBM representing over a million dollars in sales. The salient provisions of the employment contract are straightforward, and the terms used are easily comprehensible to the layman. She had the benefit of counsel.[2] Nor is this a situation in which one party to the contract is confronted by an absence of meaningful choice. The very fact that Ali had enough bargaining "clout" to successfully negotiate for more favorable terms on other provisions evidences the contrary. She admits that she was aware of the postemployment commissions clause, but did not attempt to negotiate for less onerous terms.[3] In short, this case is a far cry from those cases where fine print, complex terminology, and presentation of a contract on a take-it-or-leave-it basis constitutes the groundwork for a finding of unconscionability.

Nor do we find substantive unconscionability. Ali's arguments of substantive unconscionability rest largely on events that occurred several years after the contract was entered into—her loss of sizable commissions on sales she had solicited during her employment but where payment was delayed for various reasons so that it was not received within 30 days after her departure. However, as indicated by the very wording of California's unconscionability statute, we must analyze the circumstances as they existed "at the time [the contract] was made" to determine if gross unfairness was apparent at that time. (Civ. Code, § 1670.5, subd. (a).)

When viewed in light of the circumstances as they existed on August 23, 1991, when the instant contract was executed, we cannot say the contract provision with respect to compensation after termination was so unfair or oppressive in its mutual obligations as to "shock the conscience." (*California Grocers Assn. v. Bank of America, supra,* 22 Cal. App. 4th at p. 214.) If the official notes accompanying Uniform Commercial Code section 2-302, upon which Civil Code section 1670.5 is based, is to be relied upon as a guide, the contract terms are to be evaluated "in the light of the general commercial background and the commercial needs of the particular trade or case, . . ." (U. Com. Code, § 2-302, com. 1). Corbin suggests that the test is whether the terms are "so extreme as to appear unconscionable according to the mores and business practices of the time and place." (1 Corbin, Contracts (1963) § 128, p. 551.)

Our survey of case law indicates that the contract provision challenged here is commonplace in employment contracts with sales representatives, such as Ali, who have ongoing responsibilities to "service" the account once the sale is made. (See, e.g., *Chretian v. Donald L. Bren Co.* (1984) 151 Cal. App. 3d 385, 389 [198 Cal. Rptr. 523]; *J.S. DeWeese Co. v. Hughes-Treitler Mfg.* (Mo.App. 1994) 881 S.W.2d 638, 644-646; see also *Entis v. Atlantic Wire & Cable Corporation* (2d Cir. 1964) 335 F.2d 759, 762.) In briefing below, the rationale for deferring commissions until payment is actually received by the customer was explained by

---

[2] Some courts have considered the presence and advice of counsel to constitute circumstantial, if not conclusive, evidence that a contract is not unconscionable. (See e.g., *Resource Management Co. v. Weston Ranch* (Utah 1985) 706 P.2d 1028, 1045; *Bernina Distributors, Inc. v. Bernina Sewing Mach.* (10th Cir. 1981) 646 F.2d 434, 440.)

[3] A company representative testified at trial that a number of individuals have successfully negotiated for modification of this provision.

American Software: "[I]f the entire commission were to be deemed earned by merely obtaining buyers, the burden of servicing those buyers pending receipt of revenues would fall on American Software's other salespersons unfamiliar with the earlier transaction who would receive nothing for their efforts." In *Watson* v. *Wood Dimension, Inc.* (1989) 209 Cal. App. 3d 1359, 1363-1365 [257 Cal. Rptr. 816], the court upheld an award of posttermination commissions for a reasonable period of time based on quantum meruit in the total absence of contractual provisions governing the situation. If a court can impose these terms on parties in the absence of an agreement, then it is difficult to see how such terms can be considered "unconscionable" when the parties agree to them.

Nor do we find that the terms of this contract represent "an overly harsh allocation of risks . . . which is not justified by the circumstances under which the contract was made." (*Carboni v. Arrospide, supra,* 2 Cal. App. 4th at p. 83.) The contract terms with regard to Ali's compensation involved certain risks to both parties to the bargain. The contract in the instant case placed a risk on Ali that she would lose commissions from her customers if payment was not received by American Software within 30 days after her resignation. American Software took the risk that at the time of Ali's termination, she would not have earned sufficient commissions to cover the substantial draws "credited" to her. This is part of the bargaining process—it does not necessarily make a contract unconscionable. The contract simply does not appear to be "overly harsh or one-sided, with no justification for it at the time of the agreement." (*Vance v. Villa Park Mobilehome Estates, supra,* 36 Cal. App. 4th at p. 709.)

Much of the parties' arguments in this case revolve around *Ellis v. McKinnon Broadcasting Co.* (1993) 18 Cal. App. 4th 1796 [23 Cal. Rptr. 2d 80]. In *Ellis* the court examined a provision in an employment contract denying the plaintiff, an advertising salesperson, commissions on advertising if the employer had not yet received payment for the advertising prior to termination of the salesperson's employment. The employer collected nearly $100,000 in advertising fees from the plaintiff's sales after he voluntarily left his employment two years later, which meant that the plaintiff would have been entitled to approximately $20,000 in commissions had he continued his employment. The court described the pivotal inquiry as assessing "the substantive *reasonableness* of the challenged provision" and proceeded to find elements of procedural unconscionability, unfair surprise, and oppression, as well as substantive unconscionability. (*Id.* at pp. 1805-1806, italics added.)

Despite the many analogous facts and issues, we reach a different conclusion than *Ellis*. In this instance, the conflicting result can most easily be explained by the fact that the *Ellis* court closely followed the *A&M Produce* analytical structure in considering whether the commissions provision was "reasonable"—an approach we have specifically rejected in favor of the more rigorous "shock the conscience" standard enunciated in *California Grocers Assn.* v. Bank of America *supra,* 22 Cal. App. 4th at page 214. We also find the result in *Ellis* hard to reconcile with other California appellate decisions which have shown considerable restraint in second-guessing provisions in employment contracts governing payment of sales commissions upon termination of employment. (See, e.g., *Chretian v. Donald L. Bren, Co., supra,* 151 Cal. App. 3d at pp. 389-390; *Neal v. State Farm Ins. Cos.* (1961) 188 Cal. App. 2d 690 [10 Cal. Rptr. 781].) A critical review of *Ellis* in the legal literature observes, "[T]he test on unconscionability is not whether the parties could have written a better or more reasonable contract. The proper test in these cases is whether the bargain is so one-sided as to shock the conscience and whether there was some bargaining impropriety resulting from surprise or oppression. The *Neal* and *Chretian* courts, unlike the court in *Ellis*, displayed the proper restraint and deference to agreements that were not egregiously one-sided in the allocation of risks." (Prince, *Unconscionability in California: A Need for Restraint and Consistency* (1995) 46 Hastings L.J. 459, 545.)

In the present case, there are no unclear or hidden terms in the employment agreement and no unusual terms that would shock the conscience, all leading to the conclusion that the contract accurately reflects the reasonable expectations of the parties. Overall, the evidence establishes that this employment contract was the result of an arm's-length negotiation between two sophisticated and experienced parties of comparable bargaining power and is fairly reflective of prevailing practices in employing commissioned sales representatives. Therefore, the contract fails to qualify as unconscionable.

The judgment is reversed. Costs are awarded to American Software, Inc.

Case 7:   **Employment Noncompetition Clauses**

Edwards v. Arthur Anderson LLP
Supreme Court of California, 2008
44 Cal. 4th 937

CHIN, J.

We granted review to address the validity of noncompetition agreements in California and the permissible scope of employment release agreements. We limited our review to the following issues: (1) To what extent does *Business and Professions Code section 16600*[1] prohibit employee noncompetition agreements; and (2) is a contract provision requiring an employee to release "any and all" claims unlawful because it encompasses nonwaivable statutory protections, such as the employee indemnity protection of *Labor Code section 2802*?

FACTS

In January 1997, Raymond Edwards II (Edwards), a certified public accountant, was hired as a tax manager by the Los Angeles office of the accounting firm Arthur Andersen LLP (Andersen). Andersen's employment offer was made contingent upon Edwards's signing a noncompetition agreement, which prohibited him from working for or soliciting certain Andersen clients for limited periods following his termination. The agreement was required of all managers, and read in relevant part: "If you leave the Firm, for eighteen months after release or resignation, you agree not to perform professional services of the type you provided for any client on which you worked during the eighteen months prior to release or resignation. This does not prohibit you from accepting employment with a client. For twelve months after you leave the Firm, you agree not to solicit (to perform professional services of the type you provided) any client of the office(s) to which you were assigned during the eighteen months preceding release or resignation. You agree not to solicit away from the Firm any of its professional personnel for eighteen months after release or resignation." Edwards signed the agreement.

Between 1997 and 2002, Edwards continued to work for Andersen, moving into the firm's private client services practice group, where he handled income, gift, and estate tax planning for individuals and entities with large incomes and net worth. Over this period he was promoted to senior manager and was on track to become a partner. In March 2002, the United States government indicted Andersen in connection with the investigation into Enron

---

[1]   All further unlabeled statutory references are to the Business and Professions Code. We conclude that *section 16600* prohibits employee noncompetition agreements unless the agreement falls within a statutory exception, and that a contract provision whereby an employee releases "any and all" claims does not encompass nonwaivable statutory protections, such as the employee indemnity protection of *Labor Code section 2802*. We therefore affirm in part and reverse in part the Court of Appeal judgment.

Corporation, and in June 2002, Andersen announced that it would cease its accounting practices in the United States. In April 2002, Andersen began selling off its practice groups to various entities. In May 2002, Andersen internally announced that HSBC USA, Inc. (a New York-based banking corporation), through a new subsidiary, Wealth and Tax Advisory Services (WTAS), would purchase a portion of Andersen's tax practice, including Edwards's group.

In July 2002, HSBC offered Edwards employment. Before hiring any of Andersen's employees, HSBC required them to execute a "Termination of Non-compete Agreement" (TONC) in order to obtain employment with HSBC. Among other things, the TONC required employees to, inter alia, (1) voluntarily resign from Andersen; (2) release Andersen from "any and all" claims, including "claims that in any way arise from or out of, are based upon or relate to Employee's employment by, association with or compensation from" defendant; (3) continue indefinitely to preserve confidential information and trade secrets except as otherwise required by a court or governmental agency; (4) refrain from disparaging Andersen or its related entities or partners; and (5) cooperate with Andersen in connection with any investigation of, or litigation against, Andersen. In exchange, Andersen would agree to accept Edwards's resignation, agree to Edwards's employment by HSBC, and release Edwards from the 1997 noncompetition agreement.

HSBC required that Andersen provide it with a completed TONC signed by every employee on the "Restricted Employees" list before the deal went through. At least one draft of the Restricted Employees list contained Edwards's name. Andersen would not release Edwards, or any other employee, from the noncompetition agreement unless that employee signed the TONC.

Edwards signed the HSBC offer letter, but he did not sign the TONC.[2] In response, Andersen terminated Edwards's employment and withheld severance benefits. HSBC withdrew its offer of employment to Edwards.

PROCEDURAL HISTORY

On April 30, 2003, Edwards filed a complaint against Andersen, HSBC and WTAS for intentional interference with prospective economic advantage and anticompetitive business practices under the Cartwright Act (§ 16720 et seq.). Edwards alleged that the Andersen noncompetition agreement violated section 16600, which states "[e]xcept as provided in this chapter, every contract by which anyone is restrained from engaging in a lawful profession, trade, or business of any kind is to that extent void." He further alleged that the TONC's release

---

[2] Edwards's reasons for refusing to sign the TONC included the fact that he believed it required him to give up his right to indemnification, which he felt was particularly important in light of the government's investigation into the company. Edwards also believed several of Andersen's clients for whom he did work would sue Andersen and name him as a defendant, and if that were the case he wanted to ensure he retained his right to indemnification.

136

of "any and all" claims violated *Labor Code sections 2802* and *2804*, which make an employee's right to indemnification from his or her employer nonwaivable.

Edwards settled with all parties except Andersen. The trial court sustained Andersen's demurrer to Edwards's Cartwright Act claim without leave to amend, concluding Edwards lacked standing to bring the action. It then denied Andersen's subsequent motion for summary adjudication on Edwards's intentional interference with prospective economic advantage cause of action, after concluding that triable issues of fact existed on the meaning of the agreements, and whether the agreements protected trade secrets. The court then granted Andersen's motion to sever trial on the issue of the enforceability of the noncompetition agreement and the TONC. (*Code Civ. Proc. §§ 598, 1048, subd. (b).*) The court dismissed all claims against Andersen, except for those relating to intentional interference with prospective economic advantage, which it concluded presented pure questions of law.

The trial court heard argument from both parties, but took no evidence. The court determined all issues of law in favor of Andersen on the merits, and entered judgment in its favor. The court specifically decided that (1) the noncompetition agreement did not violate *section 16600* because it was narrowly tailored and did not deprive Edwards of his right to pursue his profession; and (2) the TONC did not purport to waive Edwards's right to indemnification. Thus, requiring him to sign these documents was not unlawful. Edwards appealed the trial court's decision.

At issue in the Court of Appeal was one of the elements required to prove a claim for intentional interference with prospective economic advantage. In order to prove a claim for intentional interference with prospective economic advantage, a plaintiff has the burden of proving five elements: (1) an economic relationship between the plaintiff and a third party, with the probability of future economic benefit to the plaintiff; (2) the defendant's knowledge of the relationship; (3) an intentional act by the defendant, designed to disrupt the relationship; (4) actual disruption of the relationship; and (5) economic harm to the plaintiff proximately caused by the defendant's wrongful act, including an intentional act by the defendant that is designed to disrupt the relationship between the plaintiff and a third party. (*Korea Supply Co. v. Lockheed Martin Corp.* (2003) 29 Cal.4th 1134, 1153-1154 [131 Cal. Rptr. 2d 29, 63 P.3d 937].) The plaintiff must also prove that the interference was wrongful, independent of its interfering character. (*Della Penna v. Toyota Motor Sales, U.S.A., Inc.* (1995) 11 Cal.4th 376, 392-393 [45 Cal. Rptr. 2d 436, 902 P.2d 740].) "[A]n act is independently wrongful if it is unlawful, that is, if it is proscribed by some constitutional, statutory, regulatory, common law, or other determinable legal standard." (*Korea Supply, supra,* 29 Cal.4th at p. 1159.)

At issue here is the third element of the tort. In the Court of Appeal, Edwards argued the independently wrongful acts requirement in this case was met in several ways that are pertinent here: (1) the noncompetition agreement was illegal under *section 16600*, making Andersen's demand that he give consideration to be released from it against public policy; (2) the TONC's additional release of "any and all" claims constituted a waiver of his indemnity rights in violation of *Labor Code sections 2802* and *2804*; and (3) the TONC's nondisparagement clause violated *Labor Code section 1102.5*.

In the published part of its opinion, the Court of Appeal held: (1) the noncompetition agreement was invalid under *section 16600*, and requiring Edwards to sign the TONC as consideration to be released from it was an independently wrongful act for purposes of the elements of Edwards's claim for intentional interference with prospective economic advantage; (2) the TONC purported to waive Edwards's indemnification rights under the Labor Code and was therefore in violation of public policy and an independently wrongful act; and (3) the TONC's nondisparagement provision did not violate *Labor Code section 1102.5* and so was not an independently wrongful act.

As initially discussed, we limited our review to resolve the first two issues.

DISCUSSION

A. *Section 16600*

Under the common law, as is still true in many states today, contractual restraints on the practice of a profession, business, or trade, were considered valid, as long as they were reasonably imposed. (*Bosley Medical Group v. Abramson (1984) 161 Cal.App.3d 284, 288 [207 Cal. Rptr. 477].*) This was true even in California. (*Wright v. Ryder (1868) 36 Cal. 342, 357* [relaxing original common law rule that all restraints on trade were invalid in recognition of increasing population and competition in trade].) However, in 1872 California settled public policy in favor of open competition, and rejected the common law "rule of reasonableness," when the Legislature enacted the Civil Code. (Civ. Code, former § 1673, repealed by Stats. 1941, ch. 526, § 2, p. 1847, and enacted as *Bus. & Prof. Code, § 16600*, Stats. 1941, ch. 526, § 1, p. 1834; *Bosley, supra, 161 Cal.App.3d at p. 288*.)[3] Today in California, covenants not to compete are void, subject to several exceptions discussed briefly below.

Section 16600 states: "Except as provided in this chapter, every contract by which anyone is restrained from engaging in a lawful profession, trade, or business of any kind is to that extent void." The chapter excepts noncompetition agreements in the sale or dissolution of corporations (*§ 16601*), partnerships (*ibid.*; *§ 16602*), and limited liability corporations (*§ 16602.5*). In the years since its original enactment as *Civil Code section 1673*, our courts have consistently affirmed that *section 16600* evinces a settled legislative policy in favor of open competition and employee mobility. (See *D'Sa v. Playhut, Inc. (2000) 85 Cal.App.4th 927, 933 [102 Cal. Rptr. 2d 495]*.) The law protects Californians and ensures "that every citizen shall retain the right to pursue any lawful employment and enterprise of their choice." (*Metro Traffic Control, Inc. v. Shadow Traffic Network (1994) 22 Cal.App.4th 853, 859 [27 Cal. Rptr. 2d 573]*.) It protects "the important legal right of persons to engage in businesses and occupations of their choosing." (*Morlife, Inc. v. Perry (1997) 56 Cal.App.4th 1514, 1520 [66 Cal. Rptr. 2d 731]*.)

This court has invalidated an otherwise narrowly tailored agreement as an improper

---

[3] Prior to oral argument, we granted Andersen's request that we take judicial notice of various documents providing information on the history of *section 16600* and its predecessor statutes. (*Evid. Code, §§ 452, 453, 459*.)

restraint under *section 16600* because it required a former employee to forfeit his pension rights on commencing work for a competitor. (*Muggill v. Reuben H. Donnelley Corp. (1965) 62 Cal.2d 239, 242-243 [42 Cal. Rptr. 107, 398 P.2d 147] (Muggill); Chamberlain v. Augustine (1916) 172 Cal. 285, 289 [156 P. 479]* [invalidating contract with partial trade restriction].) In *Muggill*, the court reviewed an adverse judgment against a company's retired employee whose pension plan rights were terminated after the former employee commenced work for a competitor. (*Muggill, at p. 240*.) The retired employee had sued the former employer, seeking declaratory relief on the ground that the provision in the pension plan that terminated the retirement payments because the retiree went to work for a competitor was "against public policy and unenforceable." (*Ibid.*) *Muggill* held that, with exceptions not applicable here, *section 16600* invalidates provisions in employment contracts and retirement pension plans that prohibit "an employee from working for a competitor after completion of his employment or imposing a penalty if he does so [citations] unless they are necessary to protect the employer's trade secrets [citation]." (*Muggill, at p. 242.*)[4] In sum, following the Legislature, this court generally condemns noncompetition agreements. (See, e.g., *Armendariz v. Foundation Health Psychcare Services, Inc. (2000) 24 Cal.4th 83, 123, fn. 12 [99 Cal. Rptr. 2d 745, 6 P.3d 669]* [such restraints on trade are "illegal"].)

Under the statute's plain meaning, therefore, an employer cannot by contract restrain a former employee from engaging in his or her profession, trade, or business unless the agreement falls within one of the exceptions to the rule. (*§ 16600*.) Andersen, however, asserts that we should interpret the term "restrain" under *section 16600* to mean simply to "prohibit," so that only contracts that totally prohibit an employee from engaging in his or her profession, trade, or business are illegal. It would then follow that a mere limitation on an employee's ability to practice his or her vocation would be permissible under *section 16600*, as long as it is reasonably based.

Andersen contends that some California courts have held that *section 16600* (and its predecessor statutes, Civil Code former sections 1673, 1674, and 1675) is the statutory embodiment of prior common law, and embraces the rule of reasonableness in evaluating competitive restraints. (See, e.g., *South Bay Radiology Medical Associates v. Asher (1990) 220 Cal.App.3d 1074, 1080 [269 Cal. Rptr. 15] (South Bay Radiology)* [*§ 16600* embodies common law prohibition against restraints on trade]; *Vacco Industries, Inc. v. Van Den Berg (1992) 5 Cal.App.4th 34, 47-48 [6 Cal. Rptr. 2d 602] (Vacco)* [*§ 16600* is codification of common law reasonable restraint rule].) Andersen claims that these cases show that *section 16600* "prohibits only broad agreements that prevent a person from engaging entirely in his chosen business, trade or profession. Agreements that do not have this broad effect--but merely regulate some aspect of post-employment conduct, e.g., to prevent raiding [employer's personnel]--are not within the scope of *[s]ection 16600*."

As Edwards observes, however, the cases Andersen cites to support a relaxation of the statutory rule simply recognize that the statutory exceptions to *section 16600* reflect the same

---

[4] We do not here address the applicability of the so-called trade secret exception to *section 16600*, as Edwards does not dispute that portion of his agreement or contend that the provision of the noncompetition agreement prohibiting him from recruiting Andersen's employees violated *section 16600*.

exceptions to the rule against noncompetition agreements that were implied in the common law. For example, *South Bay Radiology* acknowledged the general prohibition against restraints on trade while applying the specific partnership dissolution exception of *section 16602* to the facts of its case. (*South Bay Radiology, supra, 220 Cal.App.3d at p. 1080.*) In that case, the covenant not to compete was set forth in a partnership agreement to which the appellant doctor was a party. When the appellant's partnership with several other doctors dissolved due to his inability to work following an accident, he challenged the noncompete clause. The court found the partnership exception to *section 16600* applicable. (*South Bay Radiology, supra, at pp. 1078-1080.*)

Vacco involved the sale of shares in a business, an exception to *section 16600* found in *section 16601*. The Court of Appeal upheld an agreement not to compete made by a terminated employee who had sold all of his stock in the business for $ 500,000 prior to his termination. In applying the exception to *section 16600*, the court held that *section 16601* "permits agreements not to compete made by a party selling the goodwill of a business or *all* of the shares of stock in a corporation." (*Vacco, supra, 5 Cal.App.4th at p. 47.*) As the present Court of Appeal recognized, "Fairly read, the foregoing authorities suggest *section 16600* embodies the original, strict common law antipathy toward restraints of trade, while the *section 16601* and *16602* exceptions incorporated the later common law 'rule of reasonableness' in instances where those exceptions apply."

We conclude that Andersen's noncompetition agreement was invalid. As the Court of Appeal observed, "The first challenged clause prohibited Edwards, for an 18-month period, from performing professional services of the type he had provided while at Andersen, for any client on whose account he had worked during 18 months prior to his termination. The second challenged clause prohibited Edwards, for a year after termination, from 'soliciting,' defined by the agreement as providing professional services to any client of Andersen's Los Angeles office." The agreement restricted Edwards from performing work for Andersen's Los Angeles clients and therefore restricted his ability to practice his accounting profession. (See *Thompson v. Impaxx, Inc.* (2003) 113 Cal.App.4th 1425, 1429 [7 Cal. Rptr. 3d 427] [distinguishing "trade-route" and solicitation cases that protect trade secrets or confidential proprietary information].) The noncompetition agreement that Edwards was required to sign before commencing employment with Andersen was therefore invalid because it restrained his ability to practice his profession. (See *Muggill, supra, 62 Cal.2d at pp. 242-243.*)

B. *Ninth Circuit's Narrow-restraint Exception*

Andersen asks this court to adopt the limited or "narrow-restraint" exception to *section 16600* that the Ninth Circuit discussed in *Campbell v. Trustees of Leland Stanford Jr. Univ.* (9th Cir. 1987) 817 F.2d 499 (*Campbell*), and that the trial court relied on in this case in order to uphold the noncompetition agreement. In *Campbell*, the Ninth Circuit acknowledged that California has rejected the common law "rule of reasonableness" with respect to restraints upon the ability to pursue a profession, but concluded that *section 16600* "only makes illegal those restraints which preclude one from engaging in a lawful profession, trade, or business." (*Campbell, supra, 817 F.2d at p. 502.*) The court remanded the case to the district court in order to allow the employee to prove that the noncompetition agreement at issue completely restrained him from practicing his " 'profession, trade, or business, within the meaning of *section 16600*.' " (*Campbell, at p. 503*.)

The confusion over the Ninth Circuit's application of *section 16600* arose in a paragraph in *Campbell*, in which the court noted that some California courts have excepted application of *section 16600* " 'where one is barred from pursuing only a small or limited part of the business, trade or profession.' " (*Campbell, supra, 817 F.2d at p. 502*.) The Ninth Circuit cited two California cases that it believed may have carved out such an exception to *section 16600*. (See *Boughton v. Socony Mobil Oil Co. (1964) 231 Cal.App.2d 188 [41 Cal. Rptr. 714]* (*Boughton*) [interpreting deed restriction on land use]; *King v. Gerold (1952) 109 Cal.App.2d 316 [240 P.2d 710]* (*King*) [rejecting manufacturer's argument that clause not to produce its product after license expiration was not an illegal restraint under *§ 16600*].) Andersen relies on those cases, citing them as the underpinnings of the Ninth Circuit's exception to *section 16600*, and urges the court to adopt their reasoning here.

As the Court of Appeal observed, however, the analyses in *Boughton* and *King* do not provide persuasive support for adopting the narrow-restraint exception. In *Boughton*, the restriction was not upon the plaintiff's practice of a profession or trade, but took the form of a covenant in a deed to a parcel of land that specified the land could not be used as a gasoline service station for a specified time period. (*Boughton, supra, 231 Cal.App.2d 188*.) Because the case involved the use of the land, *section 16600* was not implicated. Of note is the fact that *Boughton* relied on *King*, an unfair competition case in which the court applied a trade secret exception to the statutory rule against noncompetition clauses. (*King, supra, 109 Cal.App.2d 316*.) In *King*, the plaintiff was not simply engaged in the manufacture and sale of goods (house trailers) but was allegedly using a trailer design substantially similar to his former employer's, the inventor of the design. (*Id. at p. 318*.)

Andersen is correct, however, that *Campbell* has been followed in some recent Ninth Circuit cases to create a narrow-restraint exception to *section 16600* in federal court. For example, *International Business Machines Corp. v. Bajorek (9th Cir. 1999) 191 F.3d 1033*, upheld an agreement mandating that an employee forfeits stock options if employed by a competitor within six months of leaving employment. *General Commercial Packaging v. TPS Package (9th Cir. 1997) 126 F.3d 1131*, held that a bargained-for contractual provision barring one party from courting a specific named customer was not an illegal restraint of trade prohibited by *section 16600*, because it did not "entirely preclude[]" the party from pursuing its trade or business. (*General Commercial Packaging v. TPS Package, supra, 126 F.3d at p. 1133*.)

Contrary to Andersen's belief, however, California courts have not embraced the Ninth Circuit's narrow-restraint exception. Indeed, no reported California state court decision has endorsed the Ninth Circuit's reasoning, and we are of the view that California courts "have been clear in their expression that *section 16600* represents a strong public policy of the state which should not be diluted by judicial fiat." (*Scott v. Snelling and Snelling, Inc. (N.D.Cal. 1990) 732 F. Supp. 1034, 1042*.)[5] *Section 16600* is unambiguous, and if the Legislature intended the statute

---

[5]   As noted, the Ninth Circuit's reading of *Boughton, supra, 231 Cal.App.2d 188*, and *King, supra, 109*

to apply only to restraints that were unreasonable or overbroad, it could have included language to that effect. We reject Andersen's contention that we should adopt a narrow-restraint exception to *section 16600* and leave it to the Legislature, if it chooses, either to relax the statutory restrictions or adopt additional exceptions to the prohibition-against-restraint rule under *section 16600*.

C. *Contract Provision Releasing "Any and All" Claims*

Edwards was not terminated from Andersen for refusing to sign the noncompetition agreement. Rather, Andersen made it a condition of Edwards's obtaining employment with HSBC that Edwards execute the TONC, releasing Andersen from, among other things, "any and all" claims, including "claims that in any way arise from or out of, are based upon or relate to [Edwards's] employment by, association with or compensation from" Andersen. As the Court of Appeal held, to the extent Andersen demanded Edwards execute the TONC as consideration for release of the invalid provisions of the noncompetition agreement, it could be considered a wrongful act for purposes of his claim for interference with prospective economic advantage. An employer "cannot lawfully make the signing of an employment agreement, which contains an unenforceable covenant not to compete, a condition of continued employment ... . [A]n employer's termination of an employee who refuses to sign such an agreement constitutes a wrongful termination in violation of public policy." (*D'Sa v. Playhut, Inc., supra, 85 Cal.App.4th at p. 929.*)

*   *   *   *   *   *

DISPOSITION

We hold that the noncompetition agreement here is invalid under *section 16600*, and we reject the narrow-restraint exception urged by Andersen. Noncompetition agreements are invalid under *section 16600* in California even if narrowly drawn, unless they fall within the applicable statutory exceptions of *section 16601, 16602, or 16602.5*. In addition, we conclude that the

TONC at issue in this case did not purport to release Andersen from any nonwaivable statutory claims and therefore is not unlawful under *Labor Code sections 2802* and *2804*.

We therefore affirm in part and reverse in part the Court of Appeal judgment, and remand the matter for proceedings consistent with the views expressed above.

Cal.App.2d 316 may be the source of that circuit's narrow-restraint exception to *section 16600*. We are not persuaded that *Boughton* or *King* provides any guidance on the issue of noncompetition agreements, largely because neither involved noncompetition agreements in the employment context. However, to the extent they are inconsistent with our analysis, we disapprove *Boughton v. Socony Mobil Oil Co., supra, 231 Cal.App.2d 188*, and *King v. Gerold, supra, 109 Cal.App.2d 316.*

142

Case 8: Parol Evidence Rule – Plain Meaning

W.W.W. Associates v. Giancontieri
Court of Appeals of New York, 1990
77 N.Y. 2d. 157

KAYE, J.

In this action for specific performance of a contract to sell real property, the issue is whether an unambiguous reciprocal cancellation provision should be read in light of extrinsic evidence, as a contingency clause for the sole benefit of plaintiff purchaser, subject to its unilateral waiver. Applying the principle that clear, complete writings should generally be enforced according to their terms, we reject plaintiff's reading of the contract and dismiss its complaint.

Defendants, owners of a two-acre parcel in Suffolk County, on October 16, 1986 contracted for the sale of the property to plaintiff, a real estate investor and developer. The purchase price was fixed at $750,000--$25,000 payable on contract execution, $225,000 to be paid in cash on closing (to take place "on or about December 1, 1986"), and the $500,000 balance secured by a purchase-money mortgage payable two years later.

The parties signed a printed form Contract of Sale, supplemented by several of their own paragraphs. Two provisions of the contract have particular relevance to the present dispute--a reciprocal cancellation provision (para 31) and a merger clause (para 19). Paragraph 31, one of the provisions the parties added to the contract form, reads: "The parties acknowledge that Sellers have been served with process instituting an action concerned with the real property which is the subject of this agreement. In the event the closing of title is delayed by reason of such litigation it is agreed that closing of title will in a like manner be adjourned until after the conclusion of such litigation provided, *in the event such litigation is not concluded, by or before 6-1-87 either party shall have the right to cancel this contract whereupon the down payment shall be returned and there shall be no further rights hereunder.*"(Emphasis supplied.) Paragraph 19 is the form merger provision, reading: "All prior understandings and agreements between seller and purchaser are merged in this contract [and it] completely expresses their full agreement. It has been entered into after full investigation, neither party relying upon any statements made by anyone else that are not set forth in this contract."

The Contract of Sale, in other paragraphs the parties added to the printed form, provided that the purchaser alone had the unconditional right to cancel the contract within 10 days of signing (para 32), and that the purchaser alone had the option to cancel if, at closing, the seller was unable to deliver building permits for 50 senior citizen housing units (para 29).

The contract in fact did not close on December 1, 1986, as originally contemplated. As

June 1, 1987 neared, with the litigation still unresolved, plaintiff on May 13 wrote defendants that it was prepared to close and would appear for closing on May 28; plaintiff also instituted the present action for specific performance. On June 2, 1987, defendants canceled the contract and returned the down payment, which plaintiff refused. Defendants thereafter sought summary judgment dismissing the specific performance action, on the ground that the contract gave them the absolute right to cancel.

Plaintiff's claim to specific performance rests upon its recitation of how paragraph 31 originated. Those facts are set forth in the affidavit of plaintiff's vice-president, submitted in opposition to defendants' summary judgment motion.

As plaintiff explains, during contract negotiations it learned that, as a result of unrelated litigation against defendants, a lis pendens had been filed against the property. Although assured by defendants that the suit was meritless, plaintiff anticipated difficulty obtaining a construction loan (including title insurance for the loan) needed to implement its plans to build senior citizen housing units. According to the affidavit, it was therefore agreed that paragraph 31 would be added for plaintiff's sole benefit, as contract vendee. As it developed, plaintiff's fears proved groundless--the lis pendens did not impede its ability to secure construction financing. However, around March 1987, plaintiff claims it learned from the broker on the transaction that one of the defendants had told him they were doing nothing to defend the litigation, awaiting June 2, 1987 to cancel the contract and suggesting the broker might get a higher price.

Defendants made no response to these factual assertions. Rather, its summary judgment motion rested entirely on the language of the Contract of Sale, which it argued was, under the law, determinative of its right to cancel.

The trial court granted defendants' motion and dismissed the complaint, holding that the agreement unambiguously conferred the right to cancel on defendants as well as plaintiff. The Appellate Division, however, reversed and, after searching the record and adopting the facts alleged by plaintiff in its affidavit, granted summary judgment to plaintiff directing specific performance of the contract. We now reverse and dismiss the complaint.

Critical to the success of plaintiff's position is consideration of the extrinsic evidence that paragraph 31 was added to the contract solely for its benefit. The Appellate Division made clear that this evidence was at the heart of its decision: "review of the record reveals that under the circumstances of this case the language of clause 31 was intended to protect the plaintiff from having to purchase the property burdened by a notice of pendency filed as a result of the underlying action which could prevent the plaintiff from obtaining clear title and would impair its ability to obtain subsequent construction financing." (152 AD2d 333, 336.)In that a party for whose sole benefit a condition is included in a contract may waive the condition prior to expiration of the time period set forth in the contract and accept the subject property "as is" *(see, e.g., Satterly v Plaisted,* 52 AD2d 1074,*affd*42 NY2d 933;*Catholic Foreign Mission Socy. v Oussani,* 215 NY 1, 8;*Born v Schrenkeisen,* 110 NY 55, 59), plaintiff's undisputed factual assertions--if material--would defeat defendants' summary judgment motion.

We conclude, however, that the extrinsic evidence tendered by plaintiff is not material. In its reliance on extrinsic evidence to bring itself within the "party benefited" cases, plaintiff ignores a vital first step in the analysis: before looking to evidence of what was in the parties' minds, a court must give due weight to what was in their contract.

A familiar and eminently sensible proposition of law is that, when parties set down their agreement in a clear, complete document, their writing should as a rule be enforced according to its terms. Evidence outside the four corners of the document as to what was really intended but unstated or misstated is generally inadmissible to add to or vary the writing *(see, e.g., Mercury Bay Boating Club v San Diego Yacht Club,* 76 NY2d 256, 269-270;*Judnick Realty Corp. v 32 W. 32nd St. Corp.,* 61 NY2d 819, 822;*Long Is. R. R. Co. v Northville Indus. Corp.,* 41 NY2d 455;*Oxford Commercial Corp. v Landau,* 12 NY2d 362, 365). That rule imparts "stability to commercial transactions by safeguarding against fraudulent claims, perjury, death of witnesses ... infirmity of memory ... [and] the fear that the jury will improperly evaluate the extrinsic evidence." (Fisch, New York Evidence § 42, at 22 [2d ed].) Such considerations are all the more compelling in the context of real property transactions, where commercial certainty is a paramount concern.

Whether or not a writing is ambiguous is a question of law to be resolved by the courts *(Van Wagner Adv. Corp. v S & M Enters.,* 67 NY2d 186, 191). In the present case, the contract, read as a whole to determine its purpose and intent *(see, e.g., Rentways, Inc. v O'Neill Milk & Cream Co.,* 308 NY 342, 347), plainly manifests the intention that defendants, as well as plaintiff, should have the right to cancel after June 1, 1987 if the litigation had not concluded by that date; and it further plainly manifests the intention that all prior understandings be merged into the contract, which expresses the parties' full agreement *(see,* 3 Corbin, Contracts § 578, at 402-403). Moreover, the face of the contract reveals a "logical reason" (152 AD2d, at 341) for the explicit provision that the cancellation right contained in paragraph 31 should run to the seller as well as the purchaser. A seller taking back a purchase-money mortgage for two thirds of the purchase price might well wish to reserve its option to sell the property for cash on an "as is" basis if third-party litigation affecting the property remained unresolved past a certain date.

Thus, we conclude there is no ambiguity as to the cancellation clause in issue, read in the context of the entire agreement, and that it confers a reciprocal right on both parties to the contract.

The question next raised is whether extrinsic evidence should be considered in order to *create* an ambiguity in the agreement. That question must be answered in the negative. It is well settled that "extrinsic and parol evidence is not admissible to create an ambiguity in a written agreement which is complete and clear and unambiguous upon its face." *(Intercontinental Planning v Daystrom, Inc.,* 24 NY2d 372, 379;*see also, Chimart Assocs. v Paul,* 66 NY2d 570, 573.)

Plaintiff's rejoinder--that defendants indeed had the specified absolute right to cancel the contract, but it was subject to plaintiff's absolute prior right of waiver--suffers from a logical inconsistency that is evident in a mere statement of the argument. But there is an even greater problem. Here, sophisticated businessmen reduced their negotiations to a clear, complete writing. In the paragraphs immediately surrounding paragraph 31, they expressly bestowed certain options on the purchaser alone, but in paragraph 31 they chose otherwise, explicitly allowing both buyer and seller to cancel in the event the litigation was unresolved by June 1, 1987. By ignoring the plain language of the contract, plaintiff effectively rewrites the bargain that was struck. An analysis that begins with consideration of extrinsic evidence of what the parties meant, instead of looking first to what they said and reaching extrinsic evidence only when required to do so because of some identified ambiguity, unnecessarily denigrates the contract and unsettles the law.

Finally, plaintiff's conclusory assertion of bad faith is supported only by its vice-president's statement that one of the defendants told the broker on the transaction, who then told him, that defendants were doing nothing to defend the action, waiting for June 2 to cancel, and suggesting that the broker might resell the property at a higher price. Where the moving party "has demonstrated its entitlement to summary judgment, the party opposing the motion must demonstrate by admissible evidence the existence of a factual issue requiring a trial of the action or tender an acceptable excuse for his failure so to do." *(Zuckerman v City of New York,* 49 NY2d 557, 560.)Even viewing the burden of a summary judgment opponent more generously than that of the summary judgment proponent, plaintiff fails to raise a triable issue of fact *(see, Friends of Animals v Associated Fur Mfrs.,* 46 NY2d 1065, 1068).

Accordingly, the Appellate Division order should be reversed, with costs, defendants' motion for summary judgment granted, and the complaint dismissed.

Case 9: Parol Evidence Rule -- Application of the Reasonably Susceptible Rule

---

Dore v. Arnold Worldwide, Inc.
Supreme Court of California, 2006
39 Cal. 4th 384

WERDEGAR, J.--Plaintiff alleges against his former employer various causes of action in connection with his termination. The trial court granted the employer summary judgment, but the Court of Appeal reversed. We agree with the trial court and, accordingly, reverse the judgment of the Court of Appeal.

Background

Plaintiff Brook Dore was employed with an advertising agency in Colorado as a regional account director specializing in automobile accounts. In late 1998, Dore discussed with his employer the possibility of relocating to the employer's Los Angeles office.

In 1999, Dore learned that a management supervisor position was available in the Los Angeles office of defendant Arnold Worldwide, Inc., formerly known as Arnold Communications, Inc., (hereafter AWI). Dore interviewed with several AWI officers and employees. According to Dore, he was never told during the interview process that his employment would be terminable without cause or "at will." Dore alleges he was told that AWI had landed a new automobile account and needed someone to handle it on a long-term basis. He also was told that, if hired, he would "play a critical role in growing the agency," that AWI was looking for "a long-term fix, not a Band-Aid," and that AWI employees were treated like family. Dore alleges he learned that the two people previously holding the position for which he was being considered had been terminated for cause--one for committing financial indiscretions, the other because his work had not satisfied a client. Dore states that AWI offered him the management supervisor position by telephone in April 1999, and he orally accepted.

Later that same month, Dore received a three-page letter from Sharon McCabe, senior vice-president of AWI, dated April 6, 1999 (AWI's letter), purporting to "confirm our offer to join us as Management Supervisor in our Los Angeles office" and to state "[t]he terms of this offer." AWI's letter then listed, in bullet-pointed sections, a commencement date, compensation details, and various benefits (including reimbursement of relocation expenses, parking at the AWI offices, various types of insurance, expense reimbursement, and vacation).

AWI's letter also stated: "You will have a 90 day assessment with your supervisor at which time you will receive initial performance feedback. This assessment will also be the time that you will work with your supervisor to set objectives against which you will be evaluated at the time of your annual review. After your assessment is complete, you and your supervisor will have the opportunity to discuss consideration for being named an officer of Arnold Communications."

In a separate paragraph central to the present dispute, AWI's letter stated: "Brook, please know that as with all of our company employees, your employment with Arnold Communications, Inc. is at will. This simply means that Arnold Communications has the right to terminate your employment at any time just as you have the right to terminate your employment with Arnold Communications, Inc. at any time."

AWI's letter requested that Dore sign and return the letter signifying his acceptance of these employment terms. Dore read and signed the letter.

AWI terminated Dore's employment in August 2001. Thereafter, Dore sued AWI and a related entity, Arnold Worldwide Partners (AWP), alleging (1) breach of contract, (2) breach of the implied covenant of good faith and fair dealing, (3) intentional infliction of emotional distress, (4) fraud, and (5) negligent misrepresentation. AWI and AWP each filed a motion for summary judgment.

The trial court granted AWI's motion on the ground that Dore could not establish the existence of either an express or an implied-in-fact agreement that his employment was terminable only for cause. The trial court granted AWP's motion on the ground that AWP could not be held liable as Dore's employer for AWI's personnel decisions and conduct. Dore appealed. The Court of Appeal affirmed in part and reversed in part. The court affirmed the judgment in favor of AWP as to liability and reversed the judgment in favor of AWI. The court remanded the matter to the trial court with directions to vacate its order granting summary judgment to AWI and enter a new order granting summary adjudication to AWI only on Dore's negligent misrepresentation cause of action. We granted AWI's petition for review.

Discussion

Dore alleges that AWI, by various oral representations, conduct, and documents, led him reasonably to understand there existed between AWI and himself an implied-in-fact contract that provided he would not be discharged from his employment except for cause. AWI contends that its oral representations, conduct, and documents could not reasonably have raised any such understanding in Dore.

We take the facts from the record that was before the trial court when it ruled on AWI's motion for summary judgment. We review the trial court's decision de novo, considering all the evidence set forth in the moving and opposing papers except that to which objections were made and sustained. We liberally construe the evidence in support of the party opposing summary judgment and resolve doubts concerning the evidence in favor of that party. (*Yanowitz v. L'Oreal USA, Inc.* (2005) 36 Cal.4th 1028, 1037 [32 Cal. Rptr. 3d 436, 116 P.3d 1123].)

Dore acknowledges that a clear and unambiguous at-will provision in a written employment contract, signed by the employee, cannot be overcome by evidence of a prior or contemporaneous implied-in-fact contract requiring good cause for termination. (See cases cited in *Guz v. Bechtel National, Inc.* (2000) 24 Cal.4th 317, 340 [100 Cal. Rptr. 2d 352, 8 P.3d 1089].) But he contends this rule cannot govern here because AWI's letter neither constitutes nor contains a clear and unambiguous agreement that his employment would be terminable without cause.

A. *Dore's Contract Claims*

   1. *"At any time"*

The Court of Appeal below agreed with Dore that AWI's letter, signed by Dore, was not clear and unambiguous with respect to cause for termination. Notwithstanding the letter's statement that "your employment with Arnold Communications, Inc. is at will," the court reasoned, by going on to define the term "at will" to mean that AWI had the right to terminate Dore's employment "at any time," AWI impliedly relinquished the right to terminate Dore without cause. We disagree.

The Courts of Appeal are in conflict over whether a provision in an employment contract providing for termination "at any time" or upon specified notice is, without more, reasonably susceptible to an interpretation allowing for the existence of an implied-in-fact agreement that termination will occur only for cause. The Court of Appeal in *Bionghi v. Metropolitan Water Dist.* (1999) 70 Cal.App.4th 1358 [83 Cal. Rptr. 2d 388] held such a provision is not thus susceptible; those in *Seubert v. McKesson Corp.* (1990) 223 Cal. App. 3d 1514 [273 Cal. Rptr. 296], *Wallis v. Farmers Group, Inc.* (1990) 220 Cal. App. 3d 718 [269 Cal. Rptr. 299], and *Bert G. Gianelli Distributing Co. v. Beck & Co.* (1985) 172 Cal. App. 3d 1020 [219 Cal. Rptr. 203] held it is. (See also *Sherman v. Mutual Benefit Life Ins. Co.* (9th Cir. 1980) 633 F.2d 782, 784 [applying California law].)

Seubert concerned a wrongful termination action brought by a regional sales manager of a computer systems company against his employer for breach of contract, misrepresentation, and breach of the implied covenant of good faith and fair dealing. Notwithstanding the plaintiff had signed an employment application stating that, " 'if hired, my employment is for no definite period and may, regardless of the date of payment of my wages and salary, be terminated at any time without any prior notice' " (*Seubert v. McKesson Corp., supra,* 223 Cal. App. 3d at p. 1517), the Court of Appeal, looking to other factors indicating the application "was not intended to be the entire employment agreement between the parties," ruled that extrinsic evidence supported the existence of an implied contract requiring cause for termination (*id.* at p. 1520).

In *Wallis,* an insurance agent entered into an agreement with the insurer she represented that provided her agency could be " 'terminated by either the Agent or [the insurance company] on three (3) months written notice.' " (*Wallis v. Farmers Group, Inc., supra,* 220 Cal. App. 3d at p. 730.) After she was terminated, the agent brought an action alleging the parties had both an express oral and an implied-in-fact agreement that she would be terminated only for cause. The Court of Appeal found that, notwithstanding the contract was integrated on the subject of termination, because its termination provision was silent as to whether good cause was required, the language was reasonably susceptible of meaning either that no cause was required or that a separate agreement requiring good cause existed. Therefore, the court held, extrinsic evidence was admissible to determine the meaning of the written agreement. (*Id.* at pp. 730-731.)

In *Gianelli*, independent local beer wholesalers and distributors brought an action against a brewer of an imported brand of beer, alleging the brewer's termination of their distribution contracts without good cause breached those contracts. Each complaining party had signed a distribution agreement providing it would " 'continue in effect unless and until terminated at any time after January 1, 1973 by thirty days written notice by either party to the other.' " (*Bert G. Gianelli Distributing Co. v. Beck & Co., supra,* 172 Cal. App. 3d at p. 1037.) The Court of Appeal held the agreements could reasonably be interpreted as consistent with an implied requirement of good cause for termination. (*Id.* at pp. 1038-1039.)

The termination clause at issue in *Bionghi* provided that the agreement "may be terminated by [the employer] hereto 30 days after notice in writing." (*Bionghi v. Metropolitan Water Dist., supra,* 70 Cal.App.4th at pp. 1361-1362.) The Court of Appeal held that the plain language of the clause was not reasonably susceptible to an interpretation requiring the employer to have good cause for termination. (*Id.* at p. 1361.) "In our view," the court stated, "a contract which provides that it may be terminated on specified notice cannot reasonably be interpreted to require good cause as well as notice for termination, unless extrinsic evidence establishes that the parties used the words in some *special sense.* Instead, such a contract allows termination with or without good cause." (*Id.* at p. 1369, italics added.)

We disagree with Dore that the verbal formulation "at any time" in the termination clause of an employment contract is per se ambiguous merely because it does not expressly speak to whether cause is required. As a matter of simple logic, rather, such a formulation ordinarily entails the notion of "with or without cause."

2. AWI's letter

That the phrase "at any time" is not in itself ambiguous with respect to cause for termination does not preclude the possibility that AWI's letter, when considered as a whole, contains ambiguity on the topic. As California courts previously have observed, the "meaning of language is to be found in its applications. An indeterminacy in the application of language signals its vagueness or ambiguity. An ambiguity arises when language is reasonably susceptible of more than one application to material facts. There cannot be an ambiguity per se, i.e. an ambiguity unrelated to an application." (*California State Auto. Assn. Inter-Ins. Bureau v. Superior Court* (1986) 177 Cal. App. 3d 855, 859, fn. 1 [223 Cal. Rptr. 246]; see also *Herzog v. National American Ins. Co.* (1970) 2 Cal.3d 192, 199, fn. 5 [84 Cal. Rptr. 705, 465 P.2d 841]

["language which might be considered ambiguous as applied to some circumstances is not necessarily ambiguous per se"].)

Accordingly, "[e]ven if a contract appears unambiguous on its face, a latent ambiguity may be exposed by extrinsic evidence which reveals more than one possible meaning to which the language of the contract is yet reasonably susceptible." (*Morey v. Vannucci* (1998) 64

Cal.App.4th 904, 912 [75 Cal. Rptr. 2d 573].) "The test of admissibility of extrinsic evidence to explain the meaning of a written instrument is not whether it appears to the court to be plain and unambiguous on its face, but whether the offered evidence is relevant to prove a meaning to which the language of the instrument is reasonably susceptible." (*Pacific Gas & E. Co. v. G. W. Thomas Drayage etc. Co.* (1968) 69 Cal.2d 33, 37 [69 Cal. Rptr. 561, 442 P.2d 641], citing numerous authorities.)

In this case, the trial court recognized that the presumption of at-will employment codified in section 2922 of the Labor Code can be overcome by an express or implied agreement to the contrary. (See *Guz v. Bechtel National, Inc., supra,* 24 Cal.4th at p. 336.) Nevertheless, the court ruled that because the express written contract--i.e., AWI's letter--controls, it need not consider whether Dore's proffered extrinsic evidence establishes the existence of an earlier implied agreement to terminate only for cause.

The Court of Appeal, in reaching the contrary conclusion, relied primarily on the fact that AWI's letter, after stating that Dore's employment is "at will," defines "at will" in a manner that refers expressly only to the duration of the contract (i.e., as meaning "that Arnold Communications has the right to terminate your employment at any time") and does not state explicitly whether cause is required.[1] The Court of Appeal also relied on evidence extrinsic to the letter, in particular, that AWI required Dore to sign a postemployment noncompetition and nondisclosure agreement.

The trial court's ruling was correct. The language of the parties' written agreement is unambiguous. AWI's letter plainly states that Dore's employment with AWI was at will. Indeed, as the trial court observed, Dore admitted as much and further admitted that he "read, signed, understood and did not disagree with the terms of the letter." Even the Court of Appeal acknowledged that the term "at will" when used in an employment contract normally conveys an intent employment may be ended by either party "at any time without cause." Although AWI's letter also states that AWI would provide Dore a "90 day assessment" and "annual review," these provisions, in describing AWI's employee evaluation schedule, neither expressly nor impliedly conferred on Dore the right to be terminated only for cause.

That AWI's letter went on to define at-will employment as employment that may be terminated at any time did not introduce ambiguity rendering the letter susceptible of being

interpreted as allowing for an implied agreement that Dore could be terminated only for cause. In defining at-will employment, AWI used language similar to the language the Legislature used in our statutory provision. Labor Code section 2922 says that an "employment, *having no specified term*, may be terminated at the will of either party on notice to the other." (Italics added.)

"An at-will employment may be ended by either party 'at any time without cause,' for any or no reason, and subject to no procedure except the statutory requirement of notice." (*Guz v.*

---

[1] The court also noted that AWI's letter states that Dore would be considered for a position as an officer of AWI after a 90-day assessment period.

Bechtel National, Inc., supra, 24 Cal.4th at p. 335.) For the parties to specify--indeed to emphasize--that Dore's employment was at will (explaining that it could be terminated at any time) would make no sense if their true meaning was that his employment could be terminated only for cause. Thus, even though AWI's letter defined "at will" as meaning "at any time," without specifying it also meant without cause or for any or no reason, the letter's meaning was clear.

Nor did Dore's proffered extrinsic evidence render AWI's letter ambiguous concerning whether he could be terminated only for cause. As noted, Dore declared that he was told his role would be "critical" because AWI "needed a long-term fix" of certain problems and wanted Dore to "build a relationship" with an important new client. He also testified that he learned in interviews that some people at AWI had been employed there for long periods and he was assured the company had a family atmosphere. Even if credited, such evidence would not support an inference that Dore reasonably understood AWI's letter as consistent with a promise not to terminate him without cause. "When a dispute arises over the meaning of contract language, the first question to be decided is whether the language is 'reasonably susceptible' to the interpretation urged by the party. If it is not, the case is over." (*Southern Cal. Edison Co. v. Superior Court* (1995) 37 Cal.App.4th 839, 847 [44 Cal. Rptr. 2d 227].)

We conclude, in sum, that AWI's letter contained no ambiguity, patent or latent, in its termination provisions. Accordingly, we agree with the trial court that no triable issues of fact exist with respect to Dore's causes of action for breach of contract and breach of the implied covenant of good faith and fair dealing.

Disposition

For the foregoing reasons, the judgment of the Court of Appeal is reversed.[2]

---

[2] *Seubert v. McKesson Corp., supra*, 223 Cal.App.3d 1514, *Wallis v. Farmers Group, Inc., supra*, 220 Cal.App.3d 718, and *Bert G. Gianelli Distributing Co. v. Beck & Co., supra*, 172 Cal.App.3d 1020, are disapproved to the extent they are inconsistent with this opinion.

Case 10:   Contract Interpretation
Parol Evidence Rule – Trade Usage

Ermolieff v. R.K.O. Radio Pictures, Inc.
Supreme Court of California, 1942
19 Cal.2d 543

CARTER, J.

Plaintiff and defendant are producers and distributors in the motion picture industry. Plaintiff was the owner and producer of a foreign language motion picture entitled "Michael Strogoff," based on a novel by Jules Verne, which prior to July 6, 1936, he had produced in the German and French languages. On that date the parties entered into a contract in which plaintiff granted to defendant the exclusive right to produce and distribute an English version of that picture in only those "countries or territories of the world" listed on an exhibit annexed to the contract. On the exhibit is listed among other places "The United Kingdom." Plaintiff reserved the rights in the picture in both foreign and English language in all countries or territories not listed in the exhibit. The contract was modified in December, 1936, and September, 1937, to add other countries or territories to the list. Plaintiff commenced the instant action on May 8, 1940, pleading the contract and its modifications and alleging that defendant had produced an English version of the picture under the title "Soldier and a Lady" in the United States and elsewhere; and that a controversy has arisen between the parties as to the countries and territories granted to defendant and those reserved by plaintiff under the contract and its modifications. Those allegations were admitted by defendant and it alleges that the only controversy between the parties is with respect to the area referred to as "The United Kingdom"; that the only dispute is whether "The United Kingdom," in which the contract grants rights to defendant, includes Eire or the Irish Free State; and that there is a custom and usage in the motion picture industry that that term does include Eire and that such usage is a part of the contract. Both the complaint and the answer pray for declaratory relief, namely, a declaration of their rights with respect to those areas embraced in the contract which are in dispute.

It was stipulated that the sole issue with respect to the territory embraced in the contract was whether defendant or plaintiff held the rights in the picture in Eire, which in turn depended upon whether The United Kingdom included Eire; that defendant did distribute the picture in Eire, and that The United Kingdom, from a political and legal viewpoint, did not include Eire, the latter being independent from it.

At the close of plaintiff's case the trial court denied defendant's motion to dismiss made on the ground that the case was not a proper one for declaratory relief under sections 1060-1062a of the Code of Civil Procedure. It granted a motion to strike all of defendant's evidence that by the custom and usage of the motion picture industry The United Kingdom included Eire on the ground that such evidence was incompetent, irrelevant, and immaterial, and entered judgment in favor of plaintiff determining that he, rather than defendant, possessed the rights with respect to the picture in Eire. From that judgment defendant appeals, claiming error in the above-mentioned rulings of the trial court.

      *   *   *   *   *   *

Defendant asserts, however, that the judgment must be reversed because of the granting of plaintiff's motion to strike defendant's evidence that according to the custom and usage of the moving picture industry Eire is included in The United Kingdom. With that contention we agree. Both plaintiff and defendant are engaged in the business of producing and distributing moving pictures and rights in connection therewith. Defendant's evidence consisted of the testimony of several witnesses familiar with the distribution of motion pictures to the effect that in contracts covering the rights to produce pictures the general custom and usage was that the term "The United Kingdom" included Eire, the Irish Free State. Plaintiff's motion to strike out all of that evidence on the ground that it was incompetent, irrelevant and immaterial was granted. Plaintiff, reserving his objection to defendant's evidence, offered contrary evidence concerning such custom and usage.

The correct rule with reference to the admissibility of evidence as to trade usage under the circumstances here presented is that while words in a contract are ordinarily to be construed according to their plain, ordinary, popular or legal meaning, as the case may be, yet if in reference to the subject matter of the contract, particular expressions have by trade usage acquired a different meaning, and both parties are engaged in that trade, the parties to the contract are deemed to have used them according to their different and peculiar sense as shown by such trade usage. Parol evidence is admissible to establish the trade usage, and that is true even though the words are in their ordinary or legal meaning entirely unambiguous, inasmuch as by reason of the usage the words are used by the parties in a different sense. (See Code of Civil Procedure, sec. 1861; Civil Code, secs. 1644, 1646, 1655; *Jenny Lind Co.* v. *Bower & Co.*, 11 Cal. 194; *Callahan* v. *Stanley*, 57 Cal. 476; *Higgins* v. *California Petroleum etc. Co.*, 120 Cal. 629, 52 Pac. 1080; *Caro* v. *Mattei*, 39 Cal. App. 253 [178 Pac. 537]; Wigmore on Evidence, vol. IX, sec. 2463, p. 204; Restatement, Contracts, secs. 246, 248; 89 A. L. R. 1228.) The basis of this rule is that to accomplish a purpose of paramount importance in interpretation of documents, namely, to ascertain the true intent of the parties, it may well be said that the usage evidence does not alter the contract of the parties, but on the contrary gives the effect to the words there used as intended by the parties. The usage becomes a part of the contract in aid of its correct interpretation.

Plaintiff relies upon such cases as *Brant* v. *California Dairies, Inc.*, 4 Cal. (2d) 128 [48 Pac. (2d) 13], and *Wells* v. *Union Oil Co.*, 25 Cal. App. (2d) 165 [76 Pac. (2d) 696], as announcing a rule contrary to the one above stated. However, in those cases evidence of custom or usage was not offered, and no contention was made therein that the words employed in the contracts there involved had any other than their ordinary, popular or legal meaning in reference to the subject matter of said contracts. That is not the case here. Plaintiff also cites other authorities. In *New York Cent. R. R. Co.* v. *Frank H. Buck Co.*, 2 Cal. (2d) 384 [41 Pac. (2d) 547], and the cases therein cited, the rule stated is merely that where the terms of the contract are expressly and directly contrary to the precise subject matter embraced in the custom or usage, parol evidence of that custom or usage is not admissible. The provision in the contract was tantamount to a clause that custom or usage shall not be a part of the contract. They did not involve a situation where the evidence was introduced to define a term in the contract. In the case at bar it cannot be said that there was a provision of that character. The contract stated that the defendant's rights existed only in the countries or territories listed in the annexed exhibit and plaintiff reserved the rights in all other countries or territories. "Territories" is a more comprehensive term than countries, and may well include more than one political entity or nation. The term "The United Kingdom" as a territory or area, does not necessarily limit that area to a political entity known as The United Kingdom. The fact that it is expressly stipulated in the contract that defendant has no rights in any countries not named in the exhibit, does not alter the situation. It falls short of being tantamount to an express and direct agreement that Eire shall not be considered as included in The United Kingdom. The door is still open to evidence of custom and usage with reference to the scope of The United Kingdom. The foregoing comments are equally applicable to the other cases cited by plaintiff, namely, *Withers* v. *Moore*, 140 Cal. 591 [74 Pac. 159]; *May* v. *American Trust Co.*, 135 Cal. App. 385 [27 Pac. (2d) 101]; *Brandenstein* v. *Jackling*, 99 Cal. App. 438 [278 Pac. 880]; *Fish* v. *Correll*, 4 Cal. App. 521 [88 Pac. 489], and *California Jewelry Co.* v. *Provident Loan Assn.*, 6 Cal. App. (2d) 506 [45 Pac. (2d) 271].

Plaintiff urges that since judicial notice may be taken and it was stipulated that Eire is independent of The United Kingdom and not a part thereof, the custom and usage evidence is not admissible to contradict that stipulation or notice. That notice and stipulation add nothing material to the situation. In any case where a word in a contract had an unquestioned common meaning there could be no dispute as to that common meaning, but the custom and usage is evidence of the peculiar sense in which it was used. The stipulation would add nothing that was not already plain on the face of the contract.

It is contended that the parties placed a practical construction on the contract which negatived presence of custom and usage as a part thereof. The contract was modified on December 1, 1936, and September 8, 1937, to include countries not mentioned in the original contract. Eire was not among the added areas and nothing was said therein with reference to the territory embraced by The United Kingdom. Malta and Gibraltar which are political subdivisions of The United Kingdom were added. It does not necessarily follow that these modifications constituted a construction of the contract by the parties to the effect that Eire was not included in the term "The United Kingdom," nor that evidence of custom or usage was removed from the picture. Indeed, it may reasonably follow from those modifications that the criterion to be used in construing the area embraced within The United Kingdom was not the political or legal boundaries thereof. It may well be said to indicate an uncertainty as to the extent of the area embraced by that term because upon plaintiff's present reasoning The United Kingdom is circumscribed by the political and legal boundaries thereof. That being the case, there would be no occasion for the modification because Malta and Gibraltar being political subdivisions of The

United Kingdom would be embraced in the contract as originally written. For those reasons, it is also a fair inference to conclude, that the parties because of the modifications, had some meaning in their mind for the term "The United Kingdom," other than that territory which is a political and legal part thereof.

Finally, plaintiff asserts that the custom and usage evidence was inadmissible because a custom and usage to be available must be known by the parties or so generally known that knowledge must be presumed, citing *Security Commercial & Savings Bank of San Diego* v. *Southern Trust & Commerce Bank*, 74 Cal. App. 734 [241 Pac. 945]. But in this case defendant's excluded evidence showed that the custom was general in the moving picture industry and both parties were engaged in the production of motion pictures. As plaintiff expresses it in his brief, "Respondent (plaintiff) is a world famous producer." It is stated in Restatement, Contracts, section 248, page 352:

"Where both parties to a transaction are engaged in the same occupation, or belong to the same group of persons, the usages of that occupation or group are operative, unless one of the parties knows or has reason to know that the other party has an inconsistent intention."

Plaintiff further urges in support of the exclusion of the evidence of usage; that the witnesses were biased, that it was a "low quality of proof," that it was insufficient and the like. These are matters that go to the weight of the evidence, rather than to its admissibility. With that we are not concerned. There is no necessity for a detailed analysis of the evidence. It is clear that the trial court did not purport to weigh or evaluate that evidence. It disregarded it in toto as is evinced by its order striking it out. On retrial of the action, if the parties so desire, the trial court may consider and give such weight to such evidence as may be introduced.

The judgment is reversed.

Case 11:   Specific Performance

Campbell Soup Co. v. Wentz
United States Court of Appeals, Third Circuit, 1948
172 F.2d 80

GOODRICH--

These are appeals from judgments of the District Court denying equitable relief to the buyer under a contract for the sale of carrots. The defendants in No. 9648 are the contract sellers. The defendant in No. 9649 is the second purchaser of part of the carrots which are the subject matter of the contract.

The transactions which raise the issues may be briefly summarized. On June 21, 1947, Campbell Soup Company (Campbell), a New Jersey corporation, entered into a written contract with George B. Wentz and Harry T. Wentz, who are Pennsylvania farmers, for delivery by the Wentzes to Campbell of all the Chantenay red cored carrots to be grown on fifteen acres of the Wentz farm during the 1947 season. Where the contract was entered into does not appear. The contract provides, however, for delivery of the carrots at the Campbell plant in Camden, New Jersey. The prices specified in the contract ranged from $ 23 to $ 30 per ton according to the time of delivery. The contract price for January, 1948 was $ 30 a ton.

The Wentzes harvested approximately 100 tons of carrots from the fifteen acres covered by the contract. Early in January, 1948, they told a Campbell representative that they would not deliver their carrots at the contract price. The market price at that time was at least $ 90 per ton, and Chantenay red cored carrots were virtually unobtainable. The Wentzes then sold approximately 62 tons of their carrots to the defendant Lojeski, a neighboring farmer. Lojeski resold about 58 tons on the open market, approximately half to Campbell and the balance to other purchasers.

On January 9, 1948, Campbell, suspecting that Lojeski was selling it 'contract carrots,' refused to purchase any more, and instituted these suits against the Wentz brothers and Lojeski to enjoin further sale of the contract carrots to others, and to compel specific performance of the contract. The trial court denied equitable relief.[1] We agree with the result reached, but on a different ground from that relied upon by the District Court.

The case has been presented by both sides as though Erie Railroad v. Tompkins, 1938, 304 U.S. 64, 58 S.Ct. 817, 82 L.Ed. 1188, 114 A.L.R. 1487, and Klaxon Company v. Stentor

---

[1] The issue is preserved on appeal by an arrangement under which Campbell received all the carrots held by the Wentzes and Lojeski, paying a stipulated market price of $ 90 per ton, $ 30 to the defendants, and the balance into the registry of the District Court pending the outcome of these appeals.

Electric Manufacturing Co., Inc., 1941, 313 U.S. 487, 61 S.Ct. 1020, 85 L.Ed. 1477, had never been decided. We are not advised as to the place of the contract, although as we have pointed out in other cases, the Pennsylvania conflict of laws rule, which binds us here, refers matters concerning the validity and extent of obligation of the contract to the place of making.[2] In this instance, however, the absence of data on which to base a rule of reference does not preclude the decision of the case. We have said several times in this Circuit that the question of the form of relief is a matter for a federal court to decide.[3] But neither federal decisions[4] nor the law of New Jersey or Pennsylvania as expressed in the Uniform Sales Act[5] differ upon this point. A party may have specific performance of a contract for the sale of chattels if the legal remedy is inadequate. Inadequacy of the legal remedy is necessarily a matter to be determined by an examination of the facts in each particular instance.

We think that on the question of adequacy of the legal remedy the case is one appropriate for specific performance. It was expressly found that at the time of the trial it was 'virtually impossible to obtain Chantenay carrots in the open market.' This Chantenay carrot is one which the plaintiff uses in large quantities, furnishing the seed to the growers with whom it makes contracts. It was not claimed that in nutritive value it is any better than other types of carrots. Its blunt shape makes it easier to handle in processing. And its color and texture differ from other varieties. The color is brighter than other carrots. The trial court found that the plaintiff failed to establish what proportion of its carrots is used for the production of soup stock and what proportion is used as identifiable physical ingredients in its soups. We do not think lack of proof on that point is material. It did appear that the plaintiff uses carrots in fifteen of its twenty-one soups. It also appeared that it uses these Chantenay carrots diced in some of them and that the appearance is uniform. The preservation of uniformity in appearance in a food article marketed throughout the country and sold under the manufacturer's name is a matter of considerable commercial significance and one which is properly considered in determining whether a substitute ingredient is just as good as the original.

The trial court concluded that the plaintiff had failed to establish that the carrots, 'judged by objective standards,' are unique goods. This we think is not a pure fact conclusion like a finding that Chantenay carrots are of uniform color. It is either a conclusion of law or of mixed fact and law and we are bound to exercise our independent judgment upon it. That the test for specific performance is not necessarily 'objective' is shown by the many cases in which equity

---

[2] A. M. Webb & Co. v. Robert P. Miller Co., 3 Cir., 1946, 157 F.2d 865; Griffin v. Metal Products Co., 1919, 264 Pa. 254, 107 A. 713; Restatement, Conflict of Laws § 332 (1934). Cf. Texas Motorcoaches v. A.C.F. Motors Co., 3 Cir., 1946, 154 F.2d 91; Restatement, Conflict of Laws § 358 (1934).

[3] Orth v. Transit Investment Corp., 3 Cir., 1942, 132 F.2d 938; Black & Yates v. Mahogany Assn., 3 Cir., 1941, 129 F.2d 227, 148 A.L.R. 841, certiorari denied, 1942, 317 U.S. 672, 63 S.Ct. 76, 87 L.Ed. 539. Cf. Note, 55 Yale L.J. 401 (1946).

[4] Gray v. Premier Investment Co., D.C.W.D. La., 1943, 51 F.Supp. 944; Texas Co. v. Central Fuel Oil Co., 8 Cir., 1912, 194 Fed. 1.

[5] Uniform Sales Act, § 68, N.J.S.A. 46:30-74; 69 P.S. § 313.

has given it to enforce contracts for articles- family heirlooms and the like- the value of which was personal to the plaintiff.[6]

Judged by the general standards applicable to determining the adequacy of the legal remedy[7] we think that on this point the case is a proper one for equitable relief. There is considerable authority, old and new, showing liberality in the granting of an equitable remedy.[8] We see no reason why a court should be reluctant to grant specific relief when it can be given without supervision of the court or other time-consuming processes against one who has deliberately broken his agreement. Here the goods of the special type contracted for were unavailable on the open market, the plaintiff had contracted for them long ahead in anticipation of its needs, and had built up a general reputation for its products as part of which reputation uniform appearance was important. We think if this were all that was involved in the case specific performance should have been granted.

The reason that we shall affirm instead of reversing with an order for specific performance is found in the contract itself. We think it is too hard a bargain and too one-sided an agreement to entitle the plaintiff to relief in a court of conscience. For each individual grower the agreement is made by filling in names and quantity and price on a printed form furnished by the buyer. This form has quite obviously been drawn by skilful draftsmen with the buyer's interests in mind.

Paragraph 2 provides for the manner of delivery. Carrots are to have their stalks cut off and be in clean sanitary bags or other containers approved by Campbell. This paragraph concludes with a statement that Campbell's determination of conformance with specifications shall be conclusive.

The defendants attack this provision as unconscionable. We do not think that it is, standing by itself. We think that the provision is comparable to the promise to perform to the satisfaction of another[9] and that Campbell would be held liable if it refused carrots which did in fact conform to the specifications.[10]

---

[6] Burr v. Bloomsburg, 1927, 101 N.J.Eq. 615, 138 A. 876; Sloane v. Clauss, 1901, 64 Ohio St. 125, 59 N.E. 884; 5 Williston, Contracts § 1419 n. 6 (Rev. ed. 1937).

[7] Restatement, Contracts § 361 (1932); 5 Williston, Contracts § 1419 (Rev. ed. 1937); 1 Pomeroy, Equity Jurisprudence § 221b (5th ed. 1941).

[8] Oreland Equipment Co. v. Copco Steel and Engineering Corp., 1944, 310 Mich. 6, 16 N.W.2d 646; Kann v. Wausau Abrasives Co., 1925, 81 N.H. 535, 129 A. 374; Mantell v. International Plastic Harmonica Corp., 1946, 138 N.J.Eq. 562, 49 A.2d 290; DeMoss v. Conart Motor Sales, Inc., Ohio Com. Pl., 1947, 72 N.E.2d 158, noted in 26 Tex.L.Rev. 351 (1948); Cochrane v. Szpakowski, 4916, 355 Pa. 357, 49 A.2d 692; Note, 152 A.L.R. 4 (1944). Professor Williston has consistently advocated a more liberal use of equitable remedies, especially under the specific performance provision of the Uniform Sales Act. 3 Williston, Sales § 601 (Rev. ed. 1948); 5 Williston, Contracts § 1419 (Rev. ed. 1937).

[9] Restatement, Contracts § 265 (1932); 3 Williston, Contracts § 675A (Rev. ed. 1937).

[10] Griffin Mfg. Co. v. Boom Boiler & Welding Co., 6 Cir., 1937, 90 F.2d 209, certiorari denied 1937, 302 U.S. 741, 58 S.Ct. 143, 82 L.Ed. 573; Lord Co. v. Industrial Dying & Finishing Works, 1916, 252 Pa. 421, 97 A. 573; 3 Williston, Contracts § 675A, n. 11 (Rev. ed. 1937).

The next paragraph allows Campbell to refuse carrots in excess of twelve tons to the acre. The next contains a covenant by the grower that he will not sell carrots to anyone else except the carrots rejected by Campbell nor will he permit anyone else to grow carrots on his land. Paragraph 10 provides liquidated damages to the extent of $ 50 per acre for any breach by the grower. There is no provision for liquidated or any other damages for breach of contract by Campbell.

The provision of the contract which we think is the hardest is paragraph 9, set out in the margin.[11] It will be noted that Campbell is excused from accepting carrots under certain circumstances. But even under such circumstances the grower, while he cannot say Campbell is liable for failure to take the carrots, is not permitted to sell them elsewhere unless Campbell agrees. This is the kind of provision which the late Francis H. Bohlen would call 'carrying a good joke too far.' What the grower may do with his product under the circumstances set out is not clear. He has covenanted not to store it anywhere except on his own farm and also not to sell to anybody else.

We are not suggesting that the contract is illegal. Nor are we suggesting any excuse for the grower in this case who has deliberately broken an agreement entered into with Campbell. We do think, however, that a party who has offered and succeeded in getting an agreement as tough as this one is, should not come to a chancellor and ask court help in the enforcement of its terms. That equity does not enforce unconscionable bargains is too well established to require elaborate citation.[12]

The plaintiff argues that the provisions of the contract are separable. We agree that they are, but do not think that decisions separating out certain provisions from illegal contracts are in point here. As already said, we do not suggest that this contract is illegal. All we say is that the sum total of its provisions drives too hard a bargain for a court of conscience to assist.

This disposition of the problem makes unnecessary further discussion of the separate liability of Lojeski, who was not a party to the contract, but who purchased some of the carrots from the Wentzes.

The judgments will be affirmed

---

[11] 'Grower shall not be obligated to deliver any Carrots which he is unable to harvest or deliver, nor shall Campbell be obligated to receive or pay for any Carrots which it is unable to inspect, grade, receive, handle, use or pack at or ship in processed form from its plants in Camden (1) because of any circumstance beyond the control of Grower or Campbell, as the case may be, or (2) because of any labor disturbance, work stoppage, slow-down, or strike involving any of Campbell's employees. Campbell shall not be liable for any delay in receiving Carrots due to any of the above contingencies. During periods when Campbell is unable to receive Grower's Carrots, Grower may with Campbell's written consent, dispose of his Carrots elsewhere. Grower may not, however, sell or otherwise dispose of any Carrots which he is unable to deliver to Campbell.'

[12] 4 Pomeroy, Equity Jurisprudence § 1405a (5th ed. 1941); 5 Williston, Contracts § 1425 (Rev. ed. 1937).

Case 12:   Reliance Damages

Security Stove v. American Ry. Express
Kansas City Court of Appeals, 1932
227 Mo.App. 175

BLAND, J.

This is an action for damages for the failure of defendant to transport, from Kansas City to Atlantic City, New Jersey, within a reasonable time, a furnace equipped with a combination oil and gas burner. The cause was tried before the court without the aid of a jury, resulting in a judgment in favor of plaintiff in the sum of $801.50 and interest, or in a total sum of $1,000.00. Defendant has appealed.

The facts show that plaintiff manufactured a furnace equipped with a special combination oil and gas burner it desired to exhibit at the American Gas Association Convention held in Atlantic City in October, 1926. The president of plaintiff testified that plaintiff engaged space for the exhibit for the reason "that the Henry L. Dougherty Company was very much interested in putting out a combination oil and gas burner; we had just developed one, after we got through, better than anything on the market and we thought this show would be the psychological time to get in contact with the Dougherty Company"; that "the thing wasn't sent there for sale but primarily to show"; that at the time the space was engaged it was too late to ship the furnace by freight so plaintiff decided to ship it by express, and, on September 18th, 1926, wrote the office of the defendant in Kansas City, stating that it had engaged a booth for exhibition purposes at Atlantic City, New Jersey, from the American Gas Association, for the week beginning October 11th; that its exhibit consisted of an oil burning furnace, together with two oil burners which weighed at least 1,500 pounds; that, "In order to get this exhibit in place on time it should be in Atlantic City not later than October the 8th. What we want you to do is to tell us how much time you will require to assure the delivery of the exhibit on time."

Mr. Bangs, chief clerk in charge of the local office of the defendant, upon receipt of the letter, sent Mr. Johnson, a commercial representative of the defendant, to see plaintiff. Johnson called upon plaintiff taking its letter with him. Johnson made a notation on the bottom of the letter giving October 4th, as the day that defendant was required to have the exhibit in order for it to reach Atlantic City on October 8th.

On October 1st, plaintiff wrote the defendant at Kansas City, referring to its letter of September 18th, concerning the fact that the furnace must be in Atlantic City not later than October 8th, and stating what Johnson had told it, saying: "Now Mr. Bangs, we want to make doubly sure that this shipment is in Atlantic City not later than October 8th and the purpose of this letter is to tell you that you can *have your truck call for the shipment between 12 and 1 o'clock on Saturday, October 2nd for this*." (Italics plaintiff's.) On October 2d, plaintiff called the office of the express company in Kansas City and told it that the shipment was ready.

Defendant came for the shipment on the last mentioned day, received it and delivered the express receipt to plaintiff. The shipment contained 21 packages. Each package was marked with stickers backed with glue and covered with silica of soda, to prevent the stickers being torn off in shipping. Each package was given a number. They ran from 1 to 21.

Plaintiff's president made arrangements to go to Atlantic City to attend the convention and install the exhibit, arriving there about October 11th. When he reached Atlantic City he found the shipment had been placed in the booth that had been assigned to plaintiff. The exhibit was set up, but it was found that one of the packages shipped was not there. This missing package contained the gas manifold, or that part of the oil and gas burner that controlled the flow of gas in the burner. This was the most important part of the exhibit and a like burner could not be obtained in Atlantic City.

Wires were sent and it was found that the stray package was at the "over and short bureau" of defendant in St. Louis. Defendant reported that the package would be forwarded to Atlantic City and would be there by Wednesday, the 13th. Plaintiff's president waited until Thursday, the day the convention closed, but the package had not arrived at the time, so he closed up the exhibit and left. About a week after he arrived in Kansas City, the package was returned by the defendant.

Bangs testified that the reasonable time for a shipment of this kind to reach Atlantic City from Kansas City would be four days; that if the shipment was received on October 4th, it would reach Atlantic City by October 8th; that plaintiff did not ask defendant for any special rate; that the rate charged was the regular one; that plaintiff asked no special advantage in the shipment; that all defendant, under its agreement with plaintiff was required to do was to deliver the shipment at Atlantic City in the ordinary course of events; that the shipment was found in St. Louis about Monday afternoon or Tuesday morning; that it was delivered at Atlantic City at the Ritz Carlton Hotel, on the 16th of the month. There was evidence on plaintiff's part that the reasonable time for a shipment of this character to reach Atlantic City from Kansas City was not more than three or four days.

The petition upon which the case was tried alleges that plaintiff, on October 2d, 1926, delivered the shipment to the defendant; that defendant agreed, in consideration of the express charges received from plaintiff, to carry the shipment from Kansas City to Atlantic City, and "to deliver the same to plaintiff at Atlantic City, New Jersey, on or before October 8th, 1926, *the same being the reasonable and proper time necessary to transport said shipment to Atlantic City*, in as good condition as when received of defendant (plaintiff) at Kansas City, Missouri; that previous to the delivery of said goods to defendant at Kansas City, Missouri, this plaintiff apprised defendant of the kind and nature of the goods and told defendant of the necessity of having the goods at Atlantic City by October 8th, 1926, and the reason therefor; that defendant knew that the goods were intended for an exhibit at the place and that they would have to be at Atlantic City by that date to be of any service to the defendant (plaintiff)." (Italics ours.)

"That this defendant through its servants and agents, after being apprised of the nature of the shipment of goods and all of the necessity of having the goods at Atlantic City at the time specified, to-wit: October 8th, 1926, agreed with plaintiff and promised and assured plaintiff that if they would transport the goods through defendant, and deliver said goods to defendant at

Kansas City by October 4th, that they would be at Atlantic City by said date, to-wit: October 8th, 1926; that relying upon the promises and assurances of the defendant's agents and servants that the goods would be in Atlantic City by October 8th, 1926, this plaintiff delivered said goods to the defendant on October 2nd, 1926, at Kansas City, Missouri, and paid defendant the express charges on same, as above set out, in packages or parcels, numbered from 1 to 21 inclusive.

That relying upon defendant's promise and the promises of its agents and servants, that said parcels would be delivered at Atlantic City by October 8th, 1926, if delivered to defendant by October 4th, 1926, plaintiff herein hired space for an exhibit at the American Gas Association Convention at Atlantic City, and planned for an exhibit at said Convention and sent men in the employ of this plaintiff to Atlantic City to install, show and operate said exhibit, and that these men were in Atlantic City ready to set up this plaintiff's exhibit at the American Gas Association Convention on October 8th, 1926."

That defendant, in violation of its agreement, failed and neglected to deliver one of the packages to its destination on October 8th, 1926.

"That the package not delivered by defendant contained the essential part of plaintiff's exhibit which plaintiff was to make at said convention on October 8th, was later discovered in St. Louis, Missouri, by the defendant herein, and that plaintiff, for this reason, could not show his exhibit."

Plaintiff asked damages, which the court in its judgment allowed as follows: $147.00 express charges (on the exhibit); $45.12 freight on the exhibit from Atlantic City to Kansas City; $101.39 railroad and pullman fares to and from Atlantic City, expended by plaintiff's president and a workman taken by him to Atlantic City; $48.00 hotel room for the two; $150.00 for the time of the president; $40.00 for wages of plaintiff's other employee and $270.00 for rental of the booth, making a total of $801.51.

Defendant contends that its instructions in the nature of demurrers to the evidence should have been given for the reason that the petition and plaintiff's evidence show that plaintiff has based its cause of action on defendant's breach of a promise to deliver the shipment at a specified time and that promise is non-enforceable and void under the Interstate Commerce Act; that the court erred in allowing plaintiff's expenses as damages; that the only damages, if any, that can be recovered in cases of this kind, are for loss of profits and that plaintiff's evidence is not sufficient to base any recovery on this ground.

No attack was made upon the petition at the trial and at this late day it must be adjudged to be sufficient if it states any cause of action whatever, however inartificially it may be drawn. Of course, the law applicable to the case is governed by the Statutes of the United States as construed by the Federal Courts. Bilby v. A., T. S. F. Ry. Co. (Mo. Sup.) 199 S. W. 1004. It is well established that a shipper cannot recover on a special contract to move a shipment within a specified time, for such would work an unjust discrimination among shippers. The only duty that the carrier is under is to carry the shipment safely and to deliver it at its destination within a reasonable time. United States v. Am. Ry. Exp. Co., 265 U. S. 425, 44 S.Ct. 560, 68 L. Ed. 1087; C. & A. R. R. Co. v. Kirby, 225 U. S. 155, 164, 32 S.Ct. 648, 56 L. Ed. 1033, Ann. Cas. 1914A,

501; A., T. & S. F. Ry. v. Robinson, 233 U. S. 173, 34 S.Ct. 556, 58 L. Ed. 901; Cicardi Bros. Fruit & Produce Co. v. Pennsylvania Co., 201 Mo. App. 609, 213 S. W. 531.

While the petition alleges that defendant agreed to deliver the shipment at Atlantic City on or before October 8th, 1926, it also alleges that this was the reasonable and proper time necessary to transport said shipment to Atlantic City. Therefore, giving the petition a liberal construction, it would appear that all that plaintiff was contending therein was that defendant had agreed to transport the shipment within a reasonable time, and that delivery on or before October 8th was necessary to comply with the agreement. The petition refers several times to the agreement that if the goods were delivered to defendant by October 4th, they would be delivered at Atlantic City not later than October 8th, but it also alleges that the goods were not delivered to defendant until October 2nd. It is quite apparent from reading the petition, as a whole, that it was not upon a contract to deliver at Atlantic City on October 8th, goods delivered by plaintiff to defendant at Kansas City on October 4th. It would appear that the purpose of plaintiff, in pleading this agreement, was to allege sufficient facts to base its claim of special damages, that is that defendant was notified that it was necessary to have the shipment at Atlantic City by October 8th, and that the damages sustained accrued as a result of plaintiff's reliance on its being so delivered and that October 8th was plenty of time for defendant to have taken to transport the shipment. Much of the petition is surplusage but we cannot adjudge it wholly insufficient at this juncture.

There is nothing in the evidence tending to show any unjust discrimination between shippers in the agreement had between plaintiff and defendant. Boiled down to its last analysis, the agreement was nothing more than that the shipment would be transported within the ordinary time. Plaintiff sought no special advantage, was asking nothing that would be denied any other shipper, was asking no particular route, no particular train, nor for any expedited service. It was simply seeking the same rights any other shipper could have enjoyed on the same terms. No special instructions were given or involved in the case. Foster v. Cleveland, C. C. & St. L. Ry. Co. (C. C.) 56 F. 434; Copper River Packing Co. v. Alaska S. S. Co. (C. C. A.) 22 F.(2d) 12.

We think, under the circumstances in this case, that it was proper to allow plaintiff's expenses as its damages. Ordinarily the measure of damages where the carrier fails to deliver a shipment at destination within a reasonable time is the difference between the market value of the goods at the time of the delivery and the time when they should have been delivered. But where the carrier has notice of peculiar circumstances under which the shipment is made, which will result in an unusual loss by the shipper in case of delay in delivery, the carrier is responsible for the real damage sustained from such delay if the notice given is of such character, and goes to such extent, in informing the carrier of the shipper's situation, that the carrier will be presumed to have contracted with reference thereto. Central Trust Co. of New York v. Savannah & W. R. Co. (C. C.) 69 F. 683, 685.

In the case at bar defendant was advised of the necessity of prompt delivery of the shipment. Plaintiff explained to Johnson the "importance of getting the exhibit there on time." Defendant knew the purpose of the exhibit and ought to respond for its negligence in failing to get it there. As we view the record this negligence is practically conceded. The undisputed testimony shows that the shipment was sent to the over and short department of the defendant in

164

St. Louis. As the packages were plainly numbered this, prima facie, shows mistake or negligence on the part of the defendant. No effort was made by it to show that it was not negligent in sending it there, or not negligent in not forwarding it within a reasonable time after it was found.

There is no evidence of claim in this case that plaintiff suffered any loss of profits by reason of the delay in the shipment. In fact defendant states in its brief:

"The plaintiff introduced not one whit of evidence showing or tending to show that he would have made any sales as a result of his exhibit but for the negligence of the defendant. On the contrary Blakesley testified that the main purpose of the exhibit was to try to interest the Henry L. Dougherty Company in plaintiff's combination oil and gas burner, yet that was all the evidence that there was as to the benefit plaintiff expected to get from the exhibit.

As a matter of evidence, it is clear that the plaintiff would not have derived a great deal of benefit from the exhibit by any stretch of the imagination. * * *

No where does plaintiff introduce evidence showing that the Henry L. Dougherty Company in all probability would have become interested in the combination oil and gas burner and made a profitable contract with the plaintiff."

There is evidence that the exhibit was not sent to make a sale.

In support of its contention that plaintiff can sue only for loss of profit, if anything, in a case of this kind, defendant, among other cases cites that of Adams Exp. Co. v. Egbert, 36 Pa. 360, 78 Am. Dec. 382. That case involved the shipment of a box containing architectural drawings or plans for a building to a building committee of the Touro Almshouse, in New Orleans. This committee had offered a premium of $500.00 to the successful competitor. These plans arrived after the various plans had been passed upon and the award made to another person. It was sought in that case to recover the value of the plans. The evidence, howover, showed that the plans would not have won the prize had they arrived on time. The court held that the plans, under the circumstances, had no appreciable value and recovery could not be had for them and there was no basis for recovery for loss of the opportunity to compete for the prize. The opinion states that in denying recovery for the plans it is contrary to the English rule in such cases. Other cases cited by defendant involve loss of profits or the loss of opportunity to compete in such events as horse racing and the like. In one case, Delta Table & Chair Co. v. R. R., 105 Miss. 861, 63 So. 272, it was held that the plaintiff could recover for loss of profits that might have been made in the sale of its commodity, as a result of exhibiting a sample at an exhibition, where the shipment was delayed too late for the exhibit. Some of the cases cited by defendant hold that such profits in those classes of cases are not recoverable, and others to the contrary.

Defendant contends that plaintiff "is endeavoring to achieve a return of the status quo in a suit based on a breach of contract. Instead of seeking to recover what he would have had, had the contract not been broken, plaintiff is trying to recover what he would have had, had there never been any contract of shipment"; that the expenses sued for would have been incurred in any event. It is no doubt, the general rule that where there is a breach of contract the party suffering the loss can recover only that which he would have had, had the contract not been broken, and this is all the cases decided upon which defendant relies, including C., M. & St. P. Ry. v. McCaull-Dinsmore Co., 253 U. S. 97, 100, 40 S.Ct. 504, 64 L. Ed. 801. But this is merely a general statement of the rule and is not inconsistent with the holdings that, in some instances, the injured party may recover expenses incurred in relying upon the contract, although such expenses would have been incurred had the contract not been breached. See Morrow v. Railroad, 140 Mo. App. 200, 212, 213, 123 S. W. 1034; Bryant v. Barton, 32 Neb. 613, 616, 49 N. W. 331; Woodbury v. Jones, 44 N. H. 206; Driggs v. Dwight, 17 Wend. (N. Y.) 71, 31 Am. Dec. 283.

In Sperry et al. v. O'Neill-Adams Co. (C. C. A.) 185 F. 231, the court held that the advantages resulting from the use of trading stamps as a means of increasing trade are so contingent that they cannot form a basis on which to rest a recovery for a breach of contract to supply them. In lieu of compensation based thereon the court directed a recovery in the sum expended in preparation for carrying on business in connection with the use of the stamps. The court said, loc. cit. 239:

> "Plaintiff in its complaint had made a claim for lost profits, but, finding it impossible to marshal any evidence which would support a finding of exact figures, abandoned that claim. Any attempt to reach a precise sum would be mere blind guesswork. Nevertheless a contract, which both sides conceded would prove a valuable one, had been broken and the party who broke it was responsible for resultant damage. In order to carry out this contract, the plaintiff made expenditures which otherwise it would not have made. * * * The trial judge held, as we think rightly, that plaintiff was entitled at least to recover these expenses to which it had been put in order to secure the benefits of a contract of which defendant's conduct deprived it."

In the case of Gilbert v. Kennedy, 22 Mich. 117, involved the question of the measure of plaintiff's damages, caused by the conduct of defendant in wrongfully feeding his cattle with plaintiff's in the latter's pasture, resulting in plaintiff's cattle suffering by the overfeeding of the pasture. The court said loc. cit. 135, 136:

> "There being practically no market value for pasturage when there was none in the market, that element of certainty is wanting, even as to those cattle which were removed from the Pitcher farm to the home farm of the plaintiff for pasturage; and, as it could not apply to the others at all, and there being no other element of certainty by which the damages can be *accurately* measured, resort must be had to such principle or basis of calculation applicable to the circumstances of the case (if any be discoverable) as will be most likely to *approximate* certainty, and which may serve as a guide in making the most probable estimate of which the nature of the case will admit; and, though it may be less certain as a scale of measurement, yet if the principle be just in itself, and more likely to approximate the *actual damages*, it is better than any rule, however certain, which must certainly produce injustice, by excluding a large portion of the damages actually sustained."

      *   *   *   *   *   *

"Compensation is a fundamental principle of damages whether the action is in contract or in tort. Wicker v. Hoppock, 6 Wall. 94, 99, 18 L. Ed. 752. One who fails to perform his contract is justly bound to make good all damages that accrue naturally from the breach: and the other party is entitled to be put in as good a position pecuniarily as he would have been by performance of the contract." Miller v. Robertson, 266 U. S. 243, 257, 258, 45 S.Ct. 73, 78, 69 L. Ed. 265.

The case at bar was to recover damages for loss of profits by reason of the failure of the defendant to transport the shipment within a reasonable time, so that it would arrive in Atlantic City for the exhibit. There were no profits contemplated. The furnace was to be shown and shipped back to Kansas City. There was no money loss, except the expenses, that was of such a nature as any court would allow as being sufficiently definite or lacking in pure speculation. Therefore, unless plaintiff is permitted to recover the expenses that it went to, which were a total loss to it by reason of its inability to exhibit the furnace and equipment, it will be deprived of any substantial compensation for its loss. The law does not contemplate any such injustice. It ought to allow plaintiff, as damages, the loss in the way of expenses that it sustained, and which it would not have been put to if it had not been for its reliance upon the defendant to perform its contract. There is no contention that the exhibit would have been entirely valueless and whatever it might have accomplished defendant knew of the circumstances and ought to respond for whatever damages plaintiff suffered. In cases of this kind the method of estimating the damages should be adopted which is the most definite and certain and which best achieves the fundamental purpose of compensation. 17 C. J. p. 846; Miller v. Robertson, 266 U. S. 243, 257, 45 S.Ct. 73, 78, 69 L. Ed. 265. Had the exhibit been shipped in order to realize a profit on sales and such profits could have been realized, or to be entered in competition for a prize, and plaintiff failed to show loss of profits with sufficient definiteness, or that he would have won the prize, defendant's cases might be in point. But as before stated, no such situation exists here.

While, it is true that plaintiff already had incurred some of these expenses, in that it had rented space at the exhibit before entering into the contract with defendant for the shipment of the exhibit and this part of plaintiff's damages, in a sense, arose out of a circumstance which transpired before the contract was even entered into, yet, plaintiff arranged for the exhibit knowing that it could call upon defendant to perform its common law duty to accept and transport the shipment with reasonable dispatch. The whole damage, therefore, was suffered in contemplation of defendant performing its contract, which it failed to do, and would not have been sustained except for the reliance by plaintiff upon defendant to perform it. It can, therefore, be fairly said that the damages or loss suffered by plaintiff grew out of the breach of the contract, for had the shipment arrived on time, plaintiff would have had the benefit of the contract, which was contemplated by all parties, defendant being advised of the purpose of the shipment.

The judgment is affirmed.

All concur.

Case 13: Foreseeable Damages

KGM Harvesting Co. v. Fresh Network
California Court of Appeals, Third District, 1995
36 Cal.App.4th 261

COTTLE, Presiding Justice.

California lettuce grower and distributor KGM Harvesting Company (hereafter seller) had a contract to deliver 14 loads of lettuce each week to Ohio lettuce broker Fresh Network (hereafter buyer). When the price of lettuce rose dramatically in May and June 1991, seller refused to deliver the required quantity of lettuce to buyer. Buyer then purchased lettuce on the open market in order to fulfill its contractual obligations to third parties. After a trial, the jury awarded buyer damages in an amount equal to the difference between the contract price and the price buyer was forced to pay for substitute lettuce on the open market. On appeal, seller argues that the damage award is excessive. We disagree and shall affirm the judgment. * * *

FACTS

In July 1989 buyer and seller entered into an agreement for the sale and purchase of lettuce. Over the years, the terms of the agreement were modified. By May 1991 the terms were that seller would sell to buyer 14 loads of lettuce each week and that buyer would pay seller 9 cents a pound for the lettuce. (A load of lettuce consists of 40 bins, each of which weighs 1,000 to 1,200 pounds. Assuming an average bin weight of 1,100 pounds, one load would equal 44,000 pounds, and the 14 loads called for in the contract would weigh 616,000 pounds. At 9 cents per pound, the cost would approximate $55,440 per week.)

Buyer sold all of the lettuce it received from seller to a lettuce broker named Castellini Company who in turn sold it to Club Chef, a company that chops and shreds lettuce for the fast food industry (specifically, Burger King, Taco Bell, and Pizza Hut). Castellini Company bought lettuce from buyer on a "cost plus" basis, meaning it would pay buyer its actual cost plus a small commission. Club Chef, in turn, bought lettuce from Castellini Company on a cost plus basis.

Seller had numerous lettuce customers other than buyer, including seller's subsidiaries Coronet East and West. Coronet East supplied all the lettuce for the McDonald's fast food chain.

In May and June 1991, when the price of lettuce went up dramatically, seller refused to supply buyer with lettuce at the contract price of nine cents per pound. Instead, it sold the lettuce to others at a profit of between $800,000 and $1,100,000. Buyer, angry at seller's breach, refused to pay seller for lettuce it had already received. Buyer then went out on the open market and purchased lettuce to satisfy its obligations to Castellini Company. Castellini covered all of buyer's extra expense except for $70,000. Castellini in turn passed on its extra costs to Club Chef which passed on at least part of its additional costs to its fast food customers.

In July 1991 buyer and seller each filed complaints under the Perishable Agricultural Commodities Act (PACA). Seller sought the balance due on its outstanding invoices ($233,000), while buyer sought damages for the difference between what it was forced to spend to buy replacement lettuce and the contract price of nine cents a pound (approximately $700,000).

Subsequently, seller filed suit for the balance due on its invoices, and buyer cross-complained for the additional cost it incurred to obtain substitute lettuce after seller's breach. At trial, the parties stipulated that seller was entitled to a directed verdict on its complaint for $233,000, the amount owing on the invoices. Accordingly, only the cross-complaint went to the jury, whose task was to determine whether buyer was entitled to damages from seller for the cost of obtaining substitute lettuce and, if so, in what amount. The jury determined that seller breached the contract, that its performance was not excused, and that buyer was entitled to $655,960.22, which represented the difference between the contract price of nine cents a pound and what it cost buyer to cover by purchasing lettuce in substitution in May and June 1991. It also determined that such an award would not result in a windfall to buyer and that buyer was obligated to the Castellini Company for the additional costs. The court subtracted from buyer's award of $655,960.22 the $233,000 buyer owed to seller on its invoices, leaving a net award in favor of buyer in the amount of $422,960.22. * * *

DISCUSSION

A. *Seller's Appeal*

Section 2711 of the California Uniform Commercial Code[1] provides a buyer with several alternative remedies for a seller's breach of contract. The buyer can " 'cover' by making in good faith and without unreasonable delay any reasonable purchase of ... goods in substitution for those due from the seller." (§ 2712, subd. (1).) In that case, the buyer "may recover from the seller as damages the difference between the cost of cover and the contract price...." (§ 2712, subd. (2).) If the buyer is unable to cover or chooses not to cover, the measure of damages is the difference between the market price and the contract price. (§ 2713.) Under either alternative, the buyer may also recover incidental and consequential damages. (§§ 2711, 2715.) In addition, in certain cases the buyer may secure specific performance or replevin "where the goods are

---

[1] Unless otherwise specified, all further statutory references are to the California Uniform Commercial Code. Section 2711 provides: "(1) Where the seller fails to make delivery or repudiates or the buyer rightfully rejects or justifiably revokes acceptance then with respect to any goods involved, and with respect to the whole if the breach goes to the whole contract (Section 2612), the buyer may cancel and whether or not he has done so may in addition to recovering so much of the price as has been paid [¶] (a) 'Cover' and have damages under the next section as to all the goods affected whether or not they have been identified to the contract; or [¶] (b) Recover damages for nondelivery as provided in this division (Section 2713). [¶] (2) Where the seller fails to deliver or repudiates the buyer may also [¶] (a) If the goods have been identified recover them as provided in this division (Section 2502); or [¶] (b) In a proper case obtain specific performance or replevy the goods as provided in this division (Section 2716). [¶] (3) On rightful rejection or justifiable revocation of acceptance a buyer has a security interest in goods in his possession or control for any payments made on their price and any expenses reasonably incurred in their inspection, receipt, transportation, care and custody and may hold such goods and resell them in like manner as an aggrieved seller (Section 2706)."

unique" (§ 2716) or may recover goods identified to a contract (§ 2502).

In the instant case, buyer "covered" as defined in section 2712 in order to fulfill its own contractual obligations to the Castellini Company. Accordingly, it was awarded the damages called for in cover cases—the difference between the contract price and the cover price. (§ 2712.)

In appeals from judgments rendered pursuant to section 2712, the dispute typically centers on whether the buyer acted in "good faith," whether the "goods in substitution" differed substantially from the contracted for goods, whether the buyer unreasonably delayed in purchasing substitute goods in the mistaken belief that the price would go down, or whether the buyer paid too much for the substitute goods. (See generally White & Summers, Uniform Commercial Code (3d ed. 1988) Buyer's Remedies, Cover, § 6–3, pp. 284–292 [hereafter White & Summers], and cases cited therein.)

In this case, however, none of these typical issues is in dispute. Seller does *not* contend that buyer paid too much for the substitute lettuce or that buyer was guilty of "unreasonable delay" or a lack of "good faith" in its attempt to obtain substitute lettuce. Nor does seller contend that the lettuce purchased was of a higher quality or grade and therefore not a reasonable substitute.

Instead, seller takes issue with section 2712 itself, contending that despite the unequivocal language of section 2712, a buyer who covers should not *necessarily* recover the difference between the cover price and the contract price. Seller points out that because of buyer's "cost plus" contract with Castellini Company, buyer was eventually able to pass on the extra expenses (except for $70,000) occasioned by seller's breach and buyer's consequent purchase of substitute lettuce on the open market. It urges this court under these circumstances not to allow buyer to obtain a "windfall."[2]

The basic premise of contract law is to effectuate the expectations of the parties to the agreement, to give them the "benefit of the bargain" they struck when they entered into the agreement. In its basic premise, contract law therefore differs significantly from tort law. As the California Supreme Court explained in *Foley v. Interactive Data Corp.* (1988) 47 Cal.3d 654, 254 Cal.Rptr. 211, 765 P.2d 373, "contract actions are created to enforce the intentions of the parties to the agreement [while] tort law is primarily designed to vindicate 'social policy.' " (*Id.* at p. 683, 254 Cal.Rptr. 211, 765 P.2d 373, citing Prosser, Law of Torts (4th ed. 1971) p. 613.)

" 'The basic object of damages is *compensation,* and in the law of contracts the theory is that the party injured by breach should receive as nearly as possible the equivalent of the benefits of performance. [Citations.]' " (*Lisec v. United Airlines, Inc.* (1992) 10 Cal.App.4th 1500, 1503,

---

[2] In answering special interrogatories, the jury found (1) that if buyer were awarded the difference between the contract price and the cost of cover, it would not result in a windfall to buyer, and (2) that buyer had an obligation to pay Castellini Company for the amount Castellini Company paid buyer to acquire the substitute lettuce. On appeal, seller contends that these findings were not supported by substantial evidence. As we shall explain, however, these findings were not necessary to justify the section 2712 award. Accordingly, we need not reach the issue whether the evidence supports the jury's findings on these two special interrogatories.

11 Cal.Rptr.2d 689.) A compensation system that gives the aggrieved party the benefit of the bargain, and no more, furthers the goal of "predictability about the cost of contractual relationships ... in our commercial system." (*Foley v. Interactive Data Corp., supra,* 47 Cal.3d at p. 683, 254 Cal.Rptr. 211, 765 P.2d 373; Putz & Klippen, *Commercial Bad Faith: Attorney Fees—Not Tort Liability—Is the Remedy for "Stonewalling"* (1987) 21 U.S.F.L.Rev. 419, 432.)

With these rules in mind, we examine the contract at issue in this case to ascertain the reasonable expectations of the parties. The contract recited that its purpose was "to supply [buyer] with a consistent quality raw product at a fair price to [seller], which also allows [buyer] profitability for his finished product." Seller promised to supply the designated quantity even if the price of lettuce went up ("We agree to supply said product and amount at stated price regardless of the market price or conditions") and buyer promised to purchase the designated quantity even if the price went down "[Buyer] agrees to purchase said product and amounts at stated price regardless of the market price or conditions, provided quality requirements are met"). The possibility that the price of lettuce would fluctuate was consequently foreseeable to both parties.

Although the contract does not recite this fact, seller was aware of buyer's contract with the Castellini Company and with the Castellini Company's contract with Club Chef. This knowledge was admitted at trial and can be inferred from the fact that seller shipped the contracted for 14 loads of lettuce directly to Club Chef each week. Thus, seller was well aware that if it failed to provide buyer with the required 14 loads of lettuce, buyer would have to obtain replacement lettuce elsewhere or would itself be in breach of contract. This was within the contemplation of the parties when they entered into their agreement.

As noted earlier, the object of contract damages is to give the aggrieved party " 'as nearly as possible the equivalent of the benefits of performance.' " (*Lisec v. United Airlines, Inc., supra,* 10 Cal.App.4th at p. 1503, 11 Cal.Rptr.2d 689; see also § 1106 ["The remedies provided by this code shall be liberally administered to the end that the aggrieved party may be put in as good a position as if the other party had fully performed...."].) In the instant case, buyer contracted for 14 loads of lettuce each week at 9 cents per pound. When seller breached its contract to provide that lettuce, buyer went out on the open market and purchased substitute lettuce to fulfill its contractual obligations to third parties. However, purchasing replacement lettuce to continue its business did not place buyer "in as good a position as if the other party had fully performed." This was because buyer paid more than nine cents per pound for the replacement lettuce. Only by reimbursing buyer for the additional costs above nine cents a pound could buyer truly receive the benefit of the bargain. This is the measure of damages set forth in section 2712.

As White and Summers point out, "Since 2–712 measures buyer's damages by the difference between his actual cover purchase and the contract price, the formula will often put buyer in the identical economic position that performance would have." (White & Summers, *supra,* § 6–3, p. 285.) Therefore, "[i]n the typical case a timely 'cover' purchase by an aggrieved buyer will preclude any 2–715 [incidental and consequential] damages." (*Ibid.*) "Not only does the damage formula in 2–712 come close to putting the aggrieved buyer in the same economic position as actual performance would have," White and Summers conclude, "but it also enables him to achieve his prime objective, namely that of acquiring his needed goods." (*Id.* at p. 292.)

In this case, the damage formula of section 2712 put buyer in the identical position performance would have: it gave buyer the contracted for 14 loads of lettuce with which to carry on its business at the contracted for price of 9 cents per pound.

Despite the obvious applicability and appropriateness of section 2712, seller argues in this appeal that the contract-cover differential of section 2712 is inappropriate in cases, as here, where the aggrieved buyer is ultimately able to pass on its additional costs to other parties. Seller contends that section 1106's remedial injunction to put the aggrieved party "in as good a position as if the other party had fully performed" demands that all subsequent events impacting on *buyer* 's ultimate profit or loss be taken into consideration (specifically, that buyer passed on all but $70,000 of its loss to Castellini Company, which passed on all of its loss to Club Chef, which passed on most of its loss to its fast food customers).[3] For this proposition, seller relies on two cases limiting a buyer's damages under a different provision of the Commercial Code, section 2713 (*Allied Canners & Packers, Inc. v. Victor Packing Co.* (1984) 162 Cal.App.3d 905, 209 Cal.Rptr. 60; *H–W–H Cattle Co., Inc. v. Schroeder* (8th Cir.1985) 767 F.2d 437), and on one section 2712 cover case in which damages were apparently limited (*Sun Maid Raisin Growers v. Victor Packing Co.* (1983) 146 Cal.App.3d 787, 194 Cal.Rptr. 612).

We begin with the cover case. In *Sun Maid Raisin Growers v. Victor Packing Co., supra,* 146 Cal.App.3d 787, 194 Cal.Rptr. 612, the seller (Victor) repudiated a contract to sell 610 tons of raisins to Sun–Maid after "disastrous" rains damaged the raisin crop and the price of raisins nearly doubled. Sun–Maid attempted to cover but was only partially successful. It was able to obtain only 200 tons of comparable raisins. For the remaining 410 tons, it had to purchase inferior raisins that had to be reconditioned at a substantial cost. Apparently the total cost of purchasing the 200 tons of high quality raisins and of purchasing and reconditioning the remaining 410 tons was $377,720 over the contract price.

The trial court awarded Sun–Maid, as consequential damages under section 2715, $295,339.40 for its lost profits. Victor appealed, arguing that the amount of lost profits was unforeseeable by either party when the contracts were formed. The Court of Appeal affirmed, noting that the evidence established that Victor knew Sun–Maid was purchasing the raisins for resale.

In its discussion, the court recounted the various measures of damages available to an aggrieved buyer under the Uniform Commercial Code for a seller's nondelivery of goods or repudiation of contract, citing sections 2712, 2713, 2715 and 2723. The court seemed to wonder why the trial court had chosen lost profits rather than the cost of cover as damages, noting that the court did not specify why it had determined damages in that manner and that neither party had requested findings. However, as neither Sun–Maid nor Victor was contesting that measure of damages on appeal (the only issue was whether lost profits were foreseeable consequential damages), the court observed that the trial court "probably found that damages should be limited to the amount that would have put Sun–Maid in 'as good a position as if the other party had fully performed.' (§ 1106.)" (*Id.* at p. 792, 194 Cal.Rptr. 612.)

---

[3] Seller, not surprisingly, does not focus on post-breach events impacting on *seller* 's ultimate profit or loss. As noted earlier, seller made a profit of between $800,000 and $1,100,000 for selling the lettuce at the higher market price rather than the lower nine cent per pound contract price.

From this simple observation, seller claims that "[i]n cases, like the instant case, involving forward contracts, *California courts hold that section 1106 limits the damages to be awarded under section 2712 (i.e.,* the cover damages statute) *and section 2713 (i.e.,* the market damages statute) *for the very reason that the non-breaching party is entitled to nothing more than to be placed in the position which would result from the breaching party's full performance of the agreement. See Sun Maid Raisin Growers v. Victor Packing Co.* (1983) 146 Cal.App.3d 787, 792, [194 Cal.Rptr. 612] (cover case); *Allied Canners & Packers, Inc. v. Victor Packing Co.* (1984) 162 Cal.App.3d 905, 915 [209 Cal.Rptr. 60] (non-cover case)." (Emphasis added.)

In fact, the *Sun Maid* court held no such thing. It simply offered one possible explanation for the trial court's award, which no one was contesting. Under the facts of that case, the cost of cover might have been unduly difficult to calculate. Sun–Maid was able to purchase only 200 tons of comparable raisins in a timely manner. There were no other Thompson seedless free tonnage raisins available within a reasonable time after seller's breach (August 1976). It was considerably later before buyer could find another 410 tons to purchase, and those raisins were damaged in part because of rains occurring *after* the breach, in September 1976.[4] Under these circumstances, the trial court and the parties may simply have chosen to focus on the easily calculable consequential damages (which buyer claimed were foreseeable and seller denied were foreseeable) and to ignore the difficult to calculate cover damages.

We now look to the "non-cover" case relied upon by seller, *Allied Canners & Packers, Inc. v. Victor Packing Co., supra,* 162 Cal.App.3d at 915, 209 Cal.Rptr. 60, which in fact does hold that section 1106 acts as a limitation on the amount of damages otherwise recoverable under *section 2713.* Before discussing the *Allied Canners* case, however, a few observations on the differences between the contract-cover differential of section 2712 and the contract-market differential of section 2713 are called for.

As noted earlier, section 2712 "will often put buyer in the identical economic position that performance would have." (White & Summers, *supra,* § 6–3, p. 285.) In contrast, the contract-market differential of section 2713 "bears no necessary relation to the change in the buyer's economic status that the breach causes. It is possible that this differential might yield the buyer a handsome sum even though the breach actually saved him money in the long run (as for example when a middleman buyer's resale markets dry up after the breach). It is also quite possible that the buyer's lost profit from resale or consumption would be greater than the contract-market difference." (*Id.,* § 6–4, at p. 294.)

White and Summers argue that the drafters of section 2713 could *not* have intended to put the buyer in the same position as performance since "[p]erformance would have given the buyer certain goods for consumption or resale" (White & Summers, *supra,* at p. 294) which would

---

[4] Section 2712's requirement that buyer purchase goods "in substitution for those due from seller" does not "envisage[ ] ... goods ... identical with those involved but commercially usable as reasonable substitutes under the circumstances of the particular case...." (U.C.C. comment 2 to § 2712.) Where, as here, the goods purchased to cover differ significantly from the contracted for goods, is the section 2712 damage formula even appropriate? Should the breaching seller be responsible for the post-breach rains in September 1976? If not, should the damage formula of section 2712 be adjusted to take these matters into consideration?

have resulted in "either a net economic gain for the buyer or a net economic loss." (*Ibid.*) The best explanation of section 2713, they suggest, is that it is a "statutory liquidated damage clause, a breach inhibitor the payout of which need bear no close relation to the plaintiff's actual loss." (*Id.* at p. 295; accord Peters, *Remedies for Breach of Contracts Relating to the Sale of Goods Under the Uniform Commercial Code: A Roadmap for Article Two* (1963) 73 Yale L.J. 199, 259.) In discussing the "problem of a buyer who has covered but who seeks to ignore 2–712 and sue for a larger contract-market differential under 2–713," the authors suggest: "If the Code's goal is to put the buyer in the same position as though there had been no breach, and if 2–712 will accomplish that goal but 2–713 will do so only by coincidence, why not force the covering buyer to use 2–712?" (*Id.* at p. 304.) Professor Robert Childres has actually called for the repeal of section 2713 and the requirement of compulsory cover. (Childres, *Buyer's Remedies: The Danger of Section 2–713* (1978) 72 Nw.U.L.Rev. 837.)

With these prefatory comments in mind, we look to the *Allied Canners* case. In *Allied Canners,* the same raisin supplier (Victor Packing Company) involved in the *Sun Maid* case breached another contract to sell raisins in 1976. The buyer, Allied Canners, had contracts to resell the raisins it bought from Victor to two Japanese companies for its cost plus 4 percent. Such a resale would have resulted in a profit of $4,462.50 to Allied. When Victor breached the contract, Allied sued for the difference between the market price and the contract price as authorized by section 2713. As the market price of raisins had soared due to the disastrous 1976 rains, the market-contract price formula would have yielded damages of approximately $150,000. Allied did not purchase substitute raisins and did not make any deliveries under its resale contracts to the Japanese buyers. One of the Japanese buyers simply released Allied from its contract because of the general unavailability of raisins. The other buyer did not release Allied, but it did not sue Allied either. By the time Allied's case against Victor went to trial, the statute of limitations on the Japanese buyer's claim had run.

Under these circumstances, the court held that the policy of section 1106 (that the aggrieved party be put in as good a position as if the other party had performed) required that the award of damages to Allied be limited to its actual loss. It noted that for this limitation to apply, three conditions must be met: (1) "the seller knew that the buyer had a resale contract"; (2) "the buyer has not been able to show that it will be liable in damages to the buyer on its forward contract";[5] and (3) "there has been no finding of bad faith on the part of the seller...." (*Allied Canners & Packers, Inc. v. Victor Packing Co., supra,* 162 Cal.App.3d at p. 915, 209 Cal.Rptr. 60.)[6]

The result in *Allied Canners* seems to have derived in large part from the court's finding that Victor had not acted in bad faith in breaching the contract. The court noted, "It does appear clear, however, that, as the trial court found, the rains caused a severe problem, and Victor made substantial efforts [to procure the raisins for Allied]. We do not deem this record one to support an inference that windfall damages must be awarded the buyer to prevent unjust enrichment to a

---

[5] The court apparently never considered anything other than whether the Japanese buyers would sue Allied Canners. For example, it did not consider whether the breach adversely affected Allied Canners' goodwill with its Japanese customers. Should the court not have also considered Allied Canners' potential loss of future contracts?

[6] The other section 2713 case on which seller relies, an Eighth Circuit case, *H–W–H Cattle Co. v. Schroeder, supra,* 767 F.2d 437, also limited a buyer's damages to its anticipated commissions on the resale of the cattle rather than the full contract-market differential.

deliberately breaching seller. (Compare *Sun Maid Raisin Growers v. Victor Packing Co., supra,* 146 Cal.App.3d 787, 194 Cal.Rptr. 612 [where, in a case coincidentally involving Victor, Victor was expressly found by the trial court to have engaged in bad faith by gambling on the market price of raisins in deciding whether to perform its contracts to sell raisins to Sun Maid].)" (162 Cal.App.3d at p. 916, 209 Cal.Rptr. 60.)[7]

We believe that this focus on the good or bad faith of the breaching party is inappropriate in a commercial sales case. As our California Supreme Court recently explained, courts should not differentiate between good and bad motives for breaching a contract in assessing the measure of the non-breaching party's damages. (*Applied Equipment Corp. v. Litton Saudi Arabia Ltd.* (1994) 7 Cal.4th 503, 513–515, 28 Cal.Rptr.2d 475, 869 P.2d 454.) Such a focus is inconsistent with the policy "to encourage contractual relations and commercial activity by enabling parties to estimate in advance the financial risks of their enterprise." (*Id.* at p. 515, 28 Cal.Rptr.2d 475, 869 P.2d 454.) " 'Courts traditionally have awarded damages for breach of contract to compensate the aggrieved party rather than to punish the breaching party.' [Citations.]" (*Foley v. Interactive Data Corp., supra,* 47 Cal.3d at p. 683, 254 Cal.Rptr. 211, 765 P.2d 373.)

The *Allied Canners* opinion has been sharply criticized in numerous law review articles and in at least one sister-state opinion. In *Tongish v. Thomas* (1992) 251 Kan. 728, 840 P.2d 471, the Kansas Supreme Court rejected the *Allied Canners* approach and instead applied the "majority view [which] would award market damages even though in excess of plaintiff's loss." (*Id.*, 840 P.2d at p. 475.) Relying on an article by Professors Simon and Novack, *Limiting the Buyer's Market Damages to Lost Profits: A Challenge to the Enforceability of Market Contracts* (1979) 92 Harv.L.Rev. 1395, the *Tongish* court explained that use of the market price/contract price damage scheme of section 2713 " 'encourages a more efficient market and discourages the breach of contracts.' " (*Tongish v. Thomas, supra,* 840 P.2d at p. 476.)

Similarly, in Schneider, *UCC Section 2–713: A Defense of Buyers' Expectancy Damages* (1986) 22 Cal.W.L.Rev. 233, 264, the author states the "[b]y limiting buyer to lost resale profits, the [*Allied Canners*] court ignored the clear language of section 2–713's compensation scheme to award expectation damages in accordance with the parties' allocation of risk as measured by the difference between contract price and market price on the date set for performance. If the court wanted to avoid giving greater damages, it would have been better for it to view what occurred to the availability and price of raisins as being beyond the risks contemplated by the parties and thus to have ruled under the doctrine of commercial impracticability as provided in

---

[7] In view of *Allied Canners* ' three part test, we assume the results would have been different here if the court had found Victor was "a deliberately breaching seller." Perhaps in that case, the court would not have focused on what the aggrieved buyer ultimately would have received on resale but might have focused on what benefits the seller reaped from breaching. In *Allied Canners,* the price of raisins went up from 30 cents a pound to 87 cents a pound. If seller had not breached, it would have had to go out on the market and buy raisins for Allied at considerably more than it was contracted to sell them for to Allied. By breaching, it avoided a loss that might have been more in the $150,000 range (market-contract differential) than the $4,000 range (Allied's lost profits). Thus, the court prevented a windfall to Allied at the cost of providing a windfall to Victor. Such a result is curious if the intent of contract damages is to effectuate the expectations of the parties to the contract. Here, the parties clearly contemplated when they entered into their fixed price agreement that the price of raisins would fluctuate and that sometimes buyer would receive a price better than the market price and that other times it would have to pay more than the market price.

section 2–615(a)."

In addition numerous New York courts have chosen not to limit a buyer's damages to actual losses. (See e.g., *Fertico Belgium v. Phosphate Chem. Export* (1987) 70 N.Y.2d 76, 517 N.Y.S.2d 465, 510 N.E.2d 334; *Apex Oil Co. v. Vanguard Oil & Service Co. Inc.* (2d Cir.1985) 760 F.2d 417; *G.A. Thompson & Co. v. Wendell J. Miller, Etc.* (S.D.N.Y.1978) 457 F.Supp. 996.)

As the foregoing discussion makes clear, we have serious reservations about whether the result in *Allied Canners,* with its emphasis on the good faith of the breaching party, is appropriate in an action seeking damages under section 2713. We have no reservations, however, in not extending the *Allied Canners* rationale to a section 2712 case. As noted earlier, no section 2712 case, including *Sun Maid Growers v. Victor Packing Co., supra,* 146 Cal.App.3d 787, 194 Cal.Rptr. 612, has ever held that cover damages must be limited by section 1106. The obvious reason is that the cover-contract differential puts a buyer who covers in the exact same position as performance would have done. This is the precisely what is called for in section 1106. In this respect, the cover/contract differential of section 2712 is very different than the market/contract differential of section 2713, which "need bear no close relation to the plaintiff's actual loss." (White & Summers, *supra,* at p. 295.)

In summary, we hold that where a buyer " 'cover[s]' by making in good faith and without unreasonable delay any reasonable purchase of ... goods in substitution for those due from the seller, ... [that buyer] may recover from the seller as damages the difference between the cost of cover and the contract price...." (§ 2712.) This gives the buyer the benefit of its bargain. What the buyer chooses to do with that bargain is not relevant to the determination of damages under section 2712.

*   *   *   *   *   *

PREMO and ELIA, JJ., concur.

Case 14:   Foreseeable Damages

Jorge Constr. v. Pomona School District
Supreme Court of California, 2004
34 Cal. 4th 960

KENNARD, J.

A school district terminates a construction contract when the contractor, four and a half months after the promised due date, still has not finished the project. The contractor's bonding company then hires another firm to complete the project, but it suspends then later reduces the amount of bonding for the contractor. The latter successfully sues the school district for breach of contract, recovering in damages some $3 million for potentially lost profits, which the contractor claimed it would have earned on prospective construction contracts it never won because of its impaired bonding capacity. The Court of Appeal concluded that those potential profits were a proper item of general damages in this action for breach of contract. We disagree.

I.

In 1994, the Pomona Unified School District (District) solicited bids for building improvements at Vejar Elementary School. The District awarded the contract to Lewis Jorge Construction Management, Inc. (Lewis Jorge), the low bidder at $6,029,000. Although the contract originally provided for completion in December of 1995, heavy rains delayed work, and the parties agreed to a revised completion date of January 22, 1996. That date came and went, but the project remained unfinished.

The District withheld payments to Lewis Jorge for work completed in April and May, 1996. On June 5, the District terminated the contract with Lewis Jorge and made a demand on the contractor's surety to finish the project under the performance bond the surety had provided for Lewis Jorge. The surety then hired another contractor to complete the school project for $164,000. That contractor completed the project between early July and mid-September, 1996.

Lewis Jorge sued the District, alleging it breached the contract by declaring Lewis Jorge in default and terminating it from the construction project. The complaint sought damages and alleged six causes of action. The first, alleging breach of contract, and the second, alleging breach of an implied warranty of sufficiency of the plans and specifications for the project, are both contractual claims naming the District as a defendant. Causes of action three through five— alleging nondisclosure of material facts, inducing breach of contract, and negligence—named a district employee as a defendant. The sixth cause of action sought equitable indemnity against both the District and the employee for claims against Lewis Jorge by its surety and its unpaid subcontractors. Lewis Jorge did not plead as special damages the profits it claimed to have lost on future contracts.

Lewis Jorge, in turn, was sued by a number of its subcontractors for nonpayment of their past due bills.

At trial, Lewis Jorge presented evidence from its bonding agent that in June 1996 it had a bonding limit of $10 million per project, with an aggregate limit of $30 million for all work in progress. By mid–1997, the only sureties willing to provide Lewis Jorge with bonding imposed a limit of $5 million per project, with an aggregate limit of $15 million, a reduction of its bonding capacity to the level its surety had imposed in the early 1990's. Sometime in 1998, Lewis Jorge ceased bidding altogether and eventually closed down.

Lewis Jorge sought to prove the extent of its lost future profits on unidentified construction projects, using as the relevant period the date of the District's breach to the date of trial, and relying on its profitability during the four years preceding the breach. Robert Knudsen, a financial analyst who specialized in calculating lost profits claims, projected that Lewis Jorge had lost $95 million in gross revenue for future contracts that, based on its past history, it would likely have been awarded. Historically, Lewis Jorge had realized a profit of about 6 percent of revenue. Knudsen calculated lost profits on unidentified projects at $4,500,000, which discounted to present value came to $3,148,107.

The jury returned special verdicts in favor of Lewis Jorge, finding the District liable for $362,671 owed on the school construction contract, of which $143,755 was attributable to the District's "breach of warranty as to the fitness of its plans or specification" (the complaint's second cause of action). It awarded $3,148,197[1] in profits Lewis Jorge did not realize "due to the loss or reduction of its bonding capacity." Having found the District's employee negligent, the jury found him and the District jointly and severally liable for $ 3,510,868.

The District and its employee appealed. Lewis Jorge also appealed, raising issues that are not material here and were rejected by the Court of Appeal. Although the Court of Appeal reversed the judgment against the District's employee, and reversed awards against the District for prejudgment interest and contractual attorney fees (Civ.Code, § 1717), it rejected the District's claim that the award to Lewis Jorge of $3,148,197 for potential profits on future projects was an improper component of *general damages* for breach of contract. The Court of Appeal granted the District's petition for rehearing on that question; after receiving additional briefing, it concluded that "the lost profit damages sought by Lewis Jorge were in the nature of general damages, [ ] not special damages as claimed by the District."

We granted the District's petition for review to resolve whether general damages for breach of a construction contract include potential profits lost on future contracts that a contractor does not win when, as a consequence of the property owner's breach, the contractor's surety reduces the contractor's bonding capacity.[2] We later solicited and received briefing from the parties on the related issue of whether an award of lost potential profits would have been proper here as special damages.

---

[1] The jury returned an award some $90 greater than the lost profit sum calculated by expert witness Knudsen.
[2] The District does not challenge either the jury's finding that the District breached the contract or its award of $362,671 in general damages for the breach.

II.

Damages awarded to an injured party for breach of contract "seek to approximate the agreed-upon performance." (*Applied Equipment Corp. v. Litton Saudi Arabia Ltd.* (1994) 7 Cal.4th 503, 515, 28 Cal.Rptr.2d 475, 869 P.2d 454 (*Applied*).) The goal is to put the plaintiff "in as good a position as he or she would have occupied" if the defendant had not breached the contract. (24 Williston on Contracts (4th ed.2002) § 64:1, p. 7.) In other words, the plaintiff is entitled to damages that are equivalent to the benefit of the plaintiff's contractual bargain. (*Id.* at pp. 9–10; 1 Witkin, Summary of Cal. Law (9th ed. 1987) Contracts, § 813, pp. 732–733; *Peterson v. Larquier* (1927) 84 Cal.App. 174, 179, 257 P. 873 [breach of lease permits injured party to recover difference between rental value at date of breach and rent specified in lease for its term].)

The injured party's damages cannot, however, exceed what it would have received if the contract had been fully performed on both sides. (Civ.Code, § 3358.) This limitation of damages for breach of a contract "serves to encourage contractual relations and commercial activity by enabling parties to estimate in advance the financial risks of their enterprise." (*Applied, supra,* 7 Cal.4th at p. 515, 28 Cal.Rptr.2d 475, 869 P.2d 454.)

Contractual damages are of two types—general damages (sometimes called direct damages) and special damages (sometimes called consequential damages). (24 Williston on Contracts, *supra,* § 64.1, pp. 11–12; 3 Dobbs, Law of Remedies (2d ed.1993) § 12.2(3), pp. 39–42; see, e.g., *Erlich v. Menezes* (1999) 21 Cal.4th 543, 558, 87 Cal.Rptr.2d 886, 981 P.2d 978.)

A. General Damages

General damages are often characterized as those that flow directly and necessarily from a breach of contract, or that are a natural result of a breach. (Civ.Code, § 3300 [damages "which, in the ordinary course of things, would be likely to result" from breach]; *Mitchell v. Clarke* (1886) 71 Cal. 163, 167–168, 11 P. 882 [general damages are those that naturally and necessarily result from breach].) Because general damages are a natural and necessary consequence of a contract breach, they are often said to be within the contemplation of the parties, meaning that because their occurrence is sufficiently predictable the parties at the time of contracting are "deemed" to have contemplated them. (Calamari & Perillo, The Law of Contracts (2d ed.1977) § 14–5, p. 525; *Hunt Bros. Co. v. San Lorenzo Water Co.* (1906) 150 Cal. 51, 56, 87 P. 1093 [parties need not "actually have contemplated the very consequence that occurred," but they would have supposed such a consequence was likely to follow a breach].)

B. Special Damages

Unlike general damages, special damages are those losses that do not arise directly and inevitably from any similar breach of any similar agreement. Instead, they are secondary or derivative losses arising from circumstances that are particular to the contract or to the parties. Special damages are recoverable if the special or particular circumstances from which they arise were actually communicated to or known by the breaching party (a subjective test) or were matters of which the breaching party should have been aware at the time of contracting (an objective test). (*Mitchell v. Clarke, supra,* 71 Cal. at pp. 164–167, 11 P. 882; 1 Witkin, Summary of Cal. Law, *supra,* § 815, p. 733.) Special damages "will not be presumed from the mere breach" but represent loss that "occurred by reason of injuries following from" the breach. (*Mitchell v. Clarke, supra,* 71 Cal. at p. 168, 11 P. 882.) Special damages are among the losses that are foreseeable and proximately caused by the breach of a contract. (Civ.Code, § 3300.)

California follows the common law rule that an English court articulated some 150 years ago in *Hadley v. Baxendale* (1854) 156 Eng.Rep. 145. After Hadley's mill shut down because of a broken crankshaft, he entered into a contract to have a new one built. When the builder asked Hadley to send him the broken shaft to use as a model, Hadley took it to Baxendale, a common carrier, for delivery to the builder. Baxendale did not deliver until seven days later. Hadley then sued Baxendale for lost profits for that period. Hadley's lost profits, the court held, were not recoverable, because he had failed to inform the carrier that the mill would be shut down until delivery of the new shaft. (*Id.* at p. 151.) Because the special circumstance—the mill's inoperability without a mill shaft—was not communicated to Baxendale, he did not assume the risk of compensating Hadley for mill profits lost as a resulting of Baxendale's late delivery of the mill shaft.

Hadley did not expressly distinguish between general and special damages. But such a distinction flows naturally from that case; hence the rule that a party assumes the risk of special damages liability for unusual losses arising from special circumstances only if it was "advised of the facts concerning special harm which might result" from breach—it is not deemed to have assumed such additional risk, however, simply by entering into the contract. (1 Witkin, Summary of Cal. Law, *supra,* § 815, p. 733; *Mitchell v. Clarke, supra,* 71 Cal. at pp. 165–169, 11 P. 882.)

The *Hadley* rule has long been applied by California courts, which view it as having been incorporated into California Civil Code section 3300's definition of the damages available for breach of a contract. (*Hunt Bros. Co. v. San Lorenzo Water Co., supra,* 150 Cal. at p. 56, 87 P. 1093; *Christensen v. Slawter* (1959) 173 Cal.App.2d 325, 334, 343 P.2d 341; *Sabraw v. Kaplan* (1962) 211 Cal.App.2d 224, 227, 27 Cal.Rptr. 81.) Contract damages, unlike damages in tort (Civ.Code, § 3333), do not permit recovery for unanticipated injury. (*Hunt Bros. Co. v. San Lorenzo Water Co., supra,* 150 Cal. at p. 56, 87 P. 1093.) Parties may voluntarily assume the risk of liability for unusual losses, but to do so they must be told, at the time the contract is made, of any special harm likely to result from a breach (*Mendoyoma, Inc. v. County of Mendocino* (1970) 8 Cal.App.3d 873, 879–880, 87 Cal.Rptr. 740; see *Erlich v. Menezes, supra,* 21 Cal.4th 543, 558–560, 87 Cal.Rptr.2d 886, 981 P.2d 978; *Brandon & Tibbs v. George Kevorkian Accountancy Corp.* (1990) 226 Cal.App.3d 442, 455–456, 277 Cal.Rptr. 40). Alternatively, the nature of the contract or the circumstances in which it is made may compel the inference that the defendant should have contemplated the fact that such a loss would be "the probable result" of the defendant's breach. (*Burnett & Doty Development Co. v. Phillips* (1978) 84 Cal.App.3d 384, 148 Cal.Rptr. 569 [the defendant's delay in preparing site for subdivision breached contract with developer and subjected the defendant to liability for profits that developer could not earn on unbuilt houses].) Not recoverable as special damages are those "beyond the expectations of the parties." (*Applied, supra,* 7 Cal.4th at p. 515, 28 Cal.Rptr.2d 475, 869 P.2d 454.) Special damages for breach of contract are limited to losses that were either actually foreseen (see, e.g., *Dallman Co. v. Southern Heater Co.* (1968) 262 Cal.App.2d 582, 586, 68 Cal.Rptr. 873 [in contract negotiations, supplier was put on notice that its failure to perform would result in lost

180

profits]) or were "reasonably foreseeable" when the contract was formed. (*Applied,* at p. 515, 28 Cal.Rptr.2d 475, 869 P.2d 454.)

III.

Here, the Court of Appeal affirmed the jury's award to Lewis Jorge of $3,148,197 in *general damages,* based on profits Lewis Jorge did not earn on future unidentified contracts because its surety had reduced its bonding capacity after the District's termination of the construction contract. The Court of Appeal concluded that such potential profits were recoverable as general damages because they followed "from the breach in the ordinary course of events" and were a "natural and probable consequence." The Court of Appeal found it significant, as did the trial court, that the contract at issue, like much of Lewis Jorge's business, was a public contract that required bonding.

The Court of Appeal reasoned: When the contract was formed, the District knew of its own bond requirements, and it knew that public works contractors must provide bonds to secure their performance. Because impaired bonding capacity "has long been recognized as a direct consequence of an owner's breach of a construction contract," the Court of Appeal concluded that the District should have known that breaching the contract and resorting to the surety to complete the project could impair Lewis Jorge's ability to obtain bonds without which it could not bid on other public contracts. Accordingly, the Court of Appeal held that the potential profits Lewis Jorge lost on contracts it did not win after the District's termination of the school construction contract were general damages attributable to the District's breach.[3]

The Court of Appeal, however, failed to consider a threshold inquiry. If the purpose of contractual damages is to give the nonbreaching party the benefit of its contractual bargain, then the first question is: What performance did the parties bargain for? General damages for breach of a contract "are based on the value of the performance itself, not on the value of some consequence that performance may produce." (3 Dobbs, Law of Remedies, *supra,* § 12.4(1), p. 62.) Profits " 'which are the direct and immediate fruits of the contract' " are " 'part and parcel of the contract itself, entering into and constituting a portion of its very elements; something stipulated for, the right to the enjoyment of which is just as clear and plain as to the fulfillment of any other stipulation.' " (*Shoemaker v. Acker* (1897) 116 Cal. 239, 245, 48 P. 62.)

Unearned profits can sometimes be used as the measure of general damages for breach of

---

[3] The District advances various public policy arguments in urging us to preclude lost future profits as a component of general damages when the hiring party is a public entity and especially when, as here, it is a school district. Lewis Jorge responds that because public contracts require bonding, profits lost on potential projects because of impaired bonding capacity after an owner's breach of a public contract will always be general damages. Whatever the merits of these arguments, we need not base our holding on the circumstance that the contract was a public contract or that a public school district was the breaching party. For bonding, although it is statutorily required for most public contracts, is also commonly imposed under contracts between private parties for larger construction projects. (See, e.g., *Cates Construction, Inc. v. Talbot Partners* (1999) 21 Cal.4th 28, 35, 40, 86 Cal.Rptr.2d 855, 980 P.2d 407 [condominium developer required contractor to furnish a labor and materials payment bond and a performance bond for the full $3.9 million contract price]; 1 Cal. Construction Contracts and Disputes (Cont.Ed.Bar 3d ed. 2003) Drafting Construction Contracts, § 2.9, p. 82 ["owner should also reserve the right to require bidders to furnish performance and payment bonds"].)

contract. Damages measured by lost profits have been upheld for breach of a construction contract when the breaching party's conduct prevented the other side from undertaking performance. (*Stark v. Shaw* (1957) 155 Cal.App.2d 171, 181, 317 P.2d 182 [contractor's delay in building subdivision prevented roofing subcontractor from performing]; *De Flavio v. Estell* (1959) 173 Cal.App.2d 226, 232–233, 343 P.2d 150 [lost profit damages below contractor's estimated profit upheld when owner repudiated contract].) The profits involved in *Stark* and *De Flavio*, however, were purely profits unearned on the very contract that was breached.

Lost profits from collateral transactions as a measure of general damages for breach of contract typically arise when the contract involves crops, goods intended for resale, or an agreement creating an exclusive sales agency. (*Nelson v. Reisner* (1958) 51 Cal.2d 161, 170–171, 331 P.2d 17 [lessor's breach of lease precluded sharecropping farmer from raising crops and realizing profit on their sale]; *Morello v. Growers Grape Prod. Assn.* (1947) 82 Cal.App.2d 365, 186 P.2d 463 [disappointed purchaser of brandy who intended to bottle and resell it]; *Brunvold v. Johnson* (1939) 36 Cal.App.2d 226, 97 P.2d 489 [termination of exclusive agent for sale of rope and twine products]; *Tahoe Ice Co. v. Union Ice Co.* (1895) 109 Cal. 242, 41 P. 1020 [termination of supply contract by ice retailer]; *Grupe v. Glick* (1945) 26 Cal.2d 680, 160 P.2d 832 [defective oil refining machines purchased for resale by exclusive agent]; see also *Brandon & Tibbs v. George Kevorkian Accountancy Corp., supra,* 226 Cal.App.3d at p. 457, 277 Cal.Rptr. 40 [where parties conceded that lost profits were the measure of damages for breach, the breach of a joint venture to expand accounting practice by acquiring an existing practice in another city supported an award of unearned profits as component of general damages for breach of contract].) The likelihood of lost profits from related or derivative transactions is so obvious in these situations that the breaching party must be deemed to have contemplated them at the inception of the contract.

We are not aware of any California authority involving a construction contract that has upheld an award of general damages against a breaching owner for profits unearned on unidentified contracts the contractor did not get when its bonding was impaired as a result of the contract breach. Lewis Jorge, nevertheless, urges us to permit such recovery, citing a Montana decision, *Laas v. Mont. Hwy. Comm'n et al* (1971) 157 Mont. 121, 483 P.2d 699. In that case the plaintiff highway contractor, who had been in business for 22 years and had made a profit on *every* construction project, claimed three years of profits lost or $250,000 for projects he was unable to win when his bonding capacity was reduced after the state breached the construction contract. The Montana Supreme Court affirmed a jury award of $78,000 in lost profits. (*Id.* at p. 130, 483 P.2d 699.) It did so without reference to the construction context, by simply applying rules for profits lost to an established business. But five years later, in *Zook Brothers Constr. Co. v. State* (1976) 171 Mont. 64, 556 P.2d 911, another case involving breach of a highway construction contract, the same court disallowed recovery of profits lost on other projects after the state's breach. The Montana court found "vague and speculative" future profits the contractor did not earn when the state's breach caused him financial woes, forcing him to sell equipment without which he was unable to take on additional work. (*Id.* at p. 76, 556 P.2d 911.) The Montana court's earlier decision in *Laas* appears to represent a singular instance of upholding lost profits on future construction projects as an item of general damages for breach of a construction contract, a holding that has not been followed in a published opinion outside

182

Montana in the 33 years it has been on the books.

The only California decision upholding damages for a contractor's lost profits on future contracts it did not win because its bonding capacity was impaired arises not, as here, from a construction contract but from a contract to provide future bonding. (*Arntz Contracting Co. v. St. Paul Fire & Marine Ins. Co.* (1996) 47 Cal.App.4th 464, 489, 54 Cal.Rptr.2d 888.) The parties to the breached contract in *Arntz* were the contractor and its surety, which agreed to provide the contractor with ongoing bonding. (*Id.* at p. 473, 54 Cal.Rptr.2d 888.) Because the contract was one for future bonding, it was entirely within the contemplation of the surety that its breach of the contract—resulting in the contractor's loss of actual bonding—would preclude the contractor from bidding on and being awarded major projects. Thus, the loss of profits on those projects were properly general damages, for they were the "direct and immediate fruits" (*Shoemaker v. Acker, supra,* 116 Cal. at p. 245, 48 P. 62) of the surety's breach of the contract to provide bonding.

Applying these rules to the school construction contract here, we cannot say that the parties' bargain included Lewis Jorge's potential profits on future construction projects it had not bid on and been awarded. Full performance by the District would have provided Lewis Jorge with full payment of the contract price. Certainly, Lewis Jorge anticipated earning a profit on the school contract with the District, but that projected profit was limited by the contract price and Lewis Jorge's costs of performance. If Lewis Jorge's bid accurately predicted its costs, the benefit of its contractual bargain for profits was capped by whatever net profit it had assumed in setting its bid price.

The District's termination of the school contract did not directly or necessarily cause Lewis Jorge's loss of potential profits on future contracts. Such loss resulted from the decision of CNA, Lewis Jorge's surety at the time of the breach, to cease bonding Lewis Jorge.

Contrary to Lewis Jorge's contention, our decision in *Warner Constr. Corp. v. City of Los Angeles* (1970) 2 Cal.3d 285, 85 Cal.Rptr. 444, 466 P.2d 996 does not compel a different result. There, a contractor sued the city for breach of a contract to construct a retaining wall. The complaint alleged four causes of action. As relevant here, the third cause of action alleged that the city had breached the contract by refusing to issue a "change order" to compensate the contractor for additional costs when soil at the site proved to be more unstable than city test holes had revealed, requiring the contractor to use special, more expensive casting methods, which did not comply with the contract's specifications. (*Id.* at p. 290, 85 Cal.Rptr. 444, 466 P.2d 996.) The fourth cause of action alleged that the city provided misleading results of two test holes it had drilled and did not disclose earlier landslides on the site. (*Id.* at pp. 290–291, 85 Cal.Rptr. 444, 466 P.2d 996.) The jury returned a general verdict for $150,000 against the city. (*Id.* at pp. 289, 300, fn. 18, 85 Cal.Rptr. 444, 466 P.2d 996.)

Of the $150,000 awarded by the jury in *Warner,* we upheld only $81,743.55 in damages.[4]

---

[4] Although the complaint in *Warner* framed the fourth cause of action as one for fraudulent concealment, which is a tort, this court treated the claim as an action in contract for breach of warranty. (*Warner Constr. Corp. v. City of Los Angeles, supra,* 2 Cal.3d at p. 294 & fn. 4, 85 Cal.Rptr. 444, 466 P.2d 996.)

(*Warner Constr. Corp. v. City of Los Angeles, supra,* 2 Cal.3d at pp. 301, 303, 85 Cal.Rptr. 444, 466 P.2d 996.) The city had challenged the $150,000 award on the ground that it included "compensation for speculative and unproven items of damages." (*Id.* at p. 300, 85 Cal.Rptr. 444, 466 P.2d 996.) The plaintiff, relying on evidence that it had suffered impairment of capital when it funded added construction costs out of pocket, argued that it was entitled to the entire $150,000 award because of its uncompensated losses, including profits it did not earn after the city's breach. This court rejected the contention that lost profits would necessarily be speculative "[f]or an established firm such as Warner." (*Id.* at p. 301, 85 Cal.Rptr. 444, 466 P.2d 996.) We went on to state that "[l]oss of business, restriction of research, reduction of bonding capacity, and destruction of a former advantageous competitive position comprise imponderable factors which may affect different companies to differing extents and amounts." (*Ibid.*) The measure of such damages, we said, "requires proof of the effect of these factors" on the plaintiff's profits. (*Ibid.*) *Warner* did not reach the merits of the contractor's lost profits claimi [sic], however, because it concluded that the contractor had failed to prove lost profits, and therefore any award for lost profits could not "be sustained." (*Ibid.*)

Warner did *not* hold that potential profits lost from future contracts are general damages that naturally flow from a breach of a construction contract. At most, it acknowledged that to recover profits lost on future contracts the plaintiff contractor must prove their occurrence and extent. (*Warner Constr. Corp. v. City of Los Angeles, supra,* 2 Cal.3d at pp. 301–302, 85 Cal.Rptr. 444, 466 P.2d 996.) Indeed, the two lost profits cases cited by *Warner* are instructive, and we briefly discuss them below.

The first, *Lucky Auto Supply v. Turner* (1966) 244 Cal.App.2d 872, 53 Cal.Rptr. 628, concerned a claim of trespass, a *tort,* for which the measure of damages is broader than for breach of a contract. (See Civ.Code, § 3333 ["all the detriment proximately caused" whether or not it could have been "anticipated"]; *Lucky Auto Supply,* at pp. 881–882, 53 Cal.Rptr. 628.)

The second case, *Dallman Co. v. Southern Heater Co.* (1968) 262 Cal.App.2d 582, 68 Cal.Rptr. 873, involved profits lost by a plumbing distributor when the supplier of its private-label water heaters breached a contract for providing a ready supply of heaters and spare parts. (*Id.* at pp. 591–592, 68 Cal.Rptr. 873.) The Court of Appeal upheld an award of lost profits because the plaintiff had specifically informed the defendant that it would suffer losses if new heaters and parts would not be readily available. (*Id.* at p. 586, 68 Cal.Rptr. 873.) In other words, the lost profits claim there met the rule of *Hadley v. Baxendale, supra,* 156 Eng. Rep. 145, allowing damages flowing from unusual circumstances communicated to the breaching party when the contract was formed.

Having here concluded that profits Lewis Jorge might have earned on future construction projects were improperly awarded as general damages, we now decide whether those lost potential profits were recoverable as special damages. Lost profits, if recoverable, are more commonly special rather than general damages (3 Dobbs, Law of Remedies, *supra,* § 12.4(3), pp. 76–77), and subject to various limitations. Not only must such damages be pled with particularity (*Mitchell v. Clarke, supra,* 71 Cal. at p. 164, 11 P. 882), but they must also be proven to be certain both as to their occurrence and their extent, albeit not with "mathematical precision."

(*Berge v. International Harvester Co.* (1983) 142 Cal.App.3d 152, 161, 190 Cal.Rptr. 815; accord, *Grupe v. Glick, supra,* 26 Cal.2d at pp. 692–693, 160 P.2d 832; *Resort Video, Ltd. v. Laser Video, Inc.* (1995) 35 Cal.App.4th 1679, 1698–1700, 42 Cal.Rptr.2d 136.) "When the contractor's claim is extended to profits allegedly lost on *other* jobs because of the defendant's breach" that "claim is clearly a claim for special damages." (3 Dobbs, Law of Remedies, *supra,* § 12.4(3), fn. 12, p. 71.) Although Lewis Jorge did not plead its lost future profits as special damages, the issue of their availability as special damages was presented to the jury, and at oral argument the District expressly stated that it was not relying on that pleading omission.

Although a few cases state that a contractor suing for breach of contract may recover as special damages any profits it might have earned on other unawarded construction contracts, such damages are frequently denied as too speculative. (See, e.g., *Hirsch Elec. Co., Inc. v. Community Services, Inc.* (1988) 145 A.D.2d 603, 605, 536 N.Y.S.2d 141, 143 [contractor's claim that breach rendered it unable to obtain bonding, without which it could not bid or win another contract on which it would have made a profit of $800,000, was rejected as consisting of "inferences piled upon inferences" that "as a matter of law, are too speculative to give rise to the recovery of damages for lost profits"]; *Manshul Constr. Corp. v. Dormitory Auth. of N.Y.* (1981) 111 Misc.2d 209, 444 N.Y.S.2d 792, 803–804.) And there are federal decisions that likewise have rejected as too remote and speculative special damages for breach consisting of profits lost on other contracts. As one circuit court explained, "even in a common-law suit there would be no recovery for general loss of business, the claimed loss of [the contractor's entire] net worth, and losses on the non-federal work—such damages are all deemed too remote." (*William Green Construction Co., Inc. v. United States* (1973) 201 Ct.Cl. 616, 477 F.2d 930, 936; accord, *Olin Jones Sand Company v. United States* (1980) 225 Ct.Cl. 741 [failure of government to make timely progress payments to contractor caused it loss of standing in the business community and occasioned denial of bonding on other contracts; lost profits on such contracts too remote and indirect]; *Rocky Mountain Constr. Co. v. United States* (1978) 218 Ct.Cl. 665, 666, 1978 WL 8468 ["wholly conjectural" whether the plaintiff contractor would have received other contracts; such speculative and remote damages not compensable as a matter of law].) These cases bar recovery of profits lost on future contracts not because the amount of the lost profits is speculative or remote, but because their occurrence is uncertain. (*Continental Car–Na–Var Corporation v. Moseley* (1944) 24 Cal.2d 104, 113, 148 P.2d 9; see 1 Dunn, Recovery of Damages for Lost Profits (5th ed.1998.) § 1.6, p. 17; 2 Bruner and O'Connor, Construction Law (2002) § 7:173, p. 945 [an impaired bonding claim is a lost business claim with the added requirement that the plaintiff must prove that the breach of contract caused the impairment of bonding capacity].)

California, likewise, has not upheld as special damages a contractor's unearned profits after breach of the construction contract. In *S.C. Anderson v. Bank of America* (1994) 24 Cal.App.4th 529, 30 Cal.Rptr.2d 286, a contractor hired to build tenant improvements did not receive timely payment from a financially strapped developer, and because of the contractor's rising receivables, its surety reduced its bonding capacity. Before the surety's action, the contractor had submitted the low bid on a public school construction project. Instead of awarding the contract to that contractor, the school district rebid the project. The contractor prepared a rebid, but could not submit its rebid because it lacked the requisite bonding capacity. Its rebid was lower than the winning bid for the school project. The contractor sued the developer's lender for fraud, seeking damages of $140,588 for profits it did not earn on the school project, amounting to 5 per cent of its rebid. The Court of Appeal affirmed nonsuit for the lender on the lost profits damages, noting there was "no evidence which would have enabled the jury to conclude it was reasonably probable" the contractor "would in fact have earned a profit" in the claimed amount. (*Id.* at p. 536, 30 Cal.Rptr.2d 286.) Although the contractor "was only obliged to demonstrate its loss with reasonable certainty" (*id.* at pp. 537–538, 30 Cal.Rptr.2d 286), the court said that the contractor had failed to show that it would be "impossible or impracticable to produce evidence relating to the accuracy of its bid, its ability to competently and efficiently perform the [school] project, or its likely net profit." (*Id.* at p. 538, 30 Cal.Rptr.2d 286.)

In contrast to *S.C. Anderson,* where the lost profits claim was for a sum certain and flowing from a particular project that the contractor would likely have won as the low bidder, the lost profits Lewis Jorge claimed it would have made on future construction projects were uncertain and speculative.

At trial, Lewis Jorge presented evidence that its bonding capacity was reduced by its surety after the District's termination of the contract. But Lewis Jorge did not establish that when the contract was formed the District could have reasonably contemplated that its breach of the contract would probably lead to a reduction of Lewis Jorge's bonding capacity by its surety, which in turn would adversely affect Lewis Jorge's ability to obtain future contracts. As the evidence at trial disclosed, Lewis Jorge's bonding agent, who had obtained the construction bonds from CNA, anticipated that CNA's suspension of Lewis Jorge's bonding capacity would only be temporary. "Damages may be awarded for breach of contract for those losses which naturally arise from the breach, or which might reasonably have been foreseen by the parties at the time they contracted, as the probable result of the breach." (*Burnett & Doty Development Co. v. Phillips, supra,* 84 Cal.App.3d at p. 389, 148 Cal.Rptr. 569.) But the breaching party "is not required to compensate the injured party for injuries that it had no reason to foresee as the probable result of its breach when it made the contract." (*Ibid.; Coughlin v. Blair* (1953) 41 Cal.2d 587, 603, 262 P.2d 305.)

Evidence at trial established that the owner's terminating a contract might or might not cause the contractor's surety to reduce its bonding capacity. As the District pointed out at oral argument, when it signed the contract it did not know what Lewis Jorge's balance sheet showed or what criteria Lewis Jorge's surety ordinarily used to evaluate a contractor's bonding limits. Absent such knowledge, the profits Lewis Jorge claimed it would have made on future, unawarded contracts were not actually foreseen nor reasonably foreseeable. Hence they are unavailable as special damages for the breach of this contract.

To summarize: It is indisputable that the District's termination of the school construction contract was the first event in a series of misfortunes that culminated in Lewis Jorge's closing down its construction business. Such disastrous consequences, however, are not the natural and necessary result of the breach of every construction contract involving bonding. Therefore, as we concluded earlier, lost profits are not general damages here. Nor were they actually foreseen or foreseeable as reasonably probable to result from the District's breach. Thus, they are not special

186
damages in this case.

*   *   *   *   *   *

WE CONCUR: GEORGE, C.J., BAXTER, WERDEGAR, CHIN, BROWN, and MORENO, JJ.

Case 15:   **Unilateral Mistake**

Grenall v. United of Omaha
California Court of Appeals, First District, 2008
165 Cal.App.4th 188

STEIN, J.

Jean M. Simes (Simes) died of cancer less than four months after purchasing an annuity that provided for monthly benefit payments as long as she lived. Plaintiffs Carol Grenall and Mike Sutton, the administrators of her estate (the Estate), sought to rescind the annuity based on a mistake of fact, namely, that Simes was unaware at the time of the contract that she was terminally ill. The trial court granted summary judgment in favor of the issuing company, defendant United of Omaha Life Insurance Company (United). We affirm because plaintiffs failed to establish an essential element for rescission based on mistake of fact.

FACTUAL AND PROCEDURAL BACKGROUND

The essential facts are undisputed for purposes of appeal:

Simes submitted a signed annuity application to United's agent on October 2, 2001, along with a single premium of $321,131. United then issued a policy for a single premium immediate annuity, effective the date of Simes's application. Simes received a copy of the policy six weeks after her application. The cover page of the annuity policy includes the following provision: "READ YOUR POLICY CAREFULLY. [¶] It includes the provisions on the following pages. [¶] If you are not satisfied with your policy, return it to us or our agent within 30 days after you receive it. We will refund the single premium and cancel the policy as of its date of issue." Among the provisions that followed, the annuity policy provided for monthly payments of $3,000 to Simes for "life only"—specifically, a "life contingent payable ... as long as the annuitant lives."

On January 25, 2002, after receiving three benefit payments, Simes was diagnosed with ovarian cancer. She died less than a week later on January 30, 2002. United stopped making annuity payments in April 2003 when it learned of her death.

The Estate filed suit against United, alleging two causes of action, for breach of contract and declaratory relief, in a form complaint. The breach of contract claim alleges that United had refused to make payments under the terms of the annuity "until the sum of the benefit payments equals the single premium." The declaratory relief cause of action seeks resolution of a dispute between the parties as to their respective rights under the annuity policy.

United moved for summary judgment, claiming the terms of the contract provided for a life annuity and did not require a refund of the premium to the Estate. Accordingly, United maintained it was entitled to summary judgment on the breach of contract and declaratory relief causes of action. In its opposition to the motion, the Estate characterized the annuity as a contract of adhesion and raised issues of procedural and substantive unconscionability.

The trial court granted summary judgment on the breach of contract cause of action, concluding that the undisputed facts showed that United had not breached the payment option to which the parties agreed, as the contract required monthly benefit payments only during Simes's lifetime.[1] The court denied the motion as to the declaratory relief cause of action, concluding that the evidence raised triable issues of material fact as to whether Simes made a unilateral mistake in agreeing to the life annuity payment option, justifying reformation, and whether surrounding circumstances justified rescission and restitution based on a mistake of fact or a mistake of law.[2]

After additional discovery, United renewed its motion for summary judgment on the declaratory relief cause of action, arguing that the Estate could not prevail on the factual issues identified in the trial court's prior order. United asserted that there was no evidence of a mistake by Simes or of what was in her mind when she purchased the annuity. In its opposition, the Estate raised a single claim for rescission based on a mistake of fact. Specifically, the Estate produced evidence that Simes did not know she had a terminal illness when she entered the annuity contract or during the statutory rescission period. The Estate also argued that the contract was procedurally and substantively unconscionable. United responded with authority rejecting rescission of annuity contracts under these circumstances.

The trial court granted summary judgment in favor of United, concluding that Simes's undetected cancer did not constitute a mistake of fact rendering enforcement unconscionable. The trial court noted that purchasers of annuities assume the risk of dying before recouping their investments and concluded it was reasonably foreseeable that Simes would die before the benefit payments matched her premium. Under these circumstances, the trial court held that it was reasonable to allocate to Simes the risk of a mistake regarding her health and life expectancy.

Judgment in favor of United was entered on June 15, 2007. The Estate filed a timely notice of appeal. United filed a motion to dismiss and for sanctions simultaneously with its respondent's brief. This court deferred a ruling on the motion pending its decision on the merits.[3]

---

[1] The trial court's interim ruling on the breach of contract cause of action is reviewable on appeal from the final judgment. (See *Jennings v. Marralle* (1994) 8 Cal.4th 121, 128, 32 Cal.Rptr.2d 275, 876 P.2d 1074.) Nonetheless, as the Estate does not assert error based on the trial court's interpretation of the contract, we deem any issues related to the interpretation of the contract waived and do not consider them. (See *Baugh v. Garl* (2006) 137 Cal.App.4th 737, 746, 40 Cal.Rptr.3d 539.)

[2] As noted, the trial court construed the Estate's declaratory relief cause of action to encompass reformation based on a unilateral mistake and rescission and restitution based on a mistake of fact or a mistake of law. United challenges this determination in its motion to dismiss and urges it as an additional ground for affirmance, arguing that the pleadings defined the issues for purposes of the motion and noting that the Estate's complaint did not seek rescission based on a mistake of fact. As we affirm the judgment on other grounds, we need not reach this issue.

[3] United seeks dismissal of the appeal for failure to provide a proper record, claiming the Estate's appendix does not contain "all essential documents" and does not comply with the California Rules of Court. United fails to identify the missing documents and has provided its own appendix, presumably curing any deficiency. The essential facts are undisputed on appeal. Accordingly, we consider the appeal on its merits.

DISCUSSION

*   *   *   *   *   *

The facts on which the Estate relied below purport to show the following: (1) Simes did not know at the time of her application and during the statutory rescission period that she had terminal ovarian cancer that would result in her death four months later; (2) Simes's illness affected her ability to make decisions; and (3) Simes did not receive a copy of the annuity policy until mid-November 2001. The sole issue argued by the Estate on appeal is whether these facts provide a legal basis for rescission of the life annuity contract based on a mistake of fact. We hold, as a matter of law, that they do not, for the following reasons.

California law permits rescission of a contract when a party's consent is given by mistake. (Civ.Code, § 1689, subd. (b)(1); *Donovan v. RRL Corp.* (2001) 26 Cal.4th 261, 278, 109 Cal.Rptr.2d 807, 27 P.3d 702 (*Donovan*).) On this basis, the Estate asserts a right to rescind the annuity policy, alleging that Simes would not have entered the contract but for a mistake of fact, specifically, the terminal illness she did not know she had. A mistake of fact may consist of a "[b]elief in the present existence of a thing material to the contract, which does not exist." (Civ.Code, § 1577.)[4] The alleged mistake therefore may be characterized as Simes's erroneous belief at the time of the contract that she was in good health and had a reasonable life expectancy.

A mistake of this nature does not support a claim for rescission. The Estate asserts a unilateral mistake and offers no evidence that United had reason to know of or caused the mistake. Accordingly, to prevail at trial, the Estate would have been required to prove the following: (1) Simes was mistaken regarding a basic assumption upon which she made the contract; (2) the mistake materially affected the agreed exchange of performances in a way that was adverse to Simes; (3) Simes did not bear the risk of the mistake; and (4) the effect of the mistake was such that enforcement of the contract would be unconscionable. (See *Donovan, supra,* 26 Cal.4th at p. 278, 109 Cal.Rptr.2d 807, 27 P.3d 702.) The facts on which the Estate relies demonstrate that it cannot establish the third of these elements.[5]

We conclude, based on the nature of the contract and the alleged mistake, that Simes bore the risk of the mistake, as a matter of law. A contracting party bears the risk of a mistake when the agreement so provides or when the party is aware of having only limited knowledge of the facts relating to the mistake but treats this limited knowledge as sufficient. (*Donovan, supra,* 26 Cal.4th at p. 283, 109 Cal.Rptr.2d 807, 27 P.3d 702, citing Rest.2d Contracts, § 154.) Additionally, the court may allocate the risk to a party because it is reasonable under the circumstances to do so. (*Donovan,* at p. 283, 109 Cal.Rptr.2d 807, 27 P.3d 702.) The contract in this case does not expressly assign the risk of the alleged mistake. Nonetheless, parties who contract for "life contingent" benefits necessarily do so based on limited knowledge of the very facts about which Simes was mistaken. We cannot fix the length of our lives or even the state of

---

[4] Under Civil Code section 1577, the mistake also must "not [be] caused by the neglect of a legal duty" by the mistaken party. This provision is not at issue here.

[5] In light of our conclusion in this regard, we need not address the remaining elements.

our health with certainty, and the parties knew that their expectations in this regard were at best an educated guess. Indeed, life annuity contracts are read "in the light of the knowledge of all mankind, that death may come tomorrow." (*Rishel v. Pacific Mut. Life Ins. Co. of California* (10th Cir.1935) 78 F.2d 881, 883 (*Rishel*).)

The allocation of this risk to Simes is reasonable because such risks are an inherent part of life annuity contracts, which reflect, at their essence, a longevity wager measured by average life expectancy. (See Rest.2d Contracts, § 154, illus. 3 [reasonable allocation of risk that annuitant has incurable disease and will live no more than a year]; see also *Stockett v. Penn Mut. Life Ins. Co.* (1954) 82 R.I. 172, 106 A.2d 741, 744 [contract not based on life expectancy of particular annuitant, but on "the average life expectancy of a specified group within which the individual may reasonably be included"].) Annuitants who survive the average life expectancy receive benefits beyond the premium; those who die earlier do not recoup their investments. Both risks are contemplated by the parties and, indeed, are an integral part of their bargain. (See *Guthrie v. Times–Mirror Co.* (1975) 51 Cal.App.3d 879, 885, 124 Cal.Rptr. 577 ["Where parties are aware at the time the contract is entered into that a doubt exists in regard to a certain matter and contract on that assumption, the risk of the existence of the doubtful matter is assumed as an element of the bargain"].)[6]

Accordingly, California courts have rejected challenges to such contracts on the ground that death came unexpectedly early. (See *Coyne v. Pacific Mut. Life Ins. Co.* (1935) 8 Cal.App.2d 104, 109, 47 P.2d 1079 (*Coyne*) [rejecting failure of consideration where annuitant committed suicide before first payment, finding he "ran the risk of such an event"]; *Gold v. Salem Lutheran Home Assn.* (1959) 53 Cal.2d 289, 291, 1 Cal.Rptr. 343, 347 P.2d 687 (*Gold*) [rejecting doctrine of frustration where resident died before performance of life care contract began, finding this was a reasonably foreseeable risk assumed by the parties]; *Sipes v. Equitable Life Assur. Society of the United States* (N.D.Cal.1996) 1996 WL 507308, at *4, 1996 U.S. Dist. LEXIS 12325, *12 [rejecting failure to disclose to woman in her 80's that life annuity was bad investment, as annuitants are presumed to know they may die before receiving substantial benefits].)

California law is consistent with that of other jurisdictions. (See, e.g., *Rishel, supra,* 78 F.2d at p. 883 ["An annuitant, for a sum certain, shares the risk of outliving his expectancy with others.... In a sense, if he lives longer than the average of his age, he wins; not so long, he loses ..."]; *Tabachinsky v. Guardian Life Insurance Company* (N.Y.Misc.1956) 147 N.Y.S.2d 719, 721 [same]; *Moses v. Manufacturers Life Insurance Company* (D.S.C.1968) 298 F.Supp. 321, 325 [the parties contemplated both the possibility that the purchaser would die before reaching her life expectancy and that she would live beyond it]; *Guthmann v. La Vida Llena* (1985) 103 N.M. 506, 513 [709 P.2d 675] [upholding retirement home's retention of residency fee on resident's death, as resident took the risk of dying sooner than expected]; see also 1 Appleman, Insurance Law and Practice (rev. ed. 1981) Annuities, § 86, pp. 306–307 ["the mere fact that the annuitant dies shortly after the contract is entered into, or after one or two payments only have been made,

---

[6] The Estate's own evidence suggests that Simes understood the nature of this exchange. Witness Michael Sutton testified at deposition that Simes told him she would be making money after 10 years of collecting on the annuity.

does not justify the setting aside of the contract, as that is one of the risks contemplated by such a form of investment"].)

The Estate does not offer any direct argument contesting allocation of the risk to Simes and simply challenges the California cases on which the trial court relied. The Estate attempts to distinguish *Coyne* and *Gold* on the basis that they involved an unknown risk of death in the future while Simes made a mistake about an *existing* fact—a fatal illness that cut her life expectancy to four months. This distinction, though factually accurate, is not significant. As noted above, the result in each of these cases turns on the nature of the contract and the risks contemplated by the parties, specifically, the risk of an early death. (See *Coyne, supra,* 8 Cal.App.2d at p. 109, 47 P.2d 1079; *Gold, supra,* 53 Cal.2d at pp. 291–292, 1 Cal.Rptr. 343, 347 P.2d 687 [parties "clearly assumed the risk of variation of the life span from that predicted by the mortality tables"].)

Although no California case directly addresses rescission based on a mistake about an annuitant's health at the time of the contract, other jurisdictions have refused to rescind in this context. For example, in *Aldrich v. Travelers Ins. Co.* (1944) 317 Mass. 86, 56 N.E.2d 888, an annuitant who had terminal cancer at the time of the contract died a little over a year later, and her estate sought to rescind based on mutual mistake and unconscionability. The Supreme Court of Massachusetts concluded that both parties had assumed the decedent's health warranted a reasonable expectation of life, but, as reasonable persons, knew this could be wrong and that she might "have within her body a condition that could cause her early death...." (See *id.* at p. 889.) The court found that the parties entered into a contract "with reference to this very risk," assumed the risks relating to the timing of her death, and were "satisfied to do business on this basis." (*Ibid.*) The court refused to allow rescission "merely because the known and assumed risk turned out to be greater than either or both [sides] expected it to be." (*Ibid.*)

Likewise, in *Woodworth v. Prudential Ins. Co. of America* (N.Y.App.Div.1939) 258 A.D. 103 [15 N.Y.S.2d 541], the annuitant's estate sought rescission based on a unilateral mistake of fact, alleging that at the time of the contract, he was "wholly unaware that he was then suffering from serious constitutional diseases which would cause his death in less than two years." (*Ibid.*) The court rejected rescission, finding that the parties had contemplated "the very possibility that here happened"—that the annuitant might die before his average life expectancy and receive a small fraction of the purchase price. (See *id.* at p. 543; see also *Rishel, supra,* 78 F.2d at p. 887 ["An annuity contract cannot be avoided because ... it develops that [the annuitant's] health was so impaired when the contract was written that his expectancy was less than the average"]; *Meyer's Executor v. Huber* (Ky.Ct.App.1955) 280 S.W.2d 157 [rejecting rescission claim based on alleged mistake about state of health and life expectancy]; *Davis v. Equitable Life Assurance Society of the United States* (1939) 280 N.Y. 656, 20 N.E.2d 1017 [although the decedent had cancer when he purchased the annuity, the "contract contemplated such contingency as arose"].)

Our sister states recognize that allocation of the risk to the annuitant in these circumstances is not only reasonable but a practical necessity. "It is difficult to see how any company could carry on an annuity business if the estate of an annuitant could rescind whenever it turned out that the condition of his health did not 'warrant a reasonable expectation of life.' " (*Aldrich v. Travelers Ins. Co., supra,* 56 N.E.2d at p. 889.) Indeed, "[i]f insurance companies

192

never profited from an annuity contract, how could [they] afford to pay those whose lives exceeded the averages upon which their rates were based?" (*Moses v. Manufacturers Life Insurance Company, supra,* 298 F.Supp. at p. 326; see *Woodworth v. Prudential Ins. Co. of America, supra,* 15 N.Y.S.2d at p. 544 [because unpaid balance becomes part of required reserve fund for the benefit of all annuitants in the class, companies would not be able to write contracts or assure proper reserves if they were required to issue refunds "upon proof after death of unknown illness when the contracts were written"].)

In light of these authorities, we hold that Simes bore the risk of the alleged mistake regarding her health and life expectancy at the time of the annuity contract. Because the Estate cannot establish an essential element of its rescission claim, summary judgment is proper. * * *

Finally, although we reject the Estate's arguments, because there is no California authority directly on point, we do not find them so wholly devoid of merit as to warrant the imposition of sanctions.

DISPOSITION

The judgment is affirmed with costs to United.

We concur: MARCHIANO, P.J., and SWAGER, J.

Case 16:   **Mutual Mistake**

Wood v. Boynton
Supreme Court of Wisconsin, 1885
64 Wis. 265

TAYLOR, J.

This action was brought in the circuit court for Milwaukee county to recover the possession of an uncut diamond of the alleged value of $ 1,000. The case was tried in the circuit court and, after hearing all the evidence in the case, the learned circuit judge directed the jury to find a verdict for the defendants. The plaintiff excepted to such instruction, and, after a verdict was rendered for the defendants, moved for a new trial upon the minutes of the judge. The motion was denied, and the plaintiff duly excepted, and, after judgment was entered in favor of the defendants, appealed to this court.

The defendants are partners in the jewelry business. On the trial it appeared that on and before the 28th of December, 1883, the plaintiff was the owner of and in the possession of a small stone of the nature and value of which she was ignorant; that on that day she sold it to one of the defendants for the sum of one dollar. Afterwards it was ascertained that the stone was a rough diamond, and of the value of about $ 700. After learning this fact the plaintiff tendered the defendants the one dollar, and ten cents as interest, and demanded a return of the stone to her. The defendants refused to deliver it, and therefore she commenced this action.

The plaintiff testified to the circumstances attending the sale of the stone to *Mr. Samuel B. Boynton,* as follows: "The first time *Boynton* saw that stone he was talking about buying the topaz, or whatever it is, in September or October. I went into his store to get a little pin mended, and I had it in a small box,--the pin,--a small ear-ring; . . . this stone, and a broken sleeve-button were in the box. *Mr. Boynton* turned to give me a check for my pin. I thought I would ask him what the stone was, and I took it out of the box and asked him to please tell me what that was. He took it in his hand and seemed some time looking at it. I told him I had been told it was a topaz, and he said it might be. He says, 'I would buy this; would you sell it?' I told him I did not know but what I would. What would it be worth? And he said he did not know; he would give me a dollar and keep it as a specimen, and I told him I would not sell it; and it was certainly pretty to look at. He asked me where I found it, and I told him in Eagle. He asked about how far out, and I said right in the village, and I went out. Afterwards, and about the 28th of December, I needed money pretty badly, and thought every dollar would help, and I took it back to *Mr. Boynton* and told him I had brought back the topaz, and he says, 'Well, yes; what did I offer you for it?' and I says, 'One dollar;' and he stepped to the change drawer and gave me the dollar, and I went out."

In another part of her testimony she says: "Before I sold the stone I had no knowledge whatever that it was a diamond. I told him that I had been advised that it was probably a topaz, and he said probably it was. The stone was about the size of a canary bird's egg, nearly the shape of an egg,--worn pointed at one end; it was nearly straw color,--a little darker." She also testified that before this action was commenced she tendered the defendants $ 1.10, and demanded the return of the stone, which they refused. This is substantially all the evidence of what took place at and before the sale to the defendants, as testified to by the plaintiff herself. She produced no other witness on that point.

The evidence on the part of the defendant is not very different from the version given by the plaintiff, and certainly is not more favorable to the plaintiff. *Mr. Samuel B. Boynton,* the defendant to whom the stone was sold, testified that at the time he bought this stone, he had never seen an uncut diamond; had seen cut diamonds, but they are quite different from the uncut ones; "he had no idea this was a diamond, and it never entered his brain at the time." Considerable evidence was given as to what took place after the sale and purchase, but that evidence has very little if any bearing upon the main point in the case.

This evidence clearly shows that the plaintiff sold the stone in question to the defendants, and delivered it to them in December, 1883, for a consideration of one dollar. The title to the stone passed by the sale and delivery to the defendants, How has that title been divested and again vested in the plaintiff? The contention of the learned counsel for the appellant is that the title became vested in the plaintiff by the tender to the *Boyntons* of the purchase money, with interest, and a demand of a return of the stone to her. Unless such tender and demand revested the title in the appellant, she cannot maintain her action.

The only question in the case is whether there was anything in the sale which entitled the vendor (the appellant) to rescind the sale and so revest the title in her. The only reasons we know of for rescinding a sale and revesting the title in the vendor so that he may maintain an action at law for the recovery of the possession against his vendee are (1) that the vendee was guilty of some fraud in procuring a sale to be made to him; (2) that there was a mistake made by the vendor in delivering an article which was not the article sold,--a mistake in fact as to the identity of the thing sold with the thing delivered upon the sale. This last is not in realty a rescission of the sale made, as the thing delivered was not the thing sold, and no title ever passed to the vendee by such delivery.

In this case, upon the plaintiff's own evidence, there can be no just ground for alleging that she was induced to make the sale she did by any fraud or unfair dealings on the part of *Mr. Boynton*. Both were entirely ignorant at the time of the character of the stone and of its intrinsic value. *Mr. Boynton* was not an expert in uncut diamonds, and had made no examination of the stone, except to take it in his hand and look at it before he made the offer of one dollar, which was refused at the time, and afterwards accepted without any comment or further examination made by *Mr. Boynton*. The appellant had the stone in her possession for a long time, and it appears from her own statement that she had made some inquiry as to its nature and qualities. If she chose to sell it without further investigation as to its intrinsic value to a person who was guilty of no fraud or unfairness which induced her to sell it for a small sum, she cannot repudiate the sale because it is afterwards ascertained that she made a bad bargain. *Kennedy v. Panama, etc., Mail Co.* L. R. 2 Q.B. 580.

There is no pretense of any mistake as to the identity of the thing sold. It was produced by the plaintiff and exhibited to the vendee before the sale was made, and the thing sold was delivered to the vendee when the purchase price was paid. *Kennedy v. Panama, etc., Mail Co.* L. R. 2 Q.B. 587; *Street v. Blay,* 2 Barn. & Adol. 456; *Gompertz v. Bartlett,* 2 El. & Bl. 849; *Gurney v. Womersley,* 4 El. & Bl. 133; *Ship's Case,* 2 De G. J. & S. 544. Suppose the appellant had produced the stone, and said she had been told that it was a diamond, and she believed it was, but had no knowledge herself as to its character or value, and *Mr. Boynton* had given her $ 500 for it, could he have rescinded the sale if it had turned out to be a topaz or any other stone of very small value? Could *Mr. Boynton* have rescinded the sale on the ground of mistake? Clearly not, nor could he rescind it on the ground that there had been a breach of warranty, because there was no warranty, nor could he rescind it on the ground of fraud, unless he could show that she falsely declared that she had been told it was a diamond, or, if she had been so told, still she knew it was not a diamond. See *Street v. Blay, supra.*

It is urged, with a good deal of earnestness, on the part of the counsel for the appellant that, because it has turned out that the stone was immensely more valuable than the parties at the time of the sale supposed it was, such fact alone is a ground for the rescission of the sale, and that fact was evidence of fraud on the part of the vendee. Whether inadequacy of price is to be received as evidence of fraud, even in a suit in equity to avoid a sale, depends upon the facts known to the parties at the time the sale is made.

When this sale was made the value of the thing sold was open to the investigation of both parties, neither knew its intrinsic value, and, so far as the evidence in this case shows, both supposed that the price paid was adequate. How can fraud be predicated upon such a sale, even though after-investigation showed that the intrinsic value of the thing sold was hundreds of times greater than the price paid? It certainly shows no such fraud as would authorize the vendor to rescind the contract and bring an action at law to recover the possession of the thing sold. Whether that fact would have any influence in an action in equity to avoid the sale we need not consider. See *Stettheimer v. Killip,* 75 N.Y. 282; *Etting v. Bank of U. S.* 11 Wheat. 59, 6 L. Ed. 419.

We can find nothing in the evidence from which it could be justly inferred that *Mr. Boynton,* at the time he offered the plaintiff one dollar for the stone, had any knowledge of the real value of the stone, or that he entertained even a belief that the stone was a diamond. It cannot, therefore, be said that there was a suppression of knowledge on the part of the defendant as to the value of the stone which a court of equity might seize upon to avoid the sale. The following cases show that, in the absence of fraud or warranty, the value of the property sold, as compared with the price paid, is no ground for a rescission of a sale. *Wheat v. Cross,* 31 Md. 99; *Lambert v. Heath,* 15 Mees. & W. 487; *Bryant v. Pember,* 45 Vt. 487; *Kuelkamp v. Hidding,* 31 Wis. 503, 511.

However unfortunate the plaintiff may have been in selling this valuable stone for a mere nominal sum, she has failed entirely to make out a case either of fraud or mistake in the sale such as will entitle her to a rescission of such sale so as to recover the property sold in an action at law.

The judgment of the circuit court is affirmed.

Case 17:   Impracticability & Frustration

Lloyd v. Murphy
Supreme Court of California, 1944
25 Cal. 2d 48

TRAYNOR, J.

On August 4, 1941, plaintiffs leased to defendant for a five-year term beginning September 15, 1941, certain premises located at the corner of Almont Drive and Wilshire Boulevard in the city of Beverly Hills, Los Angeles County, "for the sole purpose of conducting thereon the business of displaying and selling new automobiles (including the servicing and repairing thereof and of selling the petroleum products of a major oil company) and for no other purpose whatsoever without the written consent of the lessor" except "to make an occasional sale of a used automobile." Defendant agreed not to sublease or assign without plaintiffs' written consent. On January 1, 1942, the federal government ordered that the sale of new automobiles be discontinued. It modified this order on January 8, 1942, to permit sales to those engaged in military activities, and on January 20, 1942, it established a system of priorities restricting sales to persons having preferential ratings of A-1-j or higher. On March 10, 1942, defendant explained the effect of these restrictions on his business to one of the plaintiffs authorized to act for the others, who orally waived the restrictions in the lease as to use and subleasing and offered to reduce the rent if defendant should be unable to operate profitably. Nevertheless defendant vacated the premises on March 15, 1942, giving oral notice of repudiation of the lease to plaintiffs, which was followed by a written notice on March 24, 1942. Plaintiffs affirmed in writing on March 26th their oral waiver and, failing to persuade defendant to perform his obligations, they rented the property to other tenants pursuant to their powers under the lease in order to mitigate damages. On May 11, 1942, plaintiffs brought this action praying for declaratory relief to determine their rights under the lease, and for judgment for unpaid rent. Following a trial on the merits, the court found that the leased premises were located on one of the main traffic arteries of Los Angeles County; that they were equipped with gasoline pumps and in general adapted for the maintenance of an automobile service station; that they contained a one-story storeroom adapted to many commercial purposes; that plaintiffs had waived the restrictions in the lease and granted defendant the right to use the premises for any legitimate purpose and to sublease to any responsible party; that defendant continues to carry on the business of selling and servicing automobiles at two other places. Defendant testified that at one of these locations he sold new automobiles exclusively and when asked if he were aware that many new automobile dealers were continuing in business replied: "Sure. It is just the location that I couldn't make a go, though, of automobiles." Although there was no finding to that effect, defendant estimated in response to inquiry by his counsel, that 90 per cent of his gross volume of business was new car sales and 10 per cent gasoline sales. The trial court held that war conditions had not terminated defendant's obligations under the lease and gave judgment for plaintiffs, declaring the lease as modified by plaintiffs' waiver to be in full force and effect, and ordered defendant to pay the unpaid rent with interest, less amounts received by plaintiffs from re-renting. Defendant brought this appeal, contending that the purpose for which the premises were leased was frustrated by the restrictions placed on the sale of new automobiles by the federal government, thereby terminating his duties under the lease.

Although commercial frustration was first recognized as an excuse for nonperformance of a contractual duty by the courts of England (*Krell* v. *Henry* [1903] 2 K.B. 740 [C.A.]; *Blakely* v. *Muller*, 19 T.L.R. 186 [K.B.]; see McElroy and Williams, *The Coronation Cases*, 4 Mod.L.Rev. 241) its soundness has been questioned by those courts (see *Maritime National Fish, Ltd.,* v. *Ocean Trawlers, Ltd.* [1935] A.C. 524, 528-29, 56 L.Q.Rev. 324, arguing that *Krell* v. *Henry, supra,* was a misapplication of *Taylor* v. *Caldwell*, 3 B.&S 826 [1863], the leading case on impossibility as an excuse for nonperformance), and they have refused to apply the doctrine to leases on the ground that an estate is conveyed to the lessee, which carries with it all risks (*Swift* v. *McBean*, 166 L.T.Rep. 87 [1942] 1 K.B. 375; *Whitehall Court* v. *Ettlinger*, 122 L.T.Rep. 540, (1920) 1 K.B. 680, [1919] 89 L.J. [K.B.] N.S. 126; 137 A.L.R. 1199, 1224; see collection and discussion on English cases in *Wood* v. *Bartolino*, N.M. [146 P.2d 883, 886-87]). Many courts, therefore, in the United States have held that the tenant bears all risks as owner of the estate (*Cusack Co.* v. *Pratt*, 78 Colo. 28 [239 P. 22, 44 A.L.R. 55]; *Yellow Cab Co.* v. *Stafford-Smith Co.*, 320 Ill. 294 [150 N.E. 670, 43 A.L.R. 1173]), but the modern cases have recognized that the defense may be available in a proper case, even in a lease. As the author declares in 6 Williston, Contracts (rev. ed. 1938), § 1955, pp. 5485-87, "The fact that lease is a conveyance and not simply a continuing contract and the numerous authorities enforcing liability to pay rent in spite of destruction of leased premises, however, have made it difficult to give relief. That the tenant has been relieved, nevertheless, in several cases indicates the gravitation of the law toward a recognition of the principle that fortuitous destruction of the value of performance wholly outside the contemplation of the parties may excuse a promisor even in a lease. . . .

"Even more clearly with respect to leases than in regard to ordinary contracts the applicability of the doctrine of frustration depends on the total or nearly total destruction of the purpose for which, in the contemplation of both parties, the transaction was entered into."

The principles of frustration have been repeatedly applied to leases by the courts of this state (*Brown* v. *Oshiro*, 58 Cal.App.2d 190 [136 P.2d 29]; *Davidson* v. *Goldstein*, 58 Cal.App.2d Supp. 909 [136 P.2d 665]; *Grace* v. *Croninger*, 12 Cal.App.2d 603 [55 P.2d 940]; *Knoblaugh* v. *McKinney*, 5 Cal.App.2d 339 [42 P.2d 332]; *Industrial Development & Land Co.* v. *Goldschmidt*, 56 Cal.App. 507 [206 P. 134]; *Burke* v. *San Francisco Breweries, Ltd.*, 21 Cal.App. 198 [131 P. 83]) and the question is whether the excuse for nonperformance is applicable under the facts of the present case.

Although the doctrine of frustration is akin to the doctrine of impossibility of performance (see Civ. Code, § 1511; 6 Cal.Jur. 435-450; 4 Cal.Jur Ten-year Supp. 187-192; *Taylor* v. *Caldwell, supra*) since both have developed from the commercial necessity of excusing performance in cases of extreme hardship, frustration is not a form of impossibility even under

198

the modern definition of that term, which includes not only cases of physical impossibility but also cases of extreme impracticability of performance (see *Mineral Park Land Co.* v. *Howard*, 172 Cal. 289, 293 [156 P. 458, L.R.A. 1916F 1]; *Christin* v. *Superior Court*, 9 Cal.2d 526, 533 [71 P.2d 205, 112 A.L.R. 1153]; 6 Williston, *op. cit. supra*, § 1935, p. 5419; Rest., Contracts, § 454, comment a., and Cal.Ann. p. 254).

Performance remains possible but the expected value of performance to the party seeking to be excused has been destroyed by a fortuitous event, which supervenes to cause an actual but not literal failure of consideration (*Krell* v. *Henry, supra; Blakely* v. *Muller, supra; Marks Realty Co.* v. *Hotel Hermitage Co.*, 170 App.Div. 484 [156 N.Y.S. 179]; 6 Williston, *op. cit. supra*, §§ 1935, 1954, pp. 5477, 5480; Restatement, Contracts, § 288).

The question in cases involving frustration is whether the equities of the case, considered in the light of sound public policy, require placing the risk of a disruption or complete destruction of the contract equilibrium on defendant or plaintiff under the circumstances of a given case (*Fibrosa Spolka Akcyjina* v. *Fairbairn Lawson Combe Barbour, Ltd.* [1942], 167 L.T.R. [H.L.] 101, 112-113; see Smith, *Some Practical Aspects of the Doctrine of Impossibility*, 32 Ill.L.Rev. 672, 675; Patterson, *Constructive Conditions in Contracts*, 42 Columb.L.Rev. 903, 949; 27 Cal.L.Rev. 461), and the answer depends on whether an unanticipated circumstance, the risk of which should not be fairly thrown on the promisor, has made performance vitally different from what was reasonably to be expected (6 Williston, *op. cit. supra*, § 1963, p. 5511; Restatement, Contracts, § 454). The purpose of a contract is to place the risks of performance upon the promisor, and the relation of the parties, terms of the contract, and circumstances surrounding its formation must be examined to determine whether it can be fairly inferred that the risk of the event that has supervened to cause the alleged frustration was not reasonably foreseeable. If it was foreseeable there should have been provision for it in the contract, and the absence of such a provision gives rise to the inference that the risk was assumed.

The doctrine of frustration has been limited to cases of extreme hardship so that businessmen, who must make their arrangements in advance, can rely with certainty on their contracts (*Anglo-Northern Trading Co.* v. *Emlyn Jones and Williams*, 2 K.B. 78; 137 A.L.R. 1199, 1216-1221). The courts have required a promisor seeking to excuse himself from performance of his obligations to prove that the risk of the frustrating event was not reasonably foreseeable and that the value of counterperformance is totally or nearly totally destroyed, for frustration is no defense if it was foreseeable or controllable by the promisor, or if counterperformance remains valuable. (*La Cumbre Golf & Country Club* v. *Santa Barbara Hotel Co.*, 205 Cal. 422, 425 [271 P. 476]; *Johnson* v. *Atkins*, 53 Cal.App.2d 430, 434 [127 P.2d 1027]; *Grace* v. *Croninger*, 12 Cal.App.2d 603, 606-607 [55 P.2d 940]; *Industrial Development & Land Co.* v. *Goldschmidt*, 56 Cal.App. 507, 511 [206 P. 134]; *Burke* v. *San Francisco Breweries, Ltd.*, 21 Cal.App. 198, 201 [131 P. 83]; *Megan* v. *Updike Grain Corp.*, (C.C.A. 8), 94 F.2d 551, 553; *Herne Bay Steamboat Co.* v. *Hutton* [1903], 2 K.B. 683; *Leiston Gas Co.* v. *Leiston Cum Sizewell Urban District Council* [1916], 2 K.B. 428; *Raner* v. *Goldberg*, 244 N.Y.

438 [155 N.E. 733]; 6 Williston, *op. cit. supra*, §§ 1939, 1955, 1963; Restatement, Contracts, § 288.)

Thus laws or other governmental acts that make performance unprofitable or more difficult or expensive do not excuse the duty to perform a contractual obligation (*Sample* v. *Fresno Flume etc. Co.*, 129 Cal. 222, 228 [61 P. 1085]; *Klauber* v. *San Diego St. Car Co.*, 95 Cal. 353, 358 [30 P. 555]; *Texas Co.* v. *Hogarth Shipping Co.*, 256 U.S. 619, 630 [41 S.Ct. 612, 65 L.Ed. 1123]; *Columbus Ry. Power & Light Co.* v. *Columbus*, 249 U.S. 399, 414 [39 S.Ct. 349, 63 L.Ed. 669]; *Thomson* v. *Thomson*, 315 Ill. 521, 527 [146 N.E. 451]; *Commonwealth* v. *Bader*, 271 Pa. 308, 312 [114 A. 266]; *Commonwealth* v. *Neff*, 271 Pa. 312, 314 [114 A. 267]; *London & Lancashire Ind. Co.* v. *Columbiana County*, 107 Ohio St. 51, 64 [140 N.E. 672]; see 6 Williston, *op. cit. supra*, §§ 1955, 1963, pp. 5507-09). It is settled that if parties have contracted with reference to a state of war or have contemplated the risks arising from it, they may not invoke the doctrine of frustration to escape their obligations (*Northern Pac. Ry. Co.* v. *American Trading Co.*, 195 U.S. 439, 467-68 [25 S.Ct. 84, 49 L.Ed. 269]; *Primos Chemical Co.* v. *Fulton Steel Corp.* (D.C.N.Y.), 266 F. 945, 948; *Krulewitch* v. *National Importing & Trading Co.*, 195 App.Div. 544 [186 N.Y.S. 838, 840]; *Smith* v. *Morse*, 20 La.Ann. 220, 222; *Lithflux Mineral & Chem. Works* v. *Jordan*, 217 Ill.App. 64, 68; *Mederios* v. *Hill*, 8 Bing. 231, 131 Eng.Rep. 390, 392; *Bolckow V. & Co.* v. *Compania Minera de Sierra Minera*, 115 L.T.R. [K.B.] 745, 747).

At the time the lease in the present case was executed the National Defense Act (Public Act No. 671 of the 76th Congress [54 Stats. 601], § 2A), approved June 28, 1940, authorizing the President to allocate materials and mobilize industry for national defense, had been law for more than a year. The automotive industry was in the process of conversion to supply the needs of our growing mechanized army and to meet lend-lease commitments. Iceland and Greenland had been occupied by the army. Automobile sales were soaring because the public anticipated that production would soon be restricted. These facts were commonly known and it cannot be said that the risk of war and its consequences necessitating restriction of the production and sale of automobiles was so remote a contingency that its risk could not be foreseen by defendant, an experienced automobile dealer. Indeed, the conditions prevailing at the time the lease was executed, and the absence of any provision in the lease contracting against the effect of war, gives rise to the inference that the risk was assumed. Defendant has therefore failed to prove that the possibility of war and its consequences on the production and sale of new automobiles was an unanticipated circumstance wholly outside the contemplation of the parties.

Nor has defendant sustained the burden of proving that the value of the lease has been destroyed. The sale of automobiles was not made impossible or illegal but merely restricted and if governmental regulation does not entirely prohibit the business to be carried on in the leased premises but only limits or restricts it, thereby making it less profitable and more difficult to continue, the lease is not terminated or the lessee excused from further performance (*Brown* v. *Oshiro, supra*, p. 194; *Davidson* v. *Goldstein, supra*, p. 918; *Grace* v. *Croninger, supra*, p. 607;

Industrial Development & Land Co. v. *Goldschmidt, supra; Burke* v. *San Francisco Brewing Co., supra*, p. 202; *First National Bank of New Rochelle* v. *Fairchester Oil Co.*, 267 App.Div. 281 [45 N.Y.S.2d 532, 533]; *Robitzek Inv. Co., Inc.* v. *Colonial Beacon Oil Co.*, 265 App.Div. 749 [40 N.Y.S.2d 819, 824]; *Colonial Operating Corp.* v. *Hannon Sales & Service, Inc.*, 265 App. Div. 411 [39 N.Y.S.2d 217, 220]; *Byrnes* v. *Balcolm*, 265 App.Div. 268 [38 N.Y.S.2d 801, 803]; *Deibler* v. *Bernard Bros. Inc.*, 385 Ill. 610 [53 N.E.2d 450, 453]; *Wood* v. *Bartolino*, N.M. [146 P.2d 883, 886, 888, 890]). Defendant may use the premises for the purpose for which they were leased. New automobiles and gasoline continue to be sold. Indeed, defendant testified that he continued to sell new automobiles exclusively at another location in the same county.

Defendant contends that the lease is restrictive and that the government orders therefore destroyed its value and frustrated its purpose. Provisions that prohibit subleasing or other uses than those specified affect the value of a lease and are to be considered in determining whether its purpose has been frustrated or its value destroyed (see Owens, *The Effect of the War Upon the Rights and Liabilities of Parties to a Contract*, 19 California State Bar Journal 132, 143). It must not be forgotten, however, that "The landlord has not covenanted that the tenant shall have the right to carry on the contemplated business or that the business to which the premises are by their nature or by the terms of the lease restricted shall be profitable enough to enable the tenant to pay the rent but has imposed a condition for his own benefit; and, certainly, unless and until he chooses to take advantage of it, the tenant is not deprived of the use of the premises." (6 Williston, Contracts, *op. cit. supra*, § 1955, p. 5485; see, also, *People* v. *Klopstock*, 24 Cal.2d 897, 901 [151 P.2d 641].) In the present lease plaintiffs reserved the rights that defendant should not use the premises for other purposes than those specified in the lease or sublease without plaintiffs' written consent. Far from preventing other uses or subleasing they waived these rights, enabling defendant to use the premises for any legitimate purpose and to sublease them to any responsible tenant. This waiver is significant in view of the location of the premises on a main traffic artery in Los Angeles County and their adaptability for many commercial purposes. The value of these rights is attested by the fact that the premises were rented soon after defendants vacated them. It is therefore clear that the governmental restrictions on the sale of new cars have not destroyed the value of the lease. Furthermore, plaintiffs offered to lower the rent if defendant should be unable to operate profitably, and their conduct was at all times fair and cooperative.

The consequences of applying the doctrine of frustration to a leasehold involving less than a total or nearly total destruction of the value of the leased premises would be undesirable. Confusion would result from different decisions purporting to define "substantial" frustration. Litigation would be encouraged by the repudiation of leases when lessees found their businesses less profitable because of the regulations attendant upon a national emergency. Many leases have been affected in varying degrees by the widespread governmental regulations necessitated by war conditions.

The cases that defendant relies upon are consistent with the conclusion reached herein. In *Industrial Development & Land Co.* v. *Goldschmidt, supra*, the lease provided that the premises should not be used other than as a saloon. When national prohibition made the sale of alcoholic beverages illegal, the court excused the tenant from further performance on the theory of illegality or impossibility by a change in domestic law. The doctrine of frustration might have been applied, since the purpose for which the property was leased was totally destroyed and there was nothing to show that the value of the lease was not thereby totally destroyed. In the present case the purpose was not destroyed but only restricted, and plaintiffs proved that the lease was valuable to defendant. In *Grace* v. *Croninger, supra,* the lease was for the purpose of conducting a "saloon and cigar store and for no other purpose" with provision for subleasing a portion of the premises for bootblack purposes. The monthly rental was $ 650. It was clear that prohibition destroyed the main purpose of the lease, but since the premises could be used for bootblack and cigar store purposes, the lessee was not excused from his duty to pay the rent. In the present case new automobiles and gasoline may be sold under the lease as executed and any legitimate business may be conducted or the premises may be subleased under the lease as modified by plaintiff's waiver. *Colonial Operating Corp.* v. *Hannon Sales & Service, Inc.*, 34 N.Y.S.2d 116, was reversed in 265 App.Div. 411 [39 N.Y.S.2d 217], and *Signal Land Corp.* v. *Loecher*, 35 N.Y.S.2d 25; *Schantz* v. *American Auto Supply Co., Inc.*, 178 Misc. 909 [36 N.Y.S.2d 747]; and *Canrock Realty Corp.* v. *Vim Electric Co., Inc.*, 37 N.Y.S.2d 139, involved government orders that totally destroyed the possibility of selling the products for which the premises were leased. No case has been cited by defendant or disclosed by research in which an appellate court has excused a lessee from performance of his duty to pay rent when the purpose of the lease has not been totally destroyed or its accomplishment rendered extremely impracticable or where it has been shown that the lease remains valuable to the lessee.

The judgment is affirmed.

Case 18: **Third Party Beneficiary**

Schauer v. Mandarin Gems of Cal., Inc.
California Court of Appeals, Fourth District, 2005
125 Cal.App.4th 949

IKOLA, J.

Sarah Jane Schauer (plaintiff) appeals from a judgment of dismissal in favor of Mandarin Gems of California, Inc., doing business as Black, Starr & Frost (defendant) after the court sustained defendant's demurrer to plaintiff's second amended complaint without leave to amend. Plaintiff sought to recover on various theories based on her discovery that a diamond ring given to her as an engagement gift prior to her marriage to her now former husband, Darin Erstad, allegedly was not worth the $43,000 he paid defendant for it in 1999. Erstad is not a party to this action.

We reverse the judgment and remand. We conclude plaintiff has standing as a third party beneficiary of the sales contract between Erstad and defendant, and she has adequately pleaded a contract cause of action based on allegations of defendant's breach of express warranty. Defendant must answer to that claim. In all other respects, the pleading is defective and cannot be cured by amendment.

FACTS

Our factual summary "accepts as true the facts alleged in the complaint, together with facts that may be implied or inferred from those expressly alleged." (*Barnett v. Fireman's Fund Ins. Co.* (2001) 90 Cal.App.4th 500, 505 [108 Cal. Rptr. 2d 657].)

Plaintiff and Erstad went shopping for an engagement ring on August 15, 1999. After looking at diamonds in premier jewelry establishments such as Tiffany and Company and Cartier, they went to defendant's store, where they found a ring that salesperson Joy said featured a 3.01 carat diamond with a clarity grading of "SI1." Erstad bought the ring the same day for $43,121.55. The following month, for insurance purposes, defendant provided Erstad a written appraisal verifying the ring had certain characteristics, including an SI1 clarity rating and an average replacement value of $45,500. Paul Lam, a graduate gemologist with the European Gemological Laboratory (EGL), signed the appraisal.

The couple's subsequent short-term marriage was dissolved in a North Dakota judgment awarding each party, "except as otherwise set forth in this Agreement," "the exclusive right, title and possession of all personal property. . .which such party now owns, possesses, holds or hereafter acquires." Plaintiff's personal property included the engagement ring given to her by Erstad.

On June 3, 2002, after the divorce, plaintiff had the ring evaluated by the "Gem Trade Laboratory," which gave the diamond a rating of "SI2 quality," an appraisal with which "multiple other [unidentified] jewelers, including one at [defendant's store]" agreed. That was how plaintiff discovered defendant's alleged misrepresentation, concealment, and breach of express warranty regarding the true clarity of the diamond and its actual worth, which is—on plaintiff's information and belief—some $ 23,000 less than what Erstad paid for it.

Plaintiff sued defendant on several theories. Three times she attempted to plead her case. In the first cause of action of the second amended complaint, she sought to recover under the Consumers Legal Remedies Act (the Act, Civ. Code, § 1760 et seq.), stating, inter alia, that had the true clarity of the diamond been known, plaintiff would not have "acquired said diamond by causing it to be purchased for her." Thereafter, if the written verification of the clarity value sent to Erstad one month after the purchase had revealed the truth, plaintiff would have "immediately rescinded the sale based on a failure of consideration." The second cause of action, for breach of contract, alleged Erstad and defendant had a written contract under which Erstad agreed to purchase the ring "for the sole and stated purpose of giving it [to] Plaintiff," making plaintiff a third party beneficiary of the sales contract. Defendant breached the contract by delivering an engagement ring that did not conform to the promised SI1 clarity rating.

In her third cause of action, for constructive fraud, plaintiff claimed the existence of a special confidential relationship in which defendant was aware plaintiff and her "predecessor in interest," presumably Erstad, "were not knowledgeable and. . .were relying exclusively on the Defendants' integrity," but defendant falsely represented the clarity of the diamond with the intent to defraud "[p]laintiff and her predecessor in interest" to make the purchase at the inflated price. The fourth cause of action for fraud alleged defendant's malicious and deceitful conduct warranted punitive damages. In the fifth cause of action, plaintiff sought rescission under Civil Code section 1689 for defendant's alleged fraud in the inducement, mistake, and failure of consideration.

Appended to the pleading was a redacted copy of a North Dakota court's judgment filed July 19, 2001, granting Erstad and plaintiff a divorce pursuant to their "Stipulation and Agreement," entitling each party, as noted *ante*, "to the exclusive right, title and possession of all personal property of the parties, joint or several, which such party now owns, possesses, holds or hereafter acquires [*except as otherwise provided in the agreement*]," and awarding the parties their respective "personal effects, clothing and jewelry."

In its general demurrer to the second amended complaint and each cause of action, defendant asserted plaintiff had no viable claim under any theory because: (1) plaintiff was neither the purchaser of the ring nor a third party beneficiary of the contract between defendant and Erstad, who was not alleged to have assigned his rights to plaintiff; (2) the statute of limitations had expired for defendant's alleged violations of the Act; (3) plaintiff was not a buyer, and the ring tendered to Erstad conformed entirely to the contract; (4) defendant owed no special confidential or fiduciary duty to plaintiff upon which to predicate a fraud cause of action; (5) any alleged fraud was the act of EGL, not attributable to defendant; and (6) fraud was not pleaded with the required specificity.[1]

The court again sustained the demurrer, this time without further leave to amend. The judgment of dismissal followed, and plaintiff appeals. As we will explain, the court erred. Although the complaint is fatally defective in some respects, plaintiff is entitled as a matter of law to pursue her contract claim as a third party beneficiary.

DISCUSSION

Standard of Review

The trial court's decision to sustain a demurrer is a legal ruling, subject to de novo review. (*Lazar v. Hertz Corp.* (1999) 69 Cal.App.4th 1494, 1501 [82 Cal. Rptr. 2d 368].) "[W]e give the complaint a reasonable interpretation, and treat the demurrer as admitting all material facts properly pleaded, but not the truth of contentions, deductions or conclusions of law. We reverse if the plaintiff has stated a cause of action under any legal theory. [Citation.]" (*Barnett v. Fireman's Fund Ins. Co., supra,* 90 Cal.App.4th at p. 507.)

The issue before us is whether, on well-pleaded facts, plaintiff may maintain an action to recover the $23,000 difference between what Erstad paid for the diamond ring and what that gift was really worth, given its alleged inferior quality.

We begin with the rule that "[e]very action must be prosecuted in the name of the real party in interest, except as otherwise provided by statute." (Code Civ. Proc., § 367.) Where the complaint shows the plaintiff does not possess the substantive right or standing to prosecute the action, "it is vulnerable to a general demurrer on the ground that it fails to state a cause of action." (*Carsten v. Psychology Examining Com.* (1980) 27 Cal.3d 793, 796 [166 Cal. Rptr. 844, 614 P.2d 276]; *Cloud v. Northrop Grumman Corp.* (1998) 67 Cal.App.4th 995, 1004 [79 Cal. Rptr. 2d 544].)

---

[1] Defendant noted that one of the exhibits to plaintiff's complaint showed defendant's disclaimer stating the EGL appraisal "SHOULD NOT BE USED AS THE BASIS FOR THE PURCHASE OR SALE OF THE ITEM/S LISTED WITHIN AND IS PROVIDED SOLELY AS AN ESTIMATE OF THE APPROXIMATE REPLACEMENT VALUES OF THE LISTED ITEM/S AT THIS TIME FOR INSURANCE COVERAGE PURPOSES." Another section of that exhibit advised, "JEWELRY APPRAISAL AND EVALUATION IS PARTIALLY SUBJECTIVE, THEREFORE ESTIMATES OF REPLACEMENT VALUE MAY VARY FROM ONE APPRAISER TO ANOTHER." Another section stated: "THE APPRAISER AND BLACK, STARR & FROST AT SOUTH COAST PLAZA. . .DISCLAIM ALL RESPONSIBILITY AND LIABILITY RESULTING FROM ANY SUIT AT LAW WHICH MIGHT ARISE IN CONNECTION WITH THE APPRAISAL. IN NO SUCH EVENT WILL THE APPRAISER AND [defendant's] OFFICERS AND EMPLOYEES. . .BE LIABLE FOR ANY DAMAGES ARISING FROM THE USE OF OR RELIANCE ON THIS APPRAISAL, OR ANY OTHER CONSEQUENTIAL DAMAGES."

The second amended complaint alleges "[d]efendant entered into a written contract with [Erstad] to purchase the subject engagement ring." The attached exhibit shows defendant issued a written appraisal to Erstad. Erstad is clearly a real party in interest, but he has not sued.

Plaintiff contends she, too, is a real party in interest because the North Dakota divorce judgment endowed her with all of Erstad's rights and remedies. As we will explain, this theory is wrong. However, as we will also discuss, plaintiff is correct in asserting she is a third party beneficiary of the sales contract. That status enables her to proceed solely on her contract claim for breach of express warranty. For the remainder, plaintiff is without standing to recover under any legal theory alleged, and the equitable remedy of rescission is also unavailable to her.

Transfer of Erstad's Rights and Remedies to Plaintiff

Plaintiff alleges and argues the North Dakota divorce judgment granted her "the exclusive right, title and possession of all [of her] personal property," including the engagement ring, and the judgment automatically divested Erstad of his substantive rights and transferred or assigned them to her by operation of law. Such is not the case.

Plaintiff undoubtedly owns the ring. (*See* Civ. Code, § 679 ["The ownership of property is absolute when a single person has the absolute dominion over it, and may use it or dispose of it according to his [or her] pleasure, subject only to general laws"]; *see also* N.D. Cent. Code, § 47-01-01 (2003) ["The ownership of a thing shall mean the right of one or more persons to possess and use it to the exclusion of others. In this code the thing of which there may be ownership is called property"].) But ownership of gifted property, even if awarded in a divorce, does not automatically carry with it ownership of the rights of the person who bought the gift. As will be seen, contrary to plaintiff's hypothesis, the divorce judgment did not give plaintiff the ring embellished with Erstad's rights under the contract or his choses in action.

A cause of action for damages is itself personal property. (*See* Civ. Code, § 953 ["A thing in action is a right to recover money or other personal property by a judicial proceeding"]; *Parker v. Walker* (1992) 5 Cal.App.4th 1173, 1182-1183, 6 Cal. Rptr. 2d 908 ["A cause of action to recover money in damages. . .is a chose in action and therefore a form of personal property"]; *see also Iszler v. Jordan* (N.D. 1957) 80 N.W.2d 665, 668-669 [a chose in action is property].) At the time of the divorce judgment, all causes of action that could have been asserted against the jeweler by a buyer of the ring were Erstad's personal property. He was, after all, the purchaser of the ring. The divorce agreement awarded to each party his or her respective personal property, *except as otherwise expressly provided.* The disposition of the ring was expressly provided for in the agreement, i.e., plaintiff was given her jewelry. Any extant choses in action against defendant, however, were *not* expressly provided for in the agreement; therefore, they were *retained* by Erstad as part of his personal property.

To be sure, Erstad could have transferred or assigned *his* rights to legal recourse to plaintiff (*see, e.g., Dixon-Reo Co. v. Horton Motor Co.* (1922) 49 N.D. 304 [191 N.W. 780, 782] [a right arising out of an obligation, i.e., a thing in action, is the property of the person to whom the right is due and may be transferred]), but there are no allegations Erstad either did so or manifested an intention to do so. (*See, e.g., Krusi v. S.J. Amoroso Construction Co.* (2000) 81 Cal.App.4th 995, 1005 [97 Cal. Rptr. 2d 294]; *Vaughn v. Dame Construction Co.* (1990) 223 Cal. App. 3d 144, 148 [272 Cal. Rptr. 261]; *see also Nisewanger v. W.J. Lane Co.* (1947) 75 N.D. 448, 455 [28 N.W.2d 409, 412] [under North Dakota law, when a chose in action is assignable, the clear intent to assign must be established].)

Third Party Beneficiary

The fact that Erstad did not assign or transfer his rights to plaintiff does not mean she is without recourse. For although plaintiff does not have Erstad's rights by virtue of the divorce judgment, she nonetheless has standing in her own right to sue for breach of contract as a third party beneficiary under the allegation, inter alia, that "[d]efendant entered into a written contract with Plaintiff's fiancee [*sic*] to purchase the subject engagement ring for the sole and stated purpose of giving it [to] Plaintiff."

Civil Code section 1559 provides: "A contract, made expressly for the benefit of a third person, may be enforced by him [or her] at any time before the parties thereto rescind it." Because third party beneficiary status is a matter of contract interpretation, a person seeking to enforce a contract as a third party beneficiary " 'must plead a contract which was made expressly for his [or her] benefit and one in which it clearly appears that he [or she] was a beneficiary.' " (*California Emergency Physicians Medical Group v. PacifiCare of California* (2003) 111 Cal.App.4th 1127, 1138 [4 Cal. Rptr. 3d 583].)

"'"[E]xpressly[,]" [as used in the statute and case law,] means "in an express manner; in direct or unmistakable terms; explicitly; definitely; directly." ' [Citations.] '[A]n intent to make the obligation inure to the benefit of the third party must have been clearly manifested by the contracting parties.' " (*Sofias v. Bank of America* (1985) 172 Cal. App. 3d 583, 587 [218 Cal. Rptr. 388].) Although this means persons only incidentally or remotely benefited by the contract are not entitled to enforce it, it does not mean both of the contracting parties must intend to benefit the third party: Rather, it means the promisor—in this case, defendant jeweler—"must have understood that the promisee [Erstad] had such intent. [Citations.] No specific manifestation by the promisor of an intent to benefit the third person is required." (*Lucas v. Hamm* (1961) 56 Cal.2d 583, 591 [15 Cal. Rptr. 821, 364 P.2d 685]; *see also Johnson v. Superior Court* (2000) 80 Cal.App.4th 1050, 1064-1065 [95 Cal. Rptr. 2d 864]; *Don Rose Oil Co., Inc. v. Lindsley* (1984) 160 Cal. App. 3d 752, 757 [206 Cal. Rptr. 670]; *Zigas v. Superior Court* (1981) 120 Cal. App. 3d 827, 837 [174 Cal. Rptr. 806].)

We conclude the pleading here meets the test of demonstrating plaintiff's standing as a third party beneficiary to enforce the contract between Erstad and defendant. The couple went shopping for an engagement ring. They were together when plaintiff chose the ring she wanted or, as alleged in the complaint, she "caused [the ring] to be purchased for her." Erstad allegedly bought the ring "for the sole and *stated* purpose of giving [the ring]" to plaintiff. (Italics added.) Under the alleged facts, the jeweler *must* have understood Erstad's intent to enter the sales contract for plaintiff's benefit. Thus, plaintiff has adequately pleaded her status as a third party beneficiary, and she is entitled to proceed with her contract claim against defendant to the extent it is not time-barred.

With regard to the limitations period, defendant incorrectly argued the complaint was time-barred by Code of Civil Procedure section 339's two-year statute of limitations applicable to oral contracts, i.e., the salesperson's alleged statement about the quality of the diamond. However, the applicable limitations period for breach of warranty in a contract for sale of goods is not set forth in the Code of Civil Procedure, but in California Uniform Commercial Code section 2725, which provides a four-year limitations period for "any contract for sale," regardless of whether the contract is written or oral. (*See Filmservice Laboratories, Inc. v. Harvey Bernhard Enterprises, Inc.,* (1989) 208 Cal. App. 3d 1297, 1304 [256 Cal. Rptr. 735] ["The term 'any contract for sale' " as used in California Uniform Commercial Code section 2725 "includes an oral agreement"]; *see also Hachten v. Stewart* (1974) 42 Cal.App.3d Supp. 1, 3 [116 Cal. Rptr. 631] [to the same effect].) There can be no legitimate question the complaint is timely under the apt statute.

Breach of Contract/Breach of Express Warranty

Plaintiff's breach of contract claim is based on allegations of defendant's breach of express warranty in representing the engagement diamond was of an SI1 clarity rating, when in actuality it was of an inferior quality. Other than noting the breach of express warranty claim is adequately pleaded, and that plaintiff is entitled to pursue it as a third party beneficiary, we express no opinion on its ultimate viability. It will be for the fact finder to determine from all the circumstances whether defendant's statements regarding the clarity rating of the diamond constituted an express warranty under California Uniform Commercial Code section 2313 or were merely nonactionable expressions of opinion. In any event, this is the only cause of action on which plaintiff may proceed, as we discuss more fully, *post.*

Rescission

Plaintiff has attempted to plead a separate cause of action for rescission. She is not entitled to that remedy. Civil Code section 1559 provides, "A contract, made expressly for the benefit of a third person, may be *enforced* by him [or her] at any time before *the parties thereto rescind it.*" (Italics added.) But only the parties to the contract may rescind it. Civil Code section 1689 provides, in pertinent part, "(a) A contract may be rescinded if all the *parties* thereto consent. [¶] (b) A *party to a contract* may rescind the contract in the following cases: [¶] (1) If the consent of the *party* rescinding, or of any *party jointly contracting* with him [or her], was given by mistake, or obtained through duress, menace, fraud, or undue influence, exercised by or with the connivance of the *party* as to whom he [or she] rescinds, or of any other *party to the contract jointly interested with such party.* [¶] (2) If the consideration for the obligation of the rescinding *party* fails, in whole or in part, through the fault of the *party* as to whom he [or she] rescinds." (Italics added.)

We have found no cases specifically holding the rescission remedy unavailable to a third party beneficiary, but the proposition is self-evident to a degree that might well explain the absence of precedent. Civil Code section 1559 grants a third party beneficiary the right to *enforce* the contract, not rescind it, and Civil Code section 1689 limits its grant of rescission rights to the contracting parties. Not only do the relevant statutes demand making rescission unavailable to a third party beneficiary, but common sense compels the conclusion. The interest of the third party beneficiary is as the intended recipient of the *benefits* of the contract, and a direct right to those benefits, i.e., specific performance, or damages in lieu thereof, will protect the beneficiary's interests. Rescission, on the other hand, extinguishes a contract between the parties. (Civ. Code, § 1688.) Plaintiff, not having participated in the agreement, not having undertaken any duty or given any consideration, is a stranger to the agreement, with no legitimate interest in voiding it. As a matter of law, without an assignment of Erstad's contract rights, plaintiff cannot rescind the sales contract to which she was not a party.

*   *   *   *   *   *

Actual and Constructive Fraud

Further, the absence of an assignment of rights from Erstad precludes plaintiff from maintaining a cause of action for actual fraud. It is axiomatic that plaintiff must allege she "actually relied upon the misrepresentation; i.e., that the representation was 'an immediate cause of [her] conduct which alter[ed] [her] legal relations,' and that without such representation, '[she] would not, in all reasonable probability, have entered into the contract or other transaction.' " (5 Witkin, *Summary of Cal. Law* (9th ed. 1988) Torts, § 711, p. 810; *Wilhelm v. Pray, Price, Williams & Russell* (1986) 186 Cal. App. 3d 1324, 1331-1332 [231 Cal. Rptr. 355].) Here, Erstad allegedly relied on the representation and entered into the contract of sale. As we have explained, he retained the right, if any, to sue for actual fraud.

As for constructive fraud, the complaint fails to plead facts establishing the requisite fiduciary or special confidential relationship between plaintiff and defendant. (*See, e.g., Tyler v. Children's Home Society* (1994) 29 Cal.App.4th 511, 548 [35 Cal. Rptr. 2d 291]; *Peterson Development Co. v. Torrey Pines Bank* (1991) 233 Cal. App. 3d 103, 116 [284 Cal. Rptr. 367] ["It is essential to the operation of the doctrine of constructive fraud that there exist a fiduciary or special relationship"].) And even assuming plaintiff could overcome the standing hurdle, fraud causes of action must be pleaded with specificity, meaning "(1) general pleading of the legal conclusion of fraud is insufficient; and (2) every element of the cause of action for fraud must be alleged in full, factually and specifically, and the policy of liberal construction of pleading will not usually be invoked to sustain a pleading that is defective in any material respect." (*Wilhelm v. Pray, Price, Williams & Russell, supra,* 186 Cal. App. 3d at p. 1331.) Plaintiff's complaint utterly fails the specificity test, not because she is an inartful pleader, but because those facts that are well pleaded necessarily negate the existence of the facts supporting the requisite elements of fraud.

DISPOSITION

The judgment is reversed. The case is remanded with directions to the trial court to overrule defendant's demurrer to plaintiff's cause of action for breach of contract and order defendant to answer. In all other respects, the demurrer has been properly sustained without leave to amend. Plaintiff shall recover her costs on appeal.

Rylaarsdam, Acting P. J., and Bedsworth, J., concurred.